Hans G. Hoffmann · Marion Hoffmann

Endlich Zeit für Englisch

Hueber Verlag

Wenn Sie Fragen zum englischen Sprachgebrauch oder Kommentare zum Inhalt dieses Buches haben, senden Sie uns diese bitte über unsere Website www.englishmaster.de. Dort finden Sie auch Informationen zu Grammatik, Wortschatz, Sprachgebrauch und Landeskunde sowie Übungen und Hinweise auf nützliche Lernhilfen. Alle Auskünfte erhalten Sie kostenlos.
Hans G. Hoffmann, Marion Hoffmann

In diesem Buch verwendete **Abkürzungen** sind:
AE = amerikanisches Englisch
BE = britisches Englisch
etw = etwas
sth = something

In den **Ausspracheangaben** ist die betonte Silbe durch Unterstreichung gekennzeichnet.

Das Werk und seine Teile sind urheberrechtlich geschützt.
Jede Verwertung in anderen als den gesetzlich zugelassenen
Fällen bedarf deshalb der vorherigen schriftlichen
Einwilligung des Verlags.

Hinweis zu § 52a UrhG: Weder das Werk noch seine Teile dürfen ohne
eine solche Einwilligung überspielt, gespeichert und in ein Netzwerk
eingespielt werden. Dies gilt auch für Intranets von Firmen und von Schulen
und sonstigen Bildungseinrichtungen.

| 3. 2. 1. | Die letzten Ziffern |
| 2013 12 11 10 09 | bezeichnen Zahl und Jahr des Druckes. |

Alle Drucke dieser Auflage können, da unverändert,
nebeneinander benutzt werden.
1. Auflage
© 2009 Hueber Verlag, 85737 Ismaning, Deutschland
Umschlaggestaltung: Parzhuber und Partner, München
Coverbilder: Brücke: © Image Source/Black; Paar: © Corbis/Jupiterimages
Redaktion: Valerio Vial, Hueber Verlag, Ismaning
Muttersprachliche Durchsicht und Beratung: John Stevens, Bad Münstereifel;
  John Greenslate, Kingston-near-Lewes
Layout und Satz: Achim Kreuzer, Augsburg
Druck und Bindung: Firmengruppe APPL, aprinta druck, Wemding
Printed in Germany
ISBN 978-3-19-009588-9
01.9588

Vorwort

„Ihr Europäer habt die Uhren, wir Afrikaner haben die Zeit", sagt man auf dem Schwarzen Erdteil und trifft damit den Nagel recht genau auf den Kopf. Schon rein mental haben wir Schwierigkeiten, uns zeitliche Freiräume zu schaffen (*to make time*), und wenn wir sie denn haben, sie so zu nutzen, dass sie unsere Lebensqualität erhöhen, uns einen Zugewinn an Glück bringen.

Aber früher oder später kommt sie, die Chance (oder die Notwendigkeit), sich dem Arbeitsstress vorübergehend oder auf Dauer zu entziehen, *to quit the rat race* – aus dem Rattenrennen auszusteigen, wie die Engländer so anschaulich sagen. In einer solchen Zeit gilt es, Versäumtes nachzuholen, Körper und Geist fit zu machen und vor allem: Freude zu finden (*to enjoy life*).

Jeder hat seine eigenen Glücksvorstellungen: gut essen gehen, Geselligkeit pflegen, in der Sonne liegen, interessante Orte besuchen, Sport, Theater, Lesen – die Liste ist lang, enthält aber bei vielen Menschen das Reisen in fremde Länder als wesentlichen Bestandteil. Damit eng verbunden ist der Wunsch, eine Sprache zu lernen oder vorhandene Sprachkenntnisse zu vertiefen. Da Englisch heute die Weltsprache schlechthin ist (→ S. 161), ist es oft das Medium der Wahl, ist es Mittel vor allem zu dem Zweck, sich beim Reisen besser verständigen zu können.

Wie sein Titel sagt, wurde dieses Buch ausdrücklich mit dem Ziel gestaltet, Ihnen die Sprache auf eine Weise nahezubringen, dass Sie sagen: Endlich ...! Dass Sie sich jedes Mal freuen, wenn Sie das Buch in die Hand nehmen, erfreuen an der Sprache, den interessanten, oft humorvollen Texten, den Sie in eine andere Welt entrückenden Bildern. *Endlich Zeit für Englisch* führt Sie in alle fünf Erdteile, macht Sie bekannt mit eigenartigen Menschen und erstaunlichen Fakten, reizt Ihren Trieb sich zu testen und zu beweisen – und hat bei alledem immer das Eine fest im Blick: *with every trick of the trade* (mit allen Mitteln) Ihr Englisch Schritt für Schritt zu verbessern.

Aufbau und Inhalt

Der Stoff ist, vom Leichteren zum Schwierigeren fortschreitend, in 15 *Units* (= Lektionen) eingeteilt. Die *Units* sind stets gleich lang (12 Seiten) und gleich aufgebaut:

A *Dialogue* (1 Seite): Hier führen zwei oder mehr Personen ein Alltagsgespräch.

B *Rules and practice* „Regeln und Übungen" (3 Seiten): Hier wird das in A eingeführte Sprachmaterial erklärt und geübt. Je weiter der Kurs fortschreitet, desto mehr wird der Stoff der aktuellen *Unit* mit dem früherer *Units* verknüpft und übergreifend behandelt.

C *Reading text* (1 Seite): Wie in A wird hier neues Sprachmaterial präsentiert, in diesem Fall aber nicht in Form eines Gesprächs, sondern in einem schriftsprachlichen, meist erzählenden Text. Im Englischen – wie im Deutschen – bestehen leichte Unterschiede zwischen den Konventionen der gesprochenen und geschriebenen Sprache, und indem wir in jeder *Unit* beide Textsorten präsentieren, können wir Ihnen ein umfassenderes Bild von Wortschatz und Grammatik des Englischen vermitteln.

D *Rules and practice* (3 Seiten): Dieser Teil entspricht in Umfang, Inhalt und Funktion dem B-Teil, bezieht sich aber in erster Linie auf den C-Text.

E *Focus on words* (1 Seite): Hier werden ausgewählte Wörter und Redensarten ausführlicher erklärt, zu Ausdrücken in früheren *Units* in Beziehung gesetzt und von ähnlichen Ausdrucksformen abgegrenzt. Vor häufig gemachten Fehlern werden Sie gewarnt.

F *Focus on culture* (1 Seite): Hier erhalten Sie Hintergrundinformationen zu den in den Texten erwähnten Namen, zur Landeskunde der englischsprachigen Länder, zu sozialen und sprachlichen Konventionen und ähnlichem.

G *Test yourself* (1 Seite): Entspannung am Ende der *Unit*! Hier wird auf besonders kurzweilige Art Sprache geübt, so durch Kreuzworträtsel, Quiz, Hörverstehenstests, Beschäftigung mit *idioms* usw.

Zu allen Aufgaben in den 15 *Units* finden Sie die Lösungen im **Schlüssel** (ab S. 187).

Auf die im Anhang abgedruckte Liste der **unregelmäßigen Verben** (→ S. 219) wird in den Erklärungen der B- und D-Teile häufig verwiesen. Es handelt sich um ca. 100, zum Teil häufig gebrauchte Verben, die ihre abgeleiteten Formen nicht mit *-ed* bilden.

Der **Wortschatz** wird auf vier Ebenen vermittelt, erklärt und wiederholt:
1. Durch vollständige Übersetzung der Texte der A- und C-Teile.
2. Durch Einzelwortübersetzungen im Randstreifen.
3. Durch genauere Erklärung und Gebrauchshinweise in den E-Teilen (s. o.).
4. Durch die alphabetische Liste „Der wichtigste Allgemeinwortschatz" (ab S. 209), die sich sowohl zum Nachschlagen als auch zum Auswendiglernen eignet. Diese 500 Wörter sind der unverzichtbare Grundbestand der Sprache.

Ratschläge für erfolgreiches Lernen

Es gibt viele unterschiedliche (und oft auch sehr individuelle und originelle) Möglichkeiten, wie Sie aus *Endlich Zeit für Englisch* Gewinn ziehen können. Wir wollen Ihnen keine Methode aufzwingen – Sie werden Ihre eigene finden. Aber wir möchten Sie auf einige hilfreiche Lerntechniken hinweisen:

▶ Ihren ersten Zugang zum Dialog (A) bzw. Lesetext (C) sollten Sie stets über die CD suchen – besonders wenn Sie Anfänger sind. Das Piktogramm 💿 sagt Ihnen, dass eine Tonaufnahme vorliegt; die Zahl 1 oder 2 vor dem Schrägstrich bezeichnet die CD und die Zahl danach den Track, den Sie ansteuern müssen. Hören Sie jede Aufnahme mehrmals, erst nur genau hinhörend, dann dabei das Schriftbild verfolgend, schließlich mitsprechend. Erst wenn Sie das Sprachmodell schon recht gut im Ohr haben, sollten Sie sich (ohne CD) mit dem Buch und dem darin gebotenen Material beschäftigen.

▶ Machen Sie die Übungen bitte in der Regel schriftlich, dann bleiben die Satzbaumuster und auch etwaige Korrekturen von falschem Sprachgebrauch besser haften.

▶ Vergleichen Sie Ihre Lösungen mit denen im Schlüssel (ab S. 187). Gibt es mehr als eine richtige Lösung, so weisen wir Sie hier darauf hin und erklären Ihnen gegebenenfalls die Unterschiede.

▶ Schließlich: Lernen Sie nie zu lange hintereinander! Wöchentlich sechsmal eine Viertelstunde sind wirksamer als auf einen Schlag mühsame anderthalb Stunden. Vertrauen Sie darauf, dass vieles sich innerhalb des Buches wiederholt; Wichtiges kommt nicht nur einmal vor, sondern immer wieder.

▶ Und wenn alle Stricke reißen, wenn Ihnen ein Stück Film fehlt, sodass Sie festhängen, teilen Sie uns Ihr Problem mit über unsere Website **www.englishmaster.de** (links ganz unten: Contact us). Sie erhalten schnell, unkompliziert und kostenlos Antwort und Hilfe.

Und nun ist es ... Endlich Zeit für Englisch!

Verfasser und Verlag

Inhaltsverzeichnis

Unit 1	Who's who • Introductions • A family of runners	am, is, are isn't it? have – has hasn't got -s-Form des Verbs	Seite	7
Unit 2	In London • In St James's Park • London for free	verneinte Frage there is – there are you can …		19
Unit 3	Hotel • Talking about the hotel • From a hotel brochure	have – has what's / what are … like? we can … will-Zukunft let's …		31
Unit 4	Bed and breakfast • Trying to make a reservation • Of beds, children and Manhattans	verneinte Frage there is – there are you can …		43
Unit 5	Down under • Chatting on the phone • Email from Sydney	Verlaufsform oder einfache Form? fancy + -ing Verlaufsform für Zukunft isn't it? – is it?		55
Unit 6	Travellers • A less than perfect holiday • You see what is inside you	Vergangenheitsform must – have to Verlaufsform der Vergangenheit will-Zukunft		67
Unit 7	Runners • Going into retirement • A marathon veteran	wie man die Zukunft ausdrückt Vergangenheit mit ago Frageanhängsel unregelmäßige Verben past perfect („had-Form")		79
Unit 8	Memory • Memory isn't everything • What's your name again?	present perfect („have-Form") unregelmäßige Verben was/were going to want to used to, should(n't), may/might Gebrauch der -ing-Form		91

Unit 9	**Food** • At a restaurant • David's blog	shall we ...? / let's ... /why don't we ...? do you want me to ...? would(n't) Hilfsverben als Stellvertreter could (have + 3. Form des Verbs)	Seite	103
Unit 10	**Golf** • A golfing holiday • Back from holiday	should have + 3. Form des Verbs it's = it is / it has -ing nach Präpositionen		115
Unit 11	**Fortune telling** • A look at the crystal ball • The fortune teller	dt. Perfekt – engl. Vergangenheit indirekte Rede betonendes do/does/did Vergangenheit mit ago Aktiv – Passiv ... shall we?		127
Unit 12	**Theft** • A car theft • A holiday experience	Aktiv – Passiv had = hätte / wäre Bedingungsform Typ 2 und 3 Frageanhängsel -ing-Form Vergangenheitszeiten		139
Unit 13	**Education** • The second life • Contentment	present perfect "unfinished" Frageanhängsel -ing nach Präpositionen Aktiv – Passiv		151
Unit 14	**Shakespeare** • Back from Stratford-upon-Avon • Shakespeare	betonendes do/does/did Aktiv – Passiv indirekte Frage have something done		163
Unit 15	**Victoria** • Victoria • Victorians	could/might/must + have + 3. Form „könnte" = could / might Gebrauch der Zeiten present perfect "unfinished" Bedingungssätze		175

Schlüssel zu den Übungen	187
Der wichtigste Allgemeinwortschatz	209
Grund- und Ordnungszahlen	217
Die wichtigsten unregelmäßigen Verben	219
Register	223

Who's who

Unit 1

> Sich und andere vorstellen
> Was Leute machen
> Pronomen
> *Am, is, are*
> *This – these*
> Plural mit *-s*
> *-s*-Form des Verbs
> *Isn't it?*
> *… and 100 dollars!*

Unit 1A Dialogue

■ = John
● = Tom
▲ = Janet
✱ = Paul
◆ = Anna
▼ = Sarah

meet = treffen, kennenlernen
suppose = annehmen
glad = froh
right = richtig
came = kamen
delighted = (hoch)erfreut
make yourself = machen Sie sich
at home = zu Hause
introduce = vorstellen
pleased = erfreut
forgot = vergaß
has made = hat gemacht
mess = Schweinerei

Leute werden einander zwanglos vorgestellt. Hören Sie den Dialog mehrfach, sprechen Sie ihn mit, klären Sie die Wortbedeutungen mit Hilfe der Übersetzung.

Introductions

■ Hello! I'm John. And you're ... um ...

● Tom, Tom Bradley.
■ Great to meet you, Tom. And I suppose you're Janet ...
▲ That's right. Hello!
■ Hello Janet! We're so glad you came.

✱ And I'm Paul. Hi!
■ Oh hello, Paul, good to meet you. – Well, we're delighted you're here. Make yourself at home. – But let me introduce our family ... This is Anna.

◆ Hello!
● Nice to meet you, Anna!
■ And these are our dear granddaughters, Sarah and Rachel. They're here with us for a week's holiday. We're always so pleased to have them.
▼ Hi!
■ And oh yes, I almost forgot – that's Toby, the new member of our family. Over here, Toby! Sit! That's a good dog! – I must tell you he's only ten weeks old and already house-trained.

▼ Look, grandad, Toby has made a mess on the rug!
■ Oh no! And our best rug too. Sarah, quick! Please run and get a cloth.

Vorstellung(en)

■ Hallo! Ich bin John. Und Sie sind ... äh ...

● Tom, Tom Bradley.
■ Prima, Sie kennenzulernen, Tom. Und Sie sind wohl Janet ...
▲ Das stimmt. Hallo!
■ Hallo, Janet! Wir freuen uns so sehr, dass Sie („kamen") gekommen sind.

✱ Und ich bin Paul. Hi! / Hallo!
■ O hallo, Paul, schön Sie kennenzulernen. – Also, wir freuen uns sehr, dass Sie hier sind. Machen Sie's sich bequem. – Aber lassen Sie mich unsere Familie vorstellen ... Dies ist Anna.

◆ Hallo!
● Schön Sie kennenzulernen, Anna!
■ Und dies sind unsere lieben Enkelinnen, Sarah und Rachel. Sie sind hier bei uns zu einem einwöchigen Urlaub. Wir freuen uns immer so, sie (bei uns) zu haben.
▼ Hallo!
■ Und, o ja, ich vergaß fast – das ist Toby, das neue Mitglied unserer Familie. Hierher, Toby! Sitz! Das ist brav! – Ich muss Ihnen sagen, er ist erst zehn Wochen alt und schon stubenrein.

▼ Schau mal, Opa, Toby hat auf den Teppich gemacht!
■ O nein! Und auch noch unser bester Teppich. Sarah, schnell! Lauf bitte und hol einen Lappen.

Unit 1B

Rules and practice

Wie viel Englisch können Sie schon? Null, ein bisschen, sechs Jahre, neun Jahre Schule vor dreißig Jahren? Wir wissen es nicht, aber wir fangen einfach mal an.
Einfach ist die Devise – locker, entspannt, aber neugierig!
In den ersten Lektionen (*Units* nennen wir sie gut englisch) wiederholen wir einfache Dinge wie Einzahl – Mehrzahl, Pronomen (solche Wörter wie *we*, *our*, *us*), einfache Verbformen wie *is* und *are* und *have*.
Wir versuchen es so zu machen, dass die schon etwas Fortgeschrittenen sich nicht langweilen und die Nullanfänger das Buch nicht frustriert in die Ecke werfen.
Seien Sie neugierig, haben Sie Geduld, üben Sie regelmäßig – sechsmal 15 Minuten pro Woche sind wirksamer als einmal eine Lernsitzung von 90 Minuten. Und üben Sie viel mit der CD!

1 Pronomen + *am* / *is* / *are*

Vollform	Kurzform	
I am	I'm	*ich bin*
you are	you're	*du bist / Sie sind / ihr seid*
he is	he's	*er ist* (männl. Person oder personifiziertes Tier)
she is	she's	*sie ist* (weibl. Person oder personifiziertes Tier)
it is	it's	*es/er/sie ist* (Sache oder nicht personifiziertes Tier)
we are	we're	*wir sind*
they are	they're	*sie sind*

Vollform – Kurzform

Die **Vollform** benutzt man in förmlichen Texten und außerdem, wenn man eines der beiden in der Kurzform zusammengezogenen Wörter betonen möchte:

So **you** are Janet.	*Du also bist Janet.*
He **is** a good dog.	*Er ist aber auch wirklich ein braver Hund.*
Is that Janet? – Yes, it **is**.	*Ist das Janet? – Ja.*

Die **Kurzform** ist die (meist unbetonte) normale Form. Sie benutzt man im täglichen Gespräch, in Briefen, E-Mails usw., zunehmend aber auch in Zeitungsartikeln, und dort nicht nur bei der Wiedergabe von wörtlicher Rede.

Unit 1B

✎ Setzen Sie *am, is, are* ein und benutzen Sie die Kurzformen.

a Hello, I _____ John Hunter.

b And you _____ Tom Bradley, I suppose.

c Is that Rachel? Yes, she _____ here with Janet.

d They _____ sisters, I suppose.

e And that _____ Toby. He _____ the new member of our family.

f We _____ all happy to have Toby. It _____ nice to have a dog.

2 I suppose

I suppose =
I guess =
ich nehme an

And **I suppose** you're Janet.
And you're Janet, **I suppose**. } *Und du bist wohl Janet.*

I suppose (= ich nehme an) drückt eine Annahme aus, der im Deutschen häufig das Wort „wohl" entspricht. Statt *I suppose* können Sie auch *I guess* sagen, das im AE häufiger als im BE vorkommt.

1/2

3 Hör-Sprech-Übung. Machen Sie jetzt eine kleine Übung mit der CD: Sie hören einen kurzen Satz und wiederholen ihn unter Hinzufügung von *I suppose*, wodurch Sie die Aussage zu einer Annahme „abmildern".

Sie hören zum Beispiel: ....You're Tom.
Sie sagen: ....You're Tom, I suppose.
Sie hören die richtige Antwort: ....You're Tom, I suppose.
Sie wiederholen die Antwort: ....You're Tom, I suppose.

4 Verben sind das A und O

Verb = Zeitwort,
Tätigkeitswort

Im Englischen gibt es, wie im Deutschen, eine ganze Reihe von verschiedenen Wortarten, zum Beispiel:
Nomen, auch Substantive oder Hauptwörter genannt: z. B. *family* oder *dog*;
Pronomen, auch Fürwörter genannt: z. B. *you* oder *yourself*;
Adverbien, auch Umstandswörter genannt: z. B. *almost* oder *always*;
Adjektive, auch Eigenschaftswörter genannt: z. B. *glad* oder *good*.

Die grammatisch vielseitigste und für einen effektiven Gebrauch der Sprache wichtigste Wortart ist das **Verb**, also zum Beispiel die Formen *is* (= ist), *are* (= bist/sind/seid) und *am* (= bin) des „Sonderverbs" *be* (= sein), die „Sonderverben" *have/has* (= haben/hat) und *must* (= muss) und „normale" Verben wie *get* (= holen), *let* (= lassen), *make* (= machen), *meet* (= kennenlernen) und *tell* (= sagen). Sie kennen auch bereits die Vergangenheitsformen *came* (= kam[en]) und *forgot* (= vergaß) sowie die Form *made* (= gemacht) des Verbs *make*.

Unit 1B

✏️ Setzen Sie die folgenden Verb(form)en ein.

came, forgot, get, let, made, make, meet, tell

a We're so glad you _____.
b Oh hello, Paul, good to _____ you.
c _____ yourself at home.
d But _____ me introduce our family ... This is Anna ...
e And oh yes, I almost _____ – that's Toby, our dog.
f I must _____ you he's only ten weeks old and already house-trained.
g Look, grandad, Toby has _____ a mess on the rug!
h Oh no! Sarah, quick! Please run and _____ a cloth.

meet = treffen, kennenlernen
let = lassen
tell = sagen

5 This – these

These ist die Mehrzahl von **this**:

This is our granddaughter.   Dies ist unsere Enkelin.
These are our granddaughters.   Dies sind unsere Enkelinnen.

✏️ Setzen Sie *this* oder *these*, *is* oder *are* ein.

a _____ _____ our dogs Ben and Toby.
b _____ _____ Tom with his wife Janet.
c _____ _____ the new member of our family.
d _____ _____ Sarah with Toby on her arm.
e _____ _____ our best rug.
f _____ rugs _____ very nice.
g _____ dogs _____ all house-trained.

wife = (Ehe-)Frau
member = Mitglied

6 Überprüfen Sie, ob Sie sich an die englischen Entsprechungen der folgenden Sätze erinnern können. Übersetzen Sie am besten schriftlich.

a Und du bist wohl Janet.   _____
b Wir freuen uns sehr, dass ihr hier seid. _____
c Toby ist ein neues Mitglied unserer Familie. _____
d Er ist erst zehn Wochen alt.   _____

Unit 1C

Reading text

A family of runners

We are a family of runners, I always say. Yes, you'll find members of our family on three continents, and they all run something.

Take my sister Ruth, she runs a German delicatessen in London. Wines, sausages (her frankfurters are popular), puddings, biscuits, chocolate, that sort of thing, all from Germany, Austria or Switzerland.

My brother Max runs a hotel in California. It's called The Blue Danube. Funny name for a hotel in California, isn't it? But it's popular, it's good, and it even has a spa.

Then there's my uncle Fred in New Zealand. Believe it or not, he runs a goat farm. Goats are his life and he has hundreds of them. The goats have lots of pasture but Uncle Fred hasn't got a house - he lives on a boat. Uncle Fred is a strange man.

And me? Well, I'm retired now but I run too - city marathons, a different city each year. Believe me it's a great hobby.

runner = Läufer(in)
always = immer
run = leiten, führen
take = nehmen
sort = Sorte, Art
called = genannt
Danube = Donau
even = sogar
spa = Wellnessbereich
believe = glauben
goat = Ziege
lots of = viel
hasn't got = hat nicht
retired = pensioniert, im Ruhestand

Eine Familie von „Rennern" / „Läufern"

Wir sind eine Familie von „Rennern", sage ich immer. Ja, Sie werden Mitglieder unserer Familie auf drei Kontinenten finden, und sie alle „rennen" (= haben / führen / leiten / betreiben) etwas.

Nehmen Sie meine Schwester Ruth, sie hat einen deutschen Feinkostladen in London. Wein, Würste (ihre Frankfurter Würstchen sind beliebt), Pudding(e), Kekse, Schokolade, solche Sachen, alles aus Deutschland, Österreich oder der Schweiz.

Mein Bruder Max hat ein Hotel in Kalifornien. Die Blaue Donau heißt es. Komischer Name für ein Hotel in Kalifornien, nicht wahr? Aber es ist beliebt, es ist gut, und es hat sogar einen Wellnessbereich.

Dann ist da mein Onkel Fred in Neuseeland. Ob Sie's glauben oder nicht, er betreibt eine Ziegenfarm. Ziegen sind sein Leben und er hat hunderte davon. Die Ziegen haben massenhaft Weide(land), aber Onkel Fred hat kein Haus – er lebt auf einem Boot / Kahn. Onkel Fred ist ein seltsamer Mann.

Und ich? Nun, ich bin jetzt im Ruhestand, aber ich laufe auch – Stadtmarathons, jedes Jahr eine andere Stadt. Glauben Sie mir, das ist ein tolles Hobby.

Rules and practice

Unit 1D

1 Der Plural (= die Mehrzahlform) wird im Englischen in aller Regel durch Anhängen von -s gebildet. (→ 2B4) Setzen Sie entsprechend dem Sinnzusammenhang die Singular- oder Pluralform ein.

a There are three marathon (runner) _____ in our family.
b One of my (granddaughter) _____ runs the London Marathon each year.
c Our little (dog) _____ Toby is not a marathon (runner) _____.
d Toby is the new (member) _____ of our (family) _____.
e He's only ten (week) _____ old.
f My (sister) _____ Ruth runs a German (delicatessen) _____ in London.
g Her German (biscuit) _____ and (cake) _____ are popular.
h My (brother) _____ Paul and Max run a (hotel) _____ in California.
i Uncle Fred in New Zealand has (hundred) _____ of (goat) _____.
j (Goat) _____ are his (hobby) _____ and his (business) _____.

-s-Plural

each year = jedes Jahr
little = klein
only ten = erst zehn
hundred = hundert
business = Geschäft

2 Die -s-Form des Verbs (→ 3B2, 4D1)

Erfahrungsgemäß macht die -s-Form des Verbs Lernenden besonders zu schaffen. Entweder hängen sie sie nicht an, wenn sie müssten, oder sie benutzen sie, wo sie nicht hingehört. Deshalb üben wir den richtigen Gebrauch dieser Form von Anfang an. Also: Wenn man im Deutschen sagt: „er/sie/es rennt", dann sagt man im Englischen *he/she/it runs*.
Nur mit *he/she/it* (oder Wörtern, die durch *he/she/it* ersetzt werden könnten) und nur in der Gegenwart (also nicht „rannte") steht die -s-Form.

✏️ Üben wir das doch gleich mal. Entscheiden Sie, ob die -s-Form oder die Form ohne -s angebracht ist.

a He (introduce) _____ his family.
b Sarah (run) _____ and (get) _____ a cloth.
c John always (say) _____ something nice.
d I (run) _____ a marathon each year.
e Our granddaughter (run) _____ the London Marathon each year.
f We (believe) _____ the dog is house-trained, but he isn't.
g The goats (live) _____ on the farm, but the farmer (live) _____ on a boat.

introduce = vorstellen
get = holen
always = immer
something nice = etwas Nettes
believe = glauben
live = leben, wohnen

Unit 1D

I have – he has

granddaughter = Enkelin
make a mess = „(hin)machen"
rug = Teppich, Brücke

3   Have – has (→3B2, 4D1)

Auch von *have* ist Ihnen die *-s*-Form schon begegnet, nämlich *has*. Für die Unterscheidung von *have* und *has* gelten die gleichen Regeln wie bei den „normalen" Verben oben in 1D2: *I/you/we/they* **have** – *he/she/it* **has**.

✏️ **Gebrauchen Sie die passende Form: *have* oder *has*.**

a   John and Anna (have) _____ two granddaughters.
b   The family (have) _____ a dog.
c   The dog (have) _____ made a mess on the rug.
d   Oh no, Toby, you (have) _____ made a mess on the rug!
e   Monica's uncle (have) _____ a boat on the Danube.
f   Our hotel (have) _____ a very nice spa.
g   Fred (have) _____ hundreds of goats and the goats (have) _____ a wonderful life.

„nicht wahr?"

4   Isn't it? = „nicht wahr?" (→5D3, 7B4)

Das Frageanhängsel *isn't it?* (verkürzt aus *is not it?*) hört man ziemlich oft, und es entspricht in etwa dem deutschen „nicht wahr?" Im Unterschied zum deutschen „nicht wahr?" ist das englische Frageanhängsel abhängig von dem, was vorne steht – *he, she* oder *it* (oder Wörter die durch *he/she/it* ersetzt werden können). Sehen Sie sich das an:

Uncle Fred is a funny man, **isn't he**?	*Onkel Fred ist ein komischer Mann, **nicht wahr**?*
Sarah is a nice girl, **isn't she**?	*Sarah ist ein nettes Mädchen, **nicht wahr**?*
That's a funny name, **isn't it**?	*Das ist ein komischer Name, **nicht wahr**?*

Uncle Fred ließe sich durch *he* ersetzen, daher *isn't he?*;
Sarah ließe sich durch *she* ersetzen, daher *isn't she?*;
that ließe sich durch *it* ersetzen, daher *isn't it?*.

1/4

retired = pensioniert, im Ruhestand

5   Hör-Sprech-Übung. Üben Sie jetzt das Anfügen des passenden Frageanhängsels (also mit *he, she* oder *it*!) mündlich.

Sie hören zum Beispiel: ....Tom is retired now.
Sie sagen: ....Tom is retired now, isn't he?
Sie hören die richtige Antwort: ....Tom is retired now, isn't he?
Sie wiederholen die Antwort: ....Tom is retired now, isn't he?

6 Hasn't got

Hasn't ist zusammengezogen aus *has not*. *Hasn't got* bedeutet „hat nicht" im Sinn von „besitzt nicht" und wird in dieser Bedeutung heute häufiger benutzt als *hasn't* allein. Mit anderen Worten: *He hasn't got a house* klingt moderner als *he hasn't a house*.

hasn't = has not

✏️ **Bilden Sie nun Sätze nach folgendem Muster.**

Uncle Fred / a family → Uncle Fred hasn't got a family.

hasn't got =
 hat nicht

a the hotel / a spa _____
b the family / a dog _____
c the goat / a name _____
d my sister / a hobby _____
e John / a sister in London _____
f she / a good computer _____

7
Little words. Im Englischen haben es die „kleinen" Wörter in sich, Wörter wie *at, for, from, of, on, to, with*. Setzen Sie diese *little words* in den folgenden Sätzen ein.

a Nice _____ meet you.
b Make yourself _____ home.
c Our granddaughters are here _____ us _____ a week's holiday.
d We're so pleased _____ have them.
e Toby is the new member _____ our family.
f The dog has made a mess _____ the rug.
g This wine is _____ Austria.
h Uncle Fred has hundreds _____ goats.
i The goats have lots _____ pasture.
j Uncle Fred lives _____ a boat.

our = unser
pasture =
 Weide(land)

8 Das Verb *run*

Das Verb *run* hat viele Bedeutungen und idiomatische Verwendungen. Die Grundbedeutung ist „rennen / laufen". In unserem *Reading text* hat es auch die Bedeutung „(einen Laden / ein Hotel / eine Farm) betreiben / führen". Mitunter kann man *run* im Deutschen auch einfach mit „haben" übersetzen:
He runs a farm in Iowa. = „Er betreibt / hat eine Farm in Iowa."

Unit 1D

Unit 1E — Focus on words

BE holiday = **AE** vacation

1. *For a week's* **holiday** (= für einen einwöchigen Urlaub): im amerikanischen Englisch *for a week's* **vacation** (→ 10E1).

2. Wendungen, mit denen man seine **Freude** ausdrückt – ungefähre Übersetzungen:

„freut mich / uns"

Nice to meet you.	Freut mich, dich kennenzulernen.
Good to meet you.	Schön, dich kennenzulernen.
Great to meet you.	Toll / Prima, dich kennenzulernen.
We're so glad you came.	Wir freuen uns so, dass du gekommen bist.
We're delighted you're here.	Wir freuen uns sehr, dass du hier bist.
We're always so pleased to have them.	Wir freuen uns immer so sehr, wenn wir sie hier haben.

Koseformen

3. *Grandad* (auch *grandpa*) ist „Opa, Opi", *dad(dy)* wäre „Papa, Vati", und dies sind Koseformen für *grandfather* und *father*.
Spricht man über seinen Vater, wählt man heute auch als Erwachsener oft das weniger förmliche Wort, also zum Beispiel: *My dad is a doctor.* (= Mein Papa ist Arzt.) „Großmutter" ist *grandmother*, „Oma" ist *grandma* oder *granny*, „Mutter" ist *mother*, und „Mutti" ist britisch *mum*, amerikanisch *mom*. Auch hier benutzen Erwachsene sehr häufig die informelle Variante: *My mum / mom is a doctor.* (= Meine Mutti / Mama ist Ärztin.)

what a mess! = das sieht ja schön aus!

4. *A mess* ist ein schmutziger, unordentlicher Zustand, ein Durcheinander, eine Schweinerei, ein Schlamassel, und davon leiten sich eine ganze Menge häufig gebrauchter Ausdrücke ab. Beispiele:

The kitchen **is a mess**.	Die Küche ist in einem fürchterlichen Zustand.
My hair **is a mess**.	Meine Haare sehen schrecklich aus.
The country is **in a mess**.	In dem Land herrscht Chaos.
There's **dog mess** all over the place.	Überall sind Hundehaufen.

rug = Teppich, Brücke

5. *A* **rug** *is a small carpet* (= ein *rug* ist ein kleiner Teppich), bei teureren Exemplaren oft „Brücke" genannt. In 1A hätte es auch heißen können: *Toby has made a mess on the carpet.*

deli(catessen)

6. *A delicatessen* (meist abgekürzt: *deli*) ist ein Feinkostladen, wo man fertig zubereitete Speisen wie *salads* (= Salate), *soups* (= Suppen), *sandwiches*, *bagels* (*a* wie in *came*), *pizzas* (langes *i*!), bzw. *cold cuts* (= Aufschnitt), *cheeses* (= Käse) usw. zum Mitnehmen (*to take away*) oder An-Ort-und-Stelle-Essen kaufen kann. *Many New York delis are open 24 hours.*

„Wellness" ist deutsch!

7. *Spa*, schon vor Jahrhunderten vom Namen eines belgischen Heilbades abgeleitet, bezeichnete zunächst Heilbäder bzw. Kurorte wie Baden-Baden oder Vichy. Heutzutage sind *spas* kommerzielle Wellnesseinrichtungen oder Wellnessbereiche in Hotels usw. Was man auf Deutsch als „Wellnesshotel" bezeichnet, wäre auf Englisch *a spa hotel*.

Focus on culture

1. Begrüßungs- und Abschiedsfloskeln

Früher war *how d'you do* die Standardbegrüßung beim ersten Kennenlernen. Die beiden „Parteien" wurden einander vorgestellt (*introduced*) und sagten *how d'you do*, um dann zu *small talk* (= oberflächliche Konversation) überzugehen. Heute wirkt *how d'you do* sehr förmlich (*very formal*), gar schon etwas altmodisch (*old-fashioned*); es werden meist (wie in 1A) legere Begrüßungen wie *hello!* oder *hi!* vorgezogen, auf die dann ein *nice / good / glad / great / pleased to meet you* (= freut mich, Sie / dich kennenzulernen) folgt. Bekannte (*acquaintances*), Freunde (*friends*) und Verwandte (*relatives*) begrüßt man ebenfalls mit *hello!* oder *hi!* und setzt gegebenenfalls ein *long time no see* (= lange nicht gesehen) hinzu oder geht gleich zu *how are you (doing)?* (= wie geht's?) über, worauf die Standardantwort lautet: *(oh) fine / very well, thank you / thanks – and you?*
Good morning / afternoon / evening ist wiederum sehr förmlich, würde also eher „Respektspersonen" gegenüber gebraucht (*good morning, sir / madam!*), ist aber gebräuchlich als Begrüßung der Zuhörer, etwa zu Beginn eines Vortrags oder einer Rede. Man verabschiedet sich mit *goodbye!* oder (vertrauter:) *bye! / bye-bye!* bzw. *bye for now!*, vielleicht auch mit *see you later!*, *so long!* oder *be seeing you* (= bis später / bis nachher!) und fügt vielleicht ein fürsorgliches *take care!* (= pass auf dich auf!) oder *safe journey!* (= gute Fahrt / Reise!) hinzu.
Grüße trägt man gegebenenfalls so auf: *Give my regards to your parents.* (= Grüßen Sie Ihre Eltern.) Oder vertrauter: *Give my love to Ann.* (= Grüß Ann schön!)

2. Anredeformen

Wie Sie wissen, unterscheidet das Englische bei der Anrede nicht zwischen „du", „Sie" und „ihr" – es gibt nur die eine universale Form *you*.
Mitunter wird gesagt, der englische Gebrauch des Vornamens entspreche dem deutschen Gebrauch von „du", aber das ist nicht so. Vielmehr ist im Englischen die Anrede mit dem Vornamen inzwischen in allen nicht ausgesprochen formellen Situationen die Regel. Im Fall einer Online-Bestellung im Internet zum Beispiel wird der englischsprachige Händler Sie in seinen Mails oft mit dem Vornamen anreden, während in solchen unpersönlichen Beziehungen (außer unter Jugendlichen) im Deutschen noch das distanzierende „Sie" vorherrscht.
Bei der Übersetzung aus dem Englischen ins Deutsche bietet sich oft die „Sie"-Anrede in Verbindung mit dem Vornamen an: „Sandra, wussten Sie schon ...?"

you = du, Sie, ihr

Unit 1G

clue = Hinweis, Anhaltspunkt
crossword (puzzle) = Kreuzworträtsel

Test yourself

Testen Sie sich! Wie gut haben Sie sich die Wörter und Gebrauchsregeln eingeprägt?
In den *clues* zum folgenden kleinen *crossword puzzle* fehlen die Verben. Setzen Sie diese in das *puzzle* ein und achten Sie dabei darauf, ob die Form ohne oder mit -s angebracht ist.
Noch ein *clue*: Nach *to* steht immer die Verbform ohne -s.
Wenn Sie das *crossword* erfolgreich gelöst haben, lassen Sie sich von dem Familienmitglied, das als erstes im Jahr Geburtstag hat, *a hundred dollars* auszahlen. (Berufen Sie sich auf uns!)

Hundred Dollar Crossword

ACROSS (= waagerecht)

3 Our goats _____ lots of pasture.
4 Oh, I almost _____ – that's Toby, our dog.
6 My sister Angela _____ a deli in New York City.
8 Toby has _____ a mess on the rug.
9 I _____ in a farmhouse.
11 Hello, Emma! We're so glad you _____.
12 The dog is only ten weeks old. He isn't house-trained, I _____.

DOWN (= senkrecht)

1 Let me _____ Sarah – she's my granddaughter.
2 Nice to _____ you.
3 My brother Max _____ a farm in California.
5 Fred and I _____ a goat farm in New Zealand.
7 Fred _____ on a boat.
10 Sarah, quick, run and _____ a cloth!

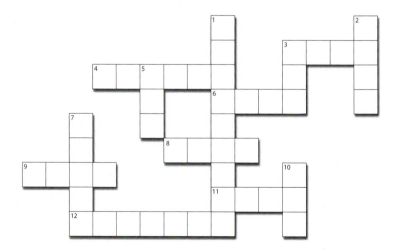

18

In London

Unit 2

- Sachen und Eigenschaften
- *It – they*
- Verneinte Frage
- Mit oder ohne *the*?
- Mehr zum Plural
- Gebrauch des Apostrophs
- *There is – there are*
- *You can ...*
- Präpositionen
- *... and a curry lunch in Soho!*

Unit 2A

Dialogue

1/6

■ = man
● = woman

Erarbeiten Sie zunächst den englischen Text (linke Spalte), indem Sie ihn hören, lesen und sprechen. Achten Sie besonders auf die Aussprache der Namen der Londoner Sehenswürdigkeiten. Erst wenn Sie die Aussprache sicher beherrschen, erschließen Sie sich die Bedeutung über die rechte Spalte.

In St James's Park

■ Isn't this park just beautiful?

● Yes it is. The lake, the ducks, the pelicans, the fine old trees, and Buckingham Palace over there.

■ And the squirrels.
● Yes, the squirrels. They're lovely.

■ It's so peaceful, and yet we're right in the middle of London.
● The government buildings of Whitehall are just a stone's throw from here ...
■ ... and so are the Houses of Parliament and Westminster Abbey.
● Trafalgar Square isn't far away either. And you can walk to Piccadilly Circus and Soho.

■ Speaking of Soho, it's lunchtime and I'm hungry. Aren't you?

● I'm very hungry.

■ Then let's go and have a nice hot curry in Soho. There's a good Indian restaurant in Denman Street.

● Is it expensive?
■ Everything in London is expensive.
● Well, not everything. Most of the museums are free.
■ OK, many museums are free, but everything else is bloody expensive.

Im St James's Park

■ Ist dieser Park nicht einfach wunderschön?

● Ja, das ist er. Der See, die Enten, die Pelikane, die schönen alten Bäume und der Buckingham-Palast da drüben.

■ Und die Eichhörnchen.
● Ja, die Eichhörnchen. Sie sind reizend / niedlich.

■ Es ist so friedlich, und doch sind wir direkt in der Mitte von London.
● Die Regierungsgebäude von Whitehall sind nur einen Steinwurf von hier (entfernt) ...
■ ... und auch die Parlamentsgebäude und die Westminster-Abtei.
● Der Trafalgar-Platz ist auch nicht weit entfernt. Und du kannst / man kann zu Fuß zum Piccadilly Circus und (nach) Soho gehen.

■ Da wir gerade von Soho sprechen / Apropos Soho, es ist Mittagszeit und ich bin hungrig. Bist du (es) nicht? / Du (etwa) nicht?

● Ich bin sehr hungrig / habe großen Hunger.

■ Dann lass uns gehen und einen schönen scharfen Curry in Soho essen. In der Denman Street ist ein gutes indisches Restaurant.

● Ist es teuer?
■ Alles in London ist teuer.
● Nun, nicht alles. Die meisten (der) Museen sind kostenlos.
■ OK, viele Museen sind kostenlos, aber alles sonst / alles andere ist sauteuer.

not ... either = auch nicht
walk = (zu Fuß) gehen
aren't (Ausspr.: „ahnt") = **are not**
let's = **let us** = lass(t) uns
hot = heiß, scharf
most of the museums = die meisten Museen
bloody (→ 8F2, 9G)

Unit 2B

Rules and practice

1 *It* oder *they*? Ersetzen Sie den fett gedruckten Satzteil durch *it* oder *they*.

Pronomen = Fürwörter

The park is beautiful. → **It**'s beautiful.
The parks are beautiful. → **They**'re beautiful.

a **Buckingham Palace** is over there. _____

b **The squirrels** are lovely. _____

c **Whitehall** is just a stone's throw from here. _____

d **The government buildings of Whitehall** are just a stone's throw from here. _____

e **The curry** is good. _____

f **Trafalgar Square** isn't far away from here. _____

g **The museums** are free. _____

2 Verneinte Frage

Beachten Sie, dass in einer verneinten Frage das *not* in der Regel zu *n't* verkürzt und anders platziert wird als im Deutschen:

Deutsch: *Ist dieser Park **nicht** wunderschön?*
Englisch: *Is**n't** this park beautiful?*

isn't it? = ist er nicht?
aren't they? = sind sie nicht?

Isn't wird zweisilbig gesprochen; *aren't* wird einsilbig („ahnt") gesprochen.

Verwandeln Sie die Aussagesätze in verneinte Fragesätze.

The park is beautiful. → Isn't the park beautiful?
The parks are beautiful. → Aren't the parks beautiful?

Unit 2B

a Buckingham Palace is over there. _____
b Everything is expensive here. _____
c Westminster Abbey is just a stone's throw from here. _____
d There's a good Indian restaurant in Denman Street. _____
e The government buildings of Whitehall are just a stone's throw from here. _____
f The squirrels are lovely. _____
g We're right in the middle of London. _____
h You're hungry. _____

3 Englisch ohne *the* – Deutsch mit Artikel („der", „die" etc.)

Namen von Parks, Plätzen, Straßen und berühmten Gebäuden stehen im Englischen oft ohne *the*.

Namen oft ohne *the*

St James's Park is beautiful.	Der St James's Park ist schön.
Buckingham Palace is over there.	Der Buckingham-Palast ist da drüben.
Westminster Abbey isn't far away.	Die Westminster-Abtei ist nicht weit weg.

✎ Entscheiden Sie, ob in die Lücke ein *the* gehört oder nicht.

a _____ squirrels in _____ St James's Park are lovely.
b There's a pelican on _____ lake.
c You can walk to _____ Piccadilly Circus.
d _____ Trafalgar Square isn't far away either.
e We're right in _____ middle of London.
f _____ Houses of Parliament are just a stone's throw from here.
g You can walk to _____ Trafalgar Square and _____ Piccadilly Circus.
h There's a good Indian restaurant in _____ Denman Street.
i Most of _____ museums in London are free.

4 Schreibung und Aussprache des Plurals (→ 1D1)

In den allermeisten Fällen wird der Plural durch Anhängen von *-s* gebildet.
Bei Wörtern wie *family* und *city* wird dabei das *-y* zu *-ie-* (*families*, *cities*); bei Wörtern wie *holiday* und *abbey* bleibt das *-y* erhalten (*holidays*, *abbeys*).

Wenn Sie genau hinhören, werden Sie feststellen, dass das Plural-*s* unterschiedlich gesprochen wird:

1. Bei den meisten Wörtern stimmhaft, d. h. weich, gesummt:

the tree – the **trees**	der Baum – die Bäume
the building – the **buildings**	das Gebäude – die Gebäude
the museum – the **museums**	das Museum – die Museen
the squirrel – the **squirrels**	das Eichhörnchen – die Eichhörnchen

2. Nach *k, t, p* und *f* stimmlos, d. h. gezischt:

the week – the **weeks**	die Woche – die Wochen
the park – the **parks**	der Park – die Parks
the biscuit – the **biscuits**	der Keks – die Kekse

3. Nach Zischlauten tritt – wenn es nicht schon vorhanden ist – ein -*e*- vor das -*s*, und die Pluralendung wird *is* gesprochen:

the bridge – the **bridges**	die Brücke – die Brücken
the palace – the **palaces**	der Palast – die Paläste
the church – the **churches**	die Kirche – die Kirchen

4. *House* ist eine Ausnahme: Aus dem gezischten -*s* des Singulars wird im Plural ein gesummtes -*s*, und das -*es* wird *is* gesprochen:

   | the house – the **houses** | das Haus – die Häuser |

Unit 2B

1/7

Plural = Mehrzahl(form)

5 Singular oder Plural, Verbformen, Pronomen. Schreiben Sie den Text ab und vervollständigen Sie ihn dabei.

The Houses of Parliament _____ beautiful. _____ are not far from St James's Park and the government (building) _____ of Whitehall.
St James's Park _____ one of the beautiful (park) _____ right in the middle of London. It is a peaceful place with fine old (tree) _____ and a lovely (lake) _____.
From St James's Park _____ is a nice walk to Soho with _____ restaurants, bars and clubs.
You _____ hungry? Then let's go and _____ a curry at an Indian restaurant. _____ are three or four Indian (restaurant) _____ in Denman Street.
Restaurants _____ expensive in London, everything _____ expensive, but most of the museums _____ free.
Ruth and Marion _____ a German delicatessen in London. Their (frankfurter) _____, puddings and biscuits _____ popular. They _____ on a boat on the Thames.

Soho and its restaurants = Soho und seine Restaurants

23

Unit 2C

1/8

a lot of = viele
(for) free = kostenlos, umsonst
look at = sich (etw) anschauen
listen to = sich (etw) anhören
interested in = interessiert an
watch = sich (etw) ansehen
I'm fond of walking = ich laufe gern

Reading text

London for free
London is a very expensive city but a lot of interesting things there are free.
Here's what you can do for free in London:
› You can visit the National Gallery in Trafalgar Square and look at the beautiful paintings.
› Also in Trafalgar Square is the Church of St-Martin-in-the-Fields, where you can listen to free lunchtime concerts.
› At the British Museum you can see wonderful collections of objects from cultures all over the world.
› If you are interested in politics, you can go to the Houses of Parliament and watch a debate in the Commons or in the Lords.
› You can go and watch a trial at the Old Bailey.
› You can go to Buckingham Palace and watch the Changing of the Guard.
› At the weekend, you can go to Speakers' Corner in Hyde Park and listen to the speakers.
› If you're fond of walking, you can walk along the south bank of the Thames from Westminster Bridge to Tower Bridge. It's one of the best ways to see London. And it's free.

London umsonst
London ist eine sehr teure Stadt, aber viele interessante Dinge dort sind kostenlos.
Hier ist, was Sie in London kostenlos tun können:
› Sie können die Nationalgalerie am Trafalgar Square besuchen und sich die schönen Gemälde ansehen.
› Auch / Ebenso am Trafalgar Square ist die Kirche St-Martin-in-the-Fields, wo Sie kostenlose Mittagskonzerte hören können.
› Im Britischen Museum können Sie herrliche Sammlungen von Gegenständen von Kulturen aus der ganzen Welt sehen.
› Wenn Sie sich für Politik interessieren, können Sie zu den Parlamentsgebäuden gehen und sich eine Debatte im Unterhaus oder im Oberhaus ansehen.
› Sie können gehen und sich eine Gerichtsverhandlung im Old Bailey ansehen.
› Sie können zum Buckingham-Palast gehen und sich die Wachablösung ansehen.
› Am Wochenende können Sie zur Rednerecke im Hyde Park gehen und den Rednern zuhören.
› Wenn Sie gern zu Fuß gehen, können Sie entlang dem Südufer der Themse von der Westminster-Brücke zur Tower-Brücke gehen. Es ist eine der besten Arten, London zu sehen. Und es ist kostenlos.

Rules and practice

Unit 2D

1 Gebrauch des Apostrophs

Der Apostroph steht, wenn zwei Wörter zusammengezogen sind:

I'm	I am	ich bin	we're	we are	wir sind
he's	he is / has	er ist / hat	they're	they are	sie sind
she's	she is / has	sie ist / hat	you'll	you will	du wirst
it's	it is / has	es ist / hat	isn't	is not	ist nicht
that's	that is / has	das ist / hat	aren't	are not	sind nicht
there's	there is	da ist	hasn't	has not	hat nicht
here's	here is	hier ist	let's	let us	lass(t) uns
you're	you are	du bist			

Der Apostroph steht, wenn Besitz oder Zugehörigkeit ausgedrückt werden soll:

a **Soho's** restaurants — Sohos Restaurants
b the **speaker's** corner — die Ecke des Redners
c **Speakers'** Corner — die Ecke der Redner / die Rednerecke
d St **James's** Park — (vgl. im Deutschen: St.-Jakobs-Park)
e a **stone's** throw away — einen Steinwurf entfernt
f a **week's** holiday — ein einwöchiger Urlaub

speaker's oder speakers'?

Beachten Sie besonders b (ein *speaker*, daher -'s) und c (mehrere *speakers*, daher -s').

✏️ Vervollständigen Sie die Sätze mit „Apostrophwörtern" aus der folgenden Liste.

aren't, city's, he's, isn't, it's, let's, Ruth's, Speakers', stone's, there's, they're, we're, you'll

a There are lots of squirrels in the park and _they're_ lovely.
b Buckingham Palace is just a _stone's_ throw from here and the Houses of Parliament _aren't_ far away either.
c _it's_ nice here and I'm glad it _isn't_ expensive.
d This is Sarah and Rachel – _there's_ our granddaughters. _We're_ always happy to have them.
e Where's Toby? Oh look, _he's_ made a mess on the rug!
f _You'll_ find lots of interesting things to see at the British Museum.
g There are some restaurants in this street but _there's_ no hotel here.
h If you're hungry, _let's_ have lunch here.
i _there's_ is one of the _Ruth's_ best delicatessens.
j The speakers at _Speakers'_ Corner _aren't_ always interesting.

there are = es gibt / sind

Unit 2D

there is / are =
es ist / sind

2 There is / are

Mit *there is* bzw. *there are* drückt man aus, dass etwas an einem Ort vorhanden ist:

There's a good Indian restaurant in Denman Street.	*In der Denman Street ist ein gutes indisches Restaurant.*
There are lots of squirrels in the park.	*Im Park sind viele Eichhörnchen.*
There are many good museums in London.	*In London gibt es viele gute Museen.*

1/9

3 Hör-Sprech-Übung. Machen Sie jetzt diese Übung mit der CD: Sie hören eine Wortgruppe, die Sie dann in einen Satz mit *There's ...* oder *There are ...* einbetten.

Sie hören zum Beispiel: .... lots of dogs in our street
Sie sagen: ....There are lots of dogs in our street.
Sie hören die richtige Antwort: ....There are lots of dogs in our street.
Sie wiederholen die Antwort: ....There are lots of dogs in our street.

4 You can ...

Subj. + *can* + Verb + Obj.

Der Text 2C enthält viele Sätze mit *you can*. Wenn Sie sie mit den deutschen Übersetzungen vergleichen, stellen Sie fest, dass die englische Wortstellung nicht nur von der deutschen abweicht, sondern im Gegensatz zur deutschen immer gleich bleibt:

> **You can visit** the National Gallery in Trafalgar Square.
> *Sie können die Nationalgalerie am Trafalgar Square besuchen.*
>
> At the British Museum **you can see** wonderful collections.
> *Im Britischen Museum können Sie herrliche Sammlungen sehen.*

 Bilden Sie nun bitte Sätze mit *can*, indem Sie die Wörter und Wortgruppen in die richtige Reihenfolge bringen.

a   a trial / at the Old Bailey / can / watch / you

_____

b   a debate / can / in the Commons / watch / you

you can watch a debate in the Commons

c   at Buckingham Palace / can / the Changing of the Guard / watch / you

you can watch

d   the beautiful paintings / can / in the National Gallery / look at / you

_____

e   can / in Hyde Park / listen to / the speakers / you

you can

f   can / free concerts / in the Church of St-Martin-in-the-Fields / listen to / you

you can listen to free concerts

5 Die Präposition *of*

Das Wörtchen *of* kommt in unseren Texten besonders häufig vor. Das ist kein Wunder, denn *of* ist (nach *the*) das zweithäufigste Wort der englischen Sprache.
Hier nun ein kleiner Test: Versuchen Sie, die folgenden Wortgruppen ins Englische zu übersetzen. Sie alle kamen in den Texten vor, und sie alle enthalten das Wort *of*.

Of hat es in sich!

a hunderte von Ziegen — hundreds of goats
b die Regierungsgebäude von Whitehall — the government buildings of Whitehall
c das Südufer der Themse — the south bank of the Thames
d die Mitte Londons — the middle of London
e die meisten der Museen — most of the museums
f die Häuser des Parlaments — the Houses of Parliament
g ein neues Mitglied unserer Familie — a new member of our family
h eine Menge interessanter Dinge — a lot of interesting things
i eine der besten Arten, London zu sehen — one of the best ways to see London
j wenn Sie gern zu Fuß gehen — if you fond of walking
k die Kirche St-Martin-in-the-Fields — the church of St. Martin
l die Wachablösung — the Changing of the Guard

6
Außer *of* haben wir noch andere Präpositionen kennengelernt: *along, at, from, in, to*. Diese Präpositionen werden im Englischen oft anders gebraucht, als man das vom Deutschen her erwartet. Welche Präpositionen gehören in die Lücken?

Präpositionen

a The National Gallery is __in__ Trafalgar Square.
b We can look __at__ the beautiful paintings there.
c __At__ the weekend we can listen __to__ the speakers in Hyde Park.
d Are you interested __in__ politics?
e We can go __to__ Buckingham Palace or watch a trial __at__ the Old Bailey.
f We can walk __along__ the south bank of the Thames __from__ Westminster Bridge __to__ Tower Bridge.

7 *Where*

Mit *where* können Sie „wo" und „wohin" ausdrücken:

where = wo, wohin

| **Where's** the Church of St-Martin-in-the-Fields? | *Wo ist die Kirche St-Martin-in-the-Fields?* |
| **Where** are you going? | *Wo gehst du hin? / Wohin gehst du?* |

Unit 2E

Adjektiv = Eigenschaftswort

Focus on words

1. In dieser *Unit* haben Sie eine ganze Reihe von **Adjektiven** kennengelernt:

nice	nett, schön, hübsch, sympathisch
beautiful	(wunder)schön (anzusehen)
good	gut
best	(der / die / das) beste
wonderful	wunderbar, herrlich
lovely	reizend, niedlich, (wunder)schön
fine	herrlich, fein
old	alt
peaceful	friedlich, ruhig
hungry	hungrig (I'm hungry = ich habe Hunger)
expensive	teuer
free	kostenlos, umsonst

Achtung, Fehlerquelle!

2. Beachten Sie den Unterschied zwischen *interesting* und *interested*:

a lot of **interesting** things	viele interessante Dinge
I'm **interested** in politics	ich („bin interessiert an") interessiere mich für Politik

3. Mit *just*, *right*, *so*, *very* und *bloody* können Sie einen Ausdruck verstärken:

isn't it **just** beautiful?	ist er nicht einfach wunderschön?
right in the middle	direkt / genau in der Mitte
we're **so** glad you came	wir freuen uns so, dass ihr gekommen seid
very expensive	sehr teuer
bloody expensive	verdammt teuer, sauteuer

Bloody (= verdammt, Scheiß-) ist ein häufig vorkommender Kraftausdruck, den man nur in lockerem Gespräch und unter seinesgleichen benutzt. (→ 8F3, 9G)

4. Für das deutsche „auch" hatten wir bisher *too*, *also* und eine Konstruktion mit *so* – und für verneintes „auch" das Wort *either*:

„auch" = too, also etc.

I run **too**	ich laufe auch
I'm **also** hungry	ich bin auch hungrig
I'm hungry – **so am** I	ich bin hungrig – ich auch
I'm not hungry **either**	ich bin auch nicht hungrig

5. Mit *speaking of* können Sie an Vorangegangenes anknüpfen, mit *if* hingegen eine Bedingung einführen:

speaking of Soho	da wir gerade von Soho sprechen, apropos Soho
if you are interested in politics	wenn du dich für Politik interessierst

Unit 2F

Focus on culture

1. *St James's Park:* der älteste (*the oldest*) und einer der schönsten (*one of the most beautiful*) der vielen Londoner Parks.

2. *Buckingham Palace:* seit 1837 offizielle Residenz der britischen Könige und Königinnen (*official residence of the British kings and queens*). Eine Haupttouristenattraktion (*main tourist attraction*) ist die Wachablösung (*Changing of the Guard*). Im August und September können Teile des Palasts besichtigt werden.

3. *Whitehall:* breite Straße mit Regierungsgebäuden, Sehenswürdigkeiten (u. a. das Gefallenendenkmal *the Cenotaph*) und der abzweigenden *Downing Street* mit *No. 10* (*Number Ten*), dem Amtssitz des Premierministers.

4. *Houses of Parliament:* gewaltiger neugotischer Gebäudekomplex an der Thames, in dem das aus Unterhaus (*House of Commons*) und Oberhaus (*House of Lords*) bestehende britische Parlament tagt.

5. *Westminster Abbey:* fast 1000 Jahre alte Krönungskirche der britischen *kings and queens* mit vielen Grabstätten britischer Monarchen und anderer Persönlichkeiten.

6. *Trafalgar Square:* größter Londoner Platz, nach der siegreichen Seeschlacht vor Trafalgar 1805 benannt, mit dem Denkmal für Admiral Nelson (*Nelson's Column*).

Admiral Nelson
1758–1805

7. *Piccadilly Circus:* zentraler Platz (Lichtreklamen, *Statue of Eros*), an dem fünf Durchgangsstraßen zusammenkommen.

8. *Soho:* kulturell durchmischter Stadtteil mit ethnischen Restaurants, Bars, Nachtklubs, *Chinatown*.

9. *Old Bailey:* zentrales Londoner Kriminalgericht (*Central Criminal Court*), Szene vieler berühmter Mordprozesse.

Unit 2G

Test yourself

Revision Crossword

ACROSS

5 da, dort
7 alles
11 Sammlung
12 scharf (gewürzt)
14 Gemälde
15 kostenlos
16 (zu Fuß) gehen
18 reizend
19 zuhören
20 Kirche
21 Baum

DOWN

1 aber
2 Ecke
3 (wunder)schön
4 Brücke
6 interessant
8 Gebäude
9 teuer
10 interessiert
13 (Straf-)Prozess
14 friedlich
17 besuchen

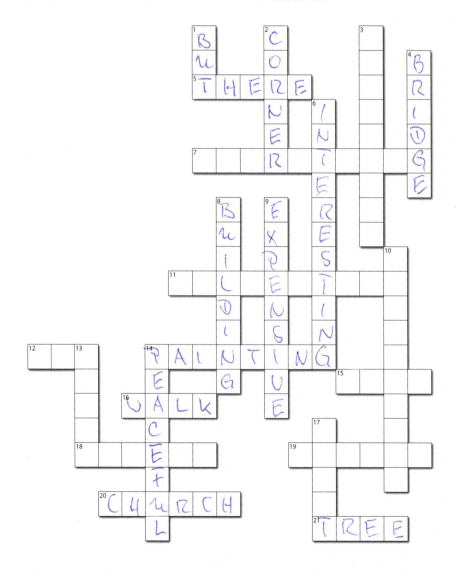

Hotel

Unit 3

- Have – has
- A – an
- What ... like?
- Can, will
- Let's ...
- „Schön"
- Wie man Bestätigung, Zustimmung, Freude ausdrückt
- ... and a souvenir from the gift shop!

Unit 3A

Dialogue

 1/10

■ = Anne
● = Paul

what ... like? = wie ... (beschaffen)?
overlooking = „überblickend"
go for a walk = einen Spaziergang machen
what about ...? = wie ist es mit ...?
your = dein, Ihr, euer
a view of = ein Ausblick auf
even = sogar

Talking about the hotel

■ What's the hotel like?
● Oh, it's old and it has charm and character. It's on a hill overlooking a lake.
■ Lovely. I suppose it's nice and quiet.
● Absolutely. It's very quiet and you can go for long walks. You can actually go swimming in the lake, but the hotel has an indoor pool too.
■ Good. What about your room – is it OK?
● Oh, it's bright and cheerful, quite large actually, and you have a view of the valley with the lake and the mountains beyond.
■ Terrific. And I suppose it has all the mod cons.
● Oh sure, a thousand TV channels, DVD, Internet, the lot. But what's really important: the bed has a duvet ...
■ Great, the best of both worlds!
● You're right. They even have a sauna and a Jacuzzi. It is an old hotel but absolutely state of the art.

Reden über das Hotel

■ Wie ist das Hotel (denn so)?
● Oh, es ist alt und hat Charme und Charakter. Es ist auf einem Berg / Hügel mit Blick auf einen See.
■ Sehr schön. Ich nehme an, es ist schön ruhig.
● Jawohl. Es ist sehr ruhig und man kann lange Spaziergänge machen. An sich kann man im See schwimmen gehen, aber das Hotel hat auch ein Hallenbad.
■ Gut! Wie ist es mit deinem Zimmer – ist es in Ordnung?
● Oh, es ist hell und freundlich, eigentlich recht groß, und man hat einen Ausblick auf das Tal mit dem See und den Bergen dahinter.
■ Toll! Und sicher hat es allen modernen Komfort.
● O ja, tausend Fernsehsender, DVD, Internet, alles. Aber was wirklich wichtig ist: das Bett hat ein Federbett ...
■ Prima, das Beste beider Welten!
● Du hast recht. Sie haben sogar eine Sauna und einen Whirlpool. Es ist ein altes Hotel, aber absolut auf dem neuesten Stand.

Rules and practice

Unit 3B

1 *It's on the tip of my tongue* (= es liegt mir auf der Zunge). Hier sind nochmal die wesentlichen Fakten über das Hotel. Können Sie die fehlenden Wörter einsetzen?

tip = Spitze
tongue = Zunge

The hotel is old and it has charm and _____. It's on a hill _____ a lake. It's _____ and quiet and you can _____ for long walks. Of course, you can go _____ in the lake, but the hotel has an indoor _____ too. My room is bright and _____ and you have a _____ of the valley with the lake and the mountains _____. The TV has _____ thousand channels, there's DVD and Internet, and what's really _____: the bed has a _____. The hotel is old _____ it has all the mod _____. It's absolutely state of the _____.

2 *Have* oder *has*?

Benutzen Sie *has* (= hat) bei *he/she/it* bzw. bei Einzahlwörtern, die durch *he/she/it* ersetzt werden können. Benutzen Sie in allen anderen Fällen *have*. (→ 1D2, 1D3)

he/she/it has –
I/you/we/they have

✎ Setzen Sie *have* oder *has* ein.

a This old hotel _____ charm and character.
b Many old hotels _____ charm and character.
c The hotel _____ an indoor pool.
d You _____ a view of the lake and the mountains.
e The room _____ a view of the mountains.
f London _____ many beautiful parks.
g Let's go and _____ a nice hot curry in a Soho restaurant.
h London's museums _____ many interesting collections.
i The British Museum _____ lots of interesting objects.
j I suppose you _____ a TV in your room.
k Paul _____ a TV in his room.
l Can I _____ a duvet?
m They _____ a sauna and a Jacuzzi.

33

Unit 3B

3 A oder an?

Der unbestimmte Artikel hat im Englischen zwei Formen: *a* oder *an*.
Die häufigere Form ist *a*:

a pool	ein Schwimmbad
a hotel	ein Hotel

Die seltenere Form *an* steht vor Wörtern, die mit einem Vokal (= Selbstlaut) beginnen:

an indoor pool	ein Hallenschwimmbad
an old hotel	ein altes Hotel

a hotel –
an old hotel

Setzen Sie *a* oder *an* ein.

a This is __a__ beautiful park.
b There's __a__ Indian restaurant in Denman Street.
c There's __a__ good Indian restaurant in Denman Street.
d There's __a__ expensive Indian restaurant in Denman Street.
e London is __a__ very expensive city.
f London is __a__ interesting city.
g I have __an__ uncle in New Zealand.
h I have __an__ strange uncle in New Zealand.

I suppose
ich vermute
davor or actually
dahinter

4 Bilden Sie Fragen mit *What's ... like?* und *What are ... like?* und beantworten Sie sie.

the hotel / very expensive → What's the hotel like? – It's very expensive.

what's the room like? = wie ist das Zimmer?
what are the rooms like? = wie sind die Zimmer?

a St James's Park / beautiful   What's it like
b the room / bright and cheerful   _____
c Tom / very nice   _____
d Sarah / a lovely girl   _____
e the Bombay Restaurant / good   _____
f Uncle Fred / a strange man   _____
g the paintings / very interesting _____
h the concerts / just wonderful   What are like
i the lake / very large and deep   _____
j the hotel / charm and character   _____

Unit 3B

5 Aussprache. Hier haben wir für Sie Wortgruppen zusammengestellt, an denen Sie die Aussprache systematisch üben können. Hören Sie genau hin und sprechen Sie mit.

1/11

Wörter, die auf der ersten Silbe betont werden:	*interesting, interested, duvet, actually*
Wörter, die auf der zweiten Silbe betont werden:	*hotel, weekend, expensive, museum*

Wörter mit stimmhaft (= weich) gelispeltem *th*:	*this, these, with, brother*
Wörter mit stimmlos (= zischend) gelispeltem *th*:	*throw, south, cloth, marathon*

Wörter mit anlautendem w, das im Englischen ähnlich einem „u" gesprochen wird:	*walk, way, well, what*
Wörter, die mit ch anfangen – achten Sie besonders auf *character*:	*cheerful, charm, chocolate* but *character*

Wörter, die mit einem ganz kurzen „a" gesprochen werden:	*bloody, curry, London, tongue*
Wörter, in denen ein bestimmter Buchstabe nicht gesprochen wird:	*building, business, interested, Buckingham*

Beachten Sie den Unterschied zwischen *quite* (1 Silbe) und *quiet* (2 Silben):	*It's quite quiet here.* (= Es ist ganz still hier.)

interesting = interessant
interested = interessiert
throw = Wurf, werfen
cheerful = fröhlich, heiter
tongue = Zunge
business = Geschäft

6 Hör-Sprech-Übung. In dieser Übung hören Sie Fragen von der CD, die Sie mit einem Satz beantworten sollen. Gelegentlich wird Ihre Antwort von der Musterantwort der CD abweichen. Das macht nichts. Wir üben hier schnelles Reagieren und Geläufigkeit. Machen Sie die Übung zwei- oder dreimal.

1/12

Sie hören zum Beispiel: ....Where's the hotel?
Sie sagen: ....It's on a hill.
Sie hören eine richtige Antwort: ....It's on a hill.
Sie wiederholen die Antwort: ....It's on a hill.

where? = wo?

Unit 3C

Reading text

1/13

From a hotel brochure

within =
  innerhalb
walking
  distance =
  „Gehentfernung"
among them =
  unter ihnen
AE center = BE
  centre
AE transportation
  = BE transport
accessible =
  zugänglich
as well = too =
  auch
will be = wird sein
available =
  erhältlich
gift = Geschenk
enjoy = genießen
excitement =
  Aufregung

The Eden Hotel is within walking distance of Broadway theatres, Fifth Avenue shopping and many famous Manhattan sights, among them Central Park, MoMA, Rockefeller Center and Times Square.
Public transportation is at our door and can take you in minutes to the Statue of Liberty, Wall Street, the Met, and the Empire State Building.
We are easily accessible from JFK, LaGuardia, and Newark airports. Penn Station and Grand Central Terminal are close by as well.
The concierge will be happy to arrange theatre tickets, restaurant reservations, transportation and sightseeing.
Souvenirs, postcards, stamps, maps, newspapers and magazines are available at the Eden Gift Shop.
At the Eden Hotel, you can enjoy all the excitement of New York at attractive prices.

Aus einem Hotelprospekt
Das Eden Hotel ist in Gehweite von Broadway-Theatern, Einkaufen auf der Fifth Avenue und vielen berühmten Sehenswürdigkeiten Manhattans, unter ihnen / darunter Central Park, MoMA, Rockefeller Center und Times Square.
Öffentliche Verkehrsmittel sind an unserer Tür und können Sie in Minuten zur Freiheitsstatue, Wall Street, dem Met (= Metropolitan Museum of Art [= Kunst]) und dem Empire State Building bringen.
Wir sind gut zu erreichen von den Flughäfen JFK, LaGuardia und Newark. (Die Bahnhöfe) Penn Station und Grand Central Terminal sind ebenfalls in der Nähe.
Der Hotelportier wird („glücklich sein zu arrangieren") sich gern kümmern um Theaterkarten, Tischreservierungen, Beförderungsmittel und Besichtigungen.
Souvenirs, Postkarten, Briefmarken, Stadtpläne/Landkarten, Zeitungen und Zeitschriften sind erhältlich im Eden-Geschenkladen.
Im Eden Hotel können Sie alle Aufregung / Spannung New Yorks bei attraktiven Preisen genießen.

Rules and practice

Unit 3D

1 Vervollständigen Sie die Sätze.

famous = berühmt
expensive = teuer
far away = weit weg

a Many of New York's famous theatres are on __Broadway__
b There are many expensive shops on __5th Avenue__
c MoMA is a __museum__ in New York City.
d JFK and LaGuardia are __Airports__ in New York City.
e Grand Central Terminal is a __Station__ in New York City.
f The Eden is an __old__ hotel in Manhattan.
g The Statue of Liberty is a famous New York __sights__ .
h St James's Park isn't __far away__ away from Buckingham Palace.
i There are many Indian ~~people~~ __lives__ in Soho.

2 Fragen mit *what* und *where* – beantworten Sie sie in ganzen Sätzen.

What's Grand Central Terminal? – It's a (big) station in New York (City).
Where's Hyde Park? – It's in London.

what = was
where = wo
big = groß
get = bekommen

a Where's Times Square? __It's in London NY__
b What's the Met? __It's a opera__
c Where are the Houses of Parliament? __the are in London__
d What are JFK and LaGuardia? __they are Airport in NY__
e What's Broadway? __It's with many theaters__
f Where are many expensive shops? __in the 5th Av__
g Where can you get souvenirs? __in a giftshop__

3 Sie und Ihr(e) Partner(in) sind als Touristen in New York City (NYC). Bilden Sie aus den nachstehenden Verben und Ergänzungen 9 *We can*-Sätze über Dinge, die Sie dort heute tun können.

We can buy / eat / go / have / take / visit ...

a bus to the Empire State Building __will take a bus__
a nice big hamburger in Times Square __will have eat__
for a walk in Central Park __will / go for a walk__
lunch at a Manhattan restaurant __will eat can have__

buy = kaufen
eat = essen
take = nehmen
visit = besuchen

Unit 3D

MoMA and the Met	will I	visit
shopping on Fifth Avenue	"	go shopping
souvenirs in the hotel gift shop	will I	can buy
swimming in the hotel pool	"	can visit
to a Broadway theatre	will I	can go to

we will eat =
  wir werden essen

4 Nun bilden Sie noch einmal 9 Sätze mit dem Sprachmaterial aus 3, diesmal aber mit *will* (= werden) statt *can*. Sie sagen also, was Sie in New York tun werden.

5 Mit den bisher gelernten Wörtern können Sie schon allerhand anfangen. Füllen Sie die Lücken im Dialog mit Wörtern aus der nachstehenden Liste.

actually, by, channels, cheerful, distance, DVD, have, Internet, isn't, it, like, place, prices, right, too, very

■ What's the Eden Hotel _like_ ?

● Oh, it's a good hotel, and it's _right_ in the middle of Manhattan, within walking _distance_ of a lot of New York sights. Many Broadway theatres are close _by_ .

■ Good. What about your room? Is it quiet?

close by =
  dicht dabei
what about …? =
  wie ist es mit …?
quiet = ruhig, still
quite large =
  recht groß

● Well, it isn't _very_ quiet. Manhattan isn't a quiet _place_ . But the room is OK. It's quite large _actually_ , and it's bright and _cheerful_ . There's _Internet_ access, a _DVD_ player, and the TV has a thousand _channels_.

■ Great. Is _it_ expensive?

● The hotel? No, it _isn't_ very expensive. And the _prices_ in the gift shop are OK too.

■ Lovely. Well, _have_ a good time in New York!

● Thanks.

6 Let's ...

Mit *let's* (= *let us* = „lass[t] uns") leitet man einen Vorschlag ein:

Let's go to Times Square.   *Lass(t) uns zum Times Square gehen / fahren.*

Übersetzen Sie alle folgenden Sätze unter Verwendung von *let's*.

a Lass uns zu Fuß gehen. — let's walk
b Lass uns einen Curry essen. —
c Lasst uns ins Britische Museum gehen. — let's go to
d Hören wir uns doch mal die Redner an! — why not we listen / let's listen to the speaker
e Lass uns einen Spaziergang machen. — let's go for a walk
f Gehen wir schwimmen! — let's go swimming
g Nehmen wir doch den Bus! — let's take the bus

walk = zu Fuß gehen
go for a walk = einen Spaziergang machen
go swimming = schwimmen gehen
take the bus = den Bus nehmen

7 Hör-Sprech-Übung. In dieser Übung üben wir Vorschläge mit *Let's ...*

Sie hören zum Beispiel: ....go shopping on Fifth Avenue
Sie sagen: ....Let's go shopping on Fifth Avenue.

1/14

Definitions Crossword

ACROSS
2 A place where you can look at old objects is a _____.
4 You can buy souvenirs in the hotel gift _____.
8 A place where you can eat is a _____.
9 A small mountain is a _____.
10 A place where you can watch a show is a _____.

DOWN
1 You can read the news in a _____.
3 An abbey is a large _____.
5 A place where travellers can sleep is a _____.
6 A sauna is a room where it's very _____.
7 The land between two mountains is a _____.

definition = Worterklärung
place = Ort
small = klein
read = lesen
news ≠ Nachrichten
abbey = Abtei
traveller = Reisende(r)
sleep = schlafen
between = zwischen

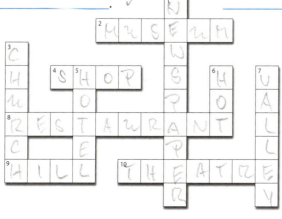

Unit 3D

Unit 3E

go = gehen, fahren
walk = (zu Fuß) gehen

Focus on words

1. Unterschied zwischen *go* und *walk*: Sowohl *go* als auch *walk* kann „gehen" heißen, aber *walk* betont, dass man zu Fuß geht:

| We can **go** to Soho. (*betont:* Soho) | Wir können (doch) nach Soho gehen. |
| We can **walk** to Soho. (*betont:* walk) | Nach Soho können wir laufen. |

Da *go* offenlässt, ob man zu Fuß geht oder mit einem Beförderungsmittel fährt, ist es auch das Verb, mit dem man „fahren" ausdrückt:

Let's **go** to an Indian restaurant.	Lass(t) uns in ein indisches Restaurant gehen.
Let's **go** to Times Square.	Lass(t) uns zum Times Square gehen / fahren.
Let's **go** to London.	Lass(t) uns nach London fahren.

2. Unterschiede zwischen *beautiful*, *fine*, *nice* und *lovely*: Jedes dieser vier Adjektive kann im Deutschen mit „schön" übersetzt werden, aber es bestehen deutliche Unterschiede zwischen den Bedeutungen:

beautiful = ästhetisch besonders ansprechend für Auge oder Ohr:

a beautiful / fine / nice / lovely girl

| a **beautiful** park / tree | ein (wunder)schöner Park / Baum |

fine = besonders eindrucksvoll für seine Art:

| a **fine** old tree | ein schöner / prächtiger alter Baum |

nice = nett, hübsch, gut, lecker:

a **nice** man	ein netter Mann
a **nice** curry	ein schöner / guter / leckerer Curry
a **nice** old house	ein schönes / hübsches / nettes altes Haus

lovely = schön, reizend, herrlich:

| what a **lovely** lake! | was für ein reizender / herrlicher See! |

3. Ausdrücke, mit denen man **Bestätigung**, **Zustimmung**, **Freude** ausdrückt. Die Beispiele zeigen Ihnen, wie Sie auf Äußerungen „positiv reagieren" können:

absolutely! = ja wirklich!
absolutely not! = nein keinesfalls!

I suppose it's nice and quiet.	Ich nehme an, es ist schön ruhig.
– **Absolutely**. It's very quiet.	– **Jawohl**, es ist sehr ruhig.
And I suppose it has all the mod cons.	Und sicher hat es allen modernen Komfort.
– **Oh sure …** / **Oh yes …**	– **O ja …**
Great, the best of both worlds!	Toll, das Beste beider Welten!
– **You're right**.	– **Du hast recht**.
The room is bright and cheerful.	Das Zimmer ist hell und freundlich.
– **Lovely**. / **Great**. / **Terrific**. / **Good**.	– **Sehr schön!** / **Prima!** / **Toll!** / **Gut!**

40

Unit 3F

Focus on culture

1. *Duvet*: (gesteppte) Bettdecke / Federbett (wie z. B. in Deutschland üblich), in GB erst in neuerer Zeit in Gebrauch statt der traditionell üblichen Kombination Wolldecke über großem Laken, die auf drei Seiten zwischen Matratze und Bettrahmen eingesteckt (*tucked in*) wird.

2. *Broadway*: älteste, 25 km lange Straße in Manhattan mit vielen Theatern, weshalb der Name oft in Verbindung mit „Theater" gebraucht wird: *a Broadway musical, a Broadway show*. Abseits vom *Broadway* befinden sich die vielen kleineren, oft experimentellen *off-Broadway theatres* (AE *theaters*).

3. *Fifth Avenue:* „Fünfte Allee", die von Osten gesehen fünfte der zwölf in Manhattan (von Südwesten nach Nordosten) verlaufenden *avenues*, die von *streets* rechtwinklig gekreuzt werden, woraus sich das für Manhattan typische Straßennetz (*grid*) ergibt.

4. *Central Park:* über 4 km langer, in der Mitte Manhattans gelegener Volkspark.

5. *MoMA: the Museum of Modern Art* (= Museum für moderne Kunst).

6. *Rockefeller Center:* architektonisch interessanter riesiger Wolkenkratzerkomplex mit *offices* (= Büros), Kultureinrichtungen, *shops* und *entertainment*-Angeboten.

7. *Times Square:* zentraler, nach der Zeitung *New York Times* benannter Platz im New Yorker *Theatre District*.

8. *Statue of Liberty:* „Freiheitsstatue" *in New York Harbour* (= im New Yorker Hafen), Geschenk Frankreichs an die USA, 1886 eingeweiht.

9. *Wall Street:* Straße in Manhattan, Zentrum des amerikanischen Finanzlebens.

10. *The Met: the Metropolitan Museum of Art*, eines der bedeutendsten *art museums* (= Kunstmuseen) der Welt.

11. *Empire State Building: famous skyscraper* (= Wolkenkratzer) mit zwei lohnenden *observation decks* (= Aussichtsplattformen), seit Zerstörung des *World Trade Center* (2001) wieder *the tallest building in New York* (= das höchste Gebäude New Yorks).

12. *JFK* (= *John F. Kennedy*), *LaGuardia*, *Newark:* die drei Großflughäfen New Yorks, der letztere nicht in New York, sondern im Staat *New Jersey*, etwa 24 km südwestlich von *Midtown Manhattan*.

13. *Penn Station, Grand Central Terminal: New York's rail stations* (= Bahnhöfe).

---

tuck in = (r)einstecken

avenue = Allee

art = Kunst

entertainment = Unterhaltung

harbour = Hafen

a tall building = ein hohes Gebäude
he's very tall = er ist sehr groß

rail = Schiene, Gleis

Unit 3G — Test yourself

Verstehen Sie Spaß? *Can you take a joke? Do you have a sense of humour?* Der folgende Test ist nämlich nicht ganz ernst gemeint.

Nicht ernst gemeint, aber gemein ist er! Also: Wir haben uns Mühe gegeben, Sie mit unseren „Ablenkantworten" kräftig zu irritieren. (Und ärgern Sie sich auch nicht darüber, dass hier einige Wörter vorkommen, die Sie noch nicht gelernt haben – sie sind in der Randleiste oder auf S. 191 erklärt.)

Wenn Sie bei allen 12 Fragen die zutreffende Antwort ankreuzen, sind Sie **sehr sehr gut**, wenn Sie es bei 10 Fragen schaffen, sind Sie **sehr gut** und bei 8 Richtigen immerhin noch **gut**.

Bei weniger als 8 Richtigen empfehlen wir Ihnen als Therapie eine Reise nach New York oder, ersatzweise, genaues Durchlesen der Erklärungen im Schlüssel (S. 191, dort finden Sie auch alle nötigen sprachlichen Erklärungen).
And now: Good luck!

Facts about New York City (NYC) – check the right answer.

Sidebar vocabulary:
- joke = Witz
- sense of humour = Sinn für Humor
- good luck! = viel Glück!
- capital = Hauptstadt
- state = (Bundes-)Staat
- population = Bevölkerung(szahl)
- bridge = Brücke
- borough = (Stadt-)Bezirk
- part = Teil
- smallest = kleinste
- black = schwarz
- pink = rosa
- island = Insel
- airport = Flughafen
- run = (Straße:) führen
- mounted police = berittene Polizei
- nickname = Spitzname
- apple = Apfel
- mammon = Reichtum (als Lebenszweck)

1. NYC is
   - [ ] the capital of the USA
   - [x] the capital of New York State
   - [x] the largest city in the USA

2. NYC is about
   - [x] 200
   - [x] 400
   - [ ] 600 years old

3. The population of NYC is about
   - [x] 8
   - [ ] 12
   - [ ] 16 million

4. NYC has about
   - [ ] 20
   - [ ] 200
   - [x] 2,000 bridges

5. Manhattan is
   - [x] a borough of NYC
   - [ ] a city
   - [ ] a part of a borough of NYC

6. The Empire State Building is the
   - [ ] oldest
   - [ ] smallest
   - [x] tallest skyscraper in NYC

7. NYC taxis are
   - [ ] black
   - [ ] pink
   - [x] yellow

8. The Statue of Liberty is
   - [ ] in Central Park
   - [x] on an island
   - [ ] on Fifth Avenue

9. Grand Central Terminal is
   - [ ] a part of an airport
   - [x] a station
   - [ ] an airport in NYC

10. [ ] 5th
    [ ] 12th
    [x] No
    Avenue runs through Central Park

11. MoMA is
    - [ ] a person
    - [x] a museum
    - [ ] the Manhattan Mounted Police

12. Which of the following is NOT a nickname of NYC?
    - [ ] the Big Apple
    - [ ] Gotham
    - [x] Mammon City

Bed and breakfast

Unit 4

- Making a reservation
- Frageform ohne *do*
- Frageform mit *do*
- Verneinte Form ohne *do*
- Verneinte Form mit *do*
- Was man (nicht) gern tut
- *-s*-Form des Verbs
- *... and no shortage of Manhattans!*

Unit 4A

Dialogue

1/15

■ = Man
● = Carol

do = tun
don't = do not = tun nicht
watch TV = „Fernsehen kucken"
by the way = übrigens
allow = erlauben
noise = Geräusch, Lärm
mean = meinen

Trying to make a reservation

■ Lovejoy Bed and Breakfast. Can I help you?
● Yes, hello. Do you have a vacancy for three nights from next Monday?

■ Single or double?
● Actually I need two rooms – a single and a double.
■ Oh I see. Let me just check … I don't have a single, but I can do two doubles – for 130 dollars, and 110 dollars.

● Hmm. – Are they non-smoking?
■ We only have non-smoking rooms.
● Good. What about TV? Can we watch the New York Jets?
■ Absolutely! We don't have TVs in the rooms, but there's a large television in the living room exclusively for our guests.
● Uh-huh. And … by the way, do you allow children?
■ No, I'm afraid we don't.
● Oh good. I don't like children's noise.
■ I see.
● But do you take dogs? We have a Yorkshire terrier.
■ Yes, if it's well-behaved. We have a German shepherd …
● Hmm. – You say in your ad you're right in the heart of Manhattan. How far are you from Grand Central Station?
■ About 1,300 miles.
● My goodness! What do you mean?
■ We're in Manhattan, Kansas.

Versuch, eine Reservierung vorzunehmen

■ Pension Lovejoy. Kann ich Ihnen helfen?
● Ja, hallo! Haben Sie ein Zimmer frei für drei Nächte von nächstem Montag an?

■ Einzelzimmer oder Doppelzimmer?
● Eigentlich brauche ich zwei Zimmer – ein Einzel- und ein Doppelzimmer.
■ Ah so. Lassen Sie mich grad mal nachsehen … Ich habe kein Einzelzimmer, aber ich kann Ihnen zwei Doppelzimmer anbieten – für 130 Dollar und 110 Dollar.

● Hm. – Sind es Nichtraucherzimmer?
■ Wir haben nur Nichtraucherzimmer.
● Gut. Wie ist es mit Fernsehen? Können wir die New York Jets sehen?
■ Ja natürlich! Wir haben keine Fernseher in den Zimmern, aber im Wohnzimmer ist ein großer Fernseher ausschließlich für unsere Gäste.
● Aha. Und … nebenbei, („erlauben") nehmen Sie Kinder?
■ Nein, leider nicht.
● O gut. Ich mag keinen Kinderlärm.
■ Ah so.
● Aber nehmen Sie Hunde? Wir haben einen Yorkshireterrier.
■ Ja, wenn er wohlerzogen ist. Wir haben einen Deutschen Schäferhund …
● Hm! – Sie sagen in Ihrer Anzeige, dass Sie direkt im Herzen Manhattans sind. Wie weit sind Sie vom Grand-Central-Bahnhof?
■ Etwa 1.300 Meilen.
● Meine Güte! Wie meinen Sie das?
■ Wir sind in Manhattan, Kansas.

Unit 4B

Rules and practice

1 Versuchen Sie sich zu erinnern, welche Wörter in die Lücken gehören.

- ■ Lovejoy Bed and Breakfast. Can I __help__ you?
- ● Yes, hello. __do__ you have a vacancy for three nights __from__ next Monday?
- ■ Single or __double__?
- ● Actually I __need__ two rooms – a single and a double.
- ■ Oh I see. __let__ me just check ... I __don't__ have a single, but I can (offer) __do__ two doubles – for 130 dollars, and 110 dollars.
- ● Hmm. – Are __they__ non-smoking?
- ■ We __only__ have non-smoking rooms.
- ● Good. What __about__ TV? Can we __watch__ the New York Jets?
- ■ Absolutely! We __don't__ have TVs in the rooms, but there's a large television in the living room __exclusively__ for our guests.
- ● Uh-huh. And ... by the way, __do__ you allow children?
- ■ No, I'm afraid we __don't__.
- ● But __do__ you take dogs? We __have__ a Yorkshire terrier.
- ■ Yes, __if__ it's well-behaved. We __have__ a German shepherd ...
- ● Hmm. – You say in your __ap__ you're right in the __heart__ of Manhattan. How __far__ are you from Grand Central Station?
- ■ About 1,300 __miles__.
- ● My goodness! What do you __mean__?
- ■ We're in Manhattan, __Kansas__

Unit 4B

are you interested in politics? = interessieren Sie sich für Politik?

2 Wie man Fragen formuliert

Bei *is*, *are*, *am* und Hilfsverben wie *can* wird die Frageform ähnlich wie im Deutschen gebildet, nämlich durch Umkehrung der Wortfolge gegenüber dem Aussagesatz:

Aussagesatz	Fragesatz
It is expensive.	**Is it** expensive?
You are interested in politics.	**Are you** interested in politics?
I can help you.	**Can I** help you?

Bei „Vollverben" (also „Nicht-Hilfsverben") hingegen bildet man die Frageform nicht durch Umstellung, sondern mit Hilfe einer Form von *do*:

Aussagesatz	Fragesatz	
You allow children.	**Do you allow** children?	*Tun Sie zulassen ...?*
You have a vacancy.	**Do you have** a vacancy?	*Tun Sie haben ...?*

like = mögen

✏️ Verwandeln Sie nun bitte die folgenden Aussagesätze in Fragen.

a The room is quiet.   *is the room quiet?*
b It's a non-smoking room.   *is it a*
c We can watch TV.   *can we*
d There's a television in the living room. *is there*
e You like children.   *do you like*
f They have a dog.   *do you have*
g You mean Grand Central Station. *do u mean*
h We can go swimming in the lake. *can we go*
i They only have non-smoking rooms. *have the*

3 Wie man Aussagen verneint

Die verneinte Form wird entsprechend der Frageform gebildet: durch Hinzufügen von *not* bzw. Anhängen von *-n't* an Hilfsverben (*is not / isn't*, *are not / aren't*, *cannot / can't* etc.) oder (bei Vollverben) durch Hinzunahme von *do not / don't* (= „tun / tut / tust nicht" etc.):

don't = do not = „tue / tun / tut / tust nicht"

Trafalgar Square **is not / isn't** far away.	*Trafalgar Square ist nicht weit entfernt.*
I **cannot / can't** see Toby. Where is he?	*Ich kann Toby nicht sehen. Wo ist er?*
I **do not / don't** like children's noise.	*Ich mag keinen Kinderlärm.*

✏️ Verneinen Sie nun bitte die folgenden Aussagen.

a The tickets are expensive.   *aren't*
b He's very well-behaved.   *he isn't*
c I can help you.   *can't*

Unit 4B

d   I watch TV a lot. — don't
e   They have a TV. — haven't
f   We allow dogs. — don't allow
g   We're in Manhattan. — aren't
h   You can swim in the lake. — can't
i   We go to concerts a lot. — don't go

4 Sprechen Sie nun über Dinge, die Sie gern tun bzw. nicht gern tun.

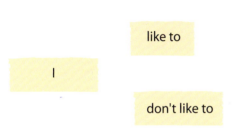

eat in restaurants.
go for long walks.
go shopping.
go to the theatre.
visit museums.
surf the Internet.
travel by bus / train / plane.
learn new things.
listen to gossip.

go shopping = einkaufen gehen
surf the Internet = im Internet surfen
travel by bus = mit dem Bus fahren
travel by plane = mit dem Flugzeug reisen
learn = lernen
gossip = Klatsch, Tratsch

5 Hör-Sprech-Übung. Machen Sie jetzt eine Übung mit der CD: Sie hören eine Frage und beantworten sie mit *No ...*

Sie hören zum Beispiel: ....Are you hungry?
Sie sagen: ....No I'm not.
Sie hören die richtige Antwort: ....No I'm not.
Sie wiederholen die Antwort: ....No I'm not.

1/16

6 Setzen Sie Präpositionen aus der folgenden Liste ein.

about, at, for, from, of, on, within

a   The hotel is __on__ a hill.
b   It's __about__ two miles __from__ here.
c   You can go __for__ long walks __from__ the hotel.
d   From my room I have a view __of__ the lake and the mountains.
e   The hotel is within walking distance __of__ the station.
f   There's a bus stop __at__ the door.
g   Souvenirs and newspapers are available __at__ the gift shop.

Unit 4C

Reading text

1/17

book a room = ein Zimmer buchen
twin = Zwilling
twin room = Zweibettzimmer
two people = zwei Personen
B&B = bed and breakfast = Frühstückspension
it's all right with her = es ist ihr recht
doesn't = does not = tut nicht
as long as = solange
bark = bellen
attack = angreifen
there are four = es gibt vier
borough = (Stadt-)Bezirk
called = genannt

Of beds, children and Manhattans
Carol wants to book a double room for three nights. There's a difference between a double room and a twin room. A double room has one large bed for two people while a twin has two single beds.
The Lovejoy B&B doesn't allow children. That's all right with Carol because she doesn't like children's noise. Carol's Yorkshire terrier, however, is welcome as long as it doesn't bark too much and doesn't attack the German shepherd.
But there's a small problem. Carol wants a room in Manhattan, New York, not in Manhattan, Kansas. The B&B is just a little too far from Grand Central.
Actually, there are four Manhattans in the United States: Apart from the borough of New York City and the city in Kansas there's the village of Manhattan in Illinois and the town of Manhattan in Montana. There's also a cocktail called manhattan, but that's another story.

Von Betten, Kindern und Manhattans
Carol möchte ein Doppelzimmer für drei Nächte reservieren/buchen. Es besteht ein Unterschied zwischen einem *double room* und einem *twin room*. Ein *double room* hat ein großes Bett für zwei Personen , während ein *twin* (wörtlich = „Zwilling") zwei Einzelbetten hat.
Das *Lovejoy B&B* („erlaubt") nimmt keine Kinder. Das ist Carol recht, da sie Kinderlärm nicht mag. Carols Yorkshireterrier ist jedoch willkommen, solange er nicht zu viel bellt und den Deutschen Schäferhund nicht angreift.
Aber es besteht ein kleines Problem. Carol möchte ein Zimmer in Manhattan, New York, nicht in Manhattan, Kansas. Das *B&B* ist einfach ein bisschen zu weit vom (New Yorker) *Grand Central*(-Bahnhof) (entfernt).
Tatsächlich / Eigentlich / An sich gibt es vier Manhattans in den Vereinigten Staaten: Abgesehen von dem Bezirk der Stadt New York und der Stadt in Kansas gibt es das Dorf Manhattan in Illinois und die (Klein-)Stadt Manhattan in Montana. Es gibt auch einen Cocktail namens Manhattan, aber das ist eine andere Geschichte.

Rules and practice

Unit 4D

1 Verb mit -s oder ohne -s? (→ 1D2, 3B2)

Wir erinnern uns: Die **-s-Form** des Verbs (*wants*, *has*, *doesn't* etc.) benutzen wir mit *he/she/it* oder Wörtern, die durch *he/she/it* ersetzt werden können; bei *I/you/we/they* oder Mehrzahlwörtern gebrauchen wir die Form **ohne -s** (*want*, *have*, *don't* etc.). Hilfsverben wie *can* und *will* haben keine -s-Form.

doesn't have = hat nicht
does he understand? = versteht er?

he / she / it / Jack / Carol / the room	**has** a double bed
I / you / we / they / these hotels only	**have** non-smoking rooms
he / she / it / Jack / Carol / the room	**doesn't have** Internet access
I / you / we / they / many B&Bs	**don't have** Internet access
does he / she / it / Jack / Carol / the dog understand English?	
do you / they / these people understand English?	
I / you / we / they / he / she / Carol	**can / will** visit the National Gallery

✎ Mit oder ohne -s?

a She always (walk) __walks__ through the park.
b We sometimes (have) __have__ a curry in an Indian restaurant.
c She (can) __can__ watch the Changing of the Guard.
d My dog never (listen) __listens__ to me.
e The hotel (overlook) __overlooks__ the lake.
f Many hotels (don't) __allow__ allow dogs.
g The Lovejoy B&B (don't) __doesn't__ allow children under twelve.
h The bus (will) __will__ take you to Grand Central in minutes.
i Some people (like) __likes__ children's noise.
j (Do) __does__ the Eden Hotel have non-smoking rooms?
k (Do) __does__ the concierge arrange theatre tickets?
l Our dog (don't) __doesn't__ bark a lot.

always = immer
sometimes = manchmal
never = nie(mals)
overlook a lake = Blick auf einen See haben

2 Aussspracheübung. Hören Sie genau hin und sprechen Sie mit.

Betonung auf der ersten Silbe:	problem, difference, vacancy, actually
Betonung auf der zweiten Silbe:	all right, attack, TV, exclusively
Betonung auf der dritten Silbe:	Illinois, well-behaved, Yorkshire terrier
Ganz kurzes *a* in der ersten Silbe:	wonderful, lunchtime, borough, double
Wörter mit der Buchstabenfolge *ea*:	eat, great, heart, breakfast

1/18

heart = Herz

Unit 4D

does she like to read? = liest sie gern?

3 Stellen Sie Fragen über Ihre(n) Partner(in) oder eine(n) Freund(in) und beantworten Sie sie. (Beispiel: *Does she like dogs? – No she doesn't like dogs.*)

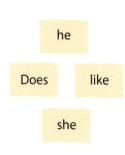

B&Bs / children / dogs / noise?
big trees / expensive hotels?
to eat in restaurants?
to go to the theatre?
to go for long walks?
to listen to classical music?
to read / to shop / to swim?
to surf the Internet?
to travel by plane?
to visit museums?
to watch TV?

Yes he/she likes …

No he/she doesn't like …

4 Antworten Sie ganz einfach, aber in ganzen Sätzen.

a What's a double room? _____

b What's a twin room? _____

c What's a Yorkshire terrier? _____

d What's Grand Central? _____

e What's Kansas? _____

f What's a manhattan? _____

g What does B&B mean? _____

h What do dogs do? _____

i What's Westminster Abbey? _____

j What can you watch at the Old Bailey? _____

5 Test zur Wiederholung. Übersetzen Sie.

a Dieses B&B hat nur Nichtraucherzimmer. _____

b Carol mag keinen Kinderlärm. _____

c Das B&B nimmt Hunde, aber es nimmt keine Kinder. _____

d Carol will kein Zweibettzimmer. _____

e Carols Hund bellt nicht sehr viel. _____

f Hat das Hotel ein Hallenschwimmbad? _____

g Hat es eine Sauna? _____

h Machen die Hunde viel Lärm? _____

make a lot of noise = viel Lärm machen
go to the theatre = ins Theater gehen

i Geht sie gern ins Theater? _____
j Gehen sie gern ins Theater? _____
k Gehen Sie gern ins Theater? _____

Unit 4D

Traveller's Crossword

airbnb

ACROSS
5 A barking dog makes a lot of _noise_.
7 A building where a train arrives is a _station_.
8 The first meal of the day is _breakfast_
9 If you travel with a dog, you can't go to a hotel where dogs are not _allowed_
11 Kansas is a US _state_.
12 A house is a kind of _building_.
13 If you want to be sure that information is correct, you have to _check_.

DOWN
1 The day of the week between Sunday and Tuesday is _monday_
2 Someone who is staying in a hotel or B&B is a _guest_.
3 Times Square, Broadway and Wall Street are all in the New York borough of _manhattan_.
4 A manhattan is a kind of _cocktail_
6 If a B&B doesn't have a room available for you, it has no _vacancies_.
10 A room for two people to stay in is a _double_.

arrive = ankommen
first = erste(r, s)
meal = Mahlzeit
allowed = erlaubt
kind = Art
want to be = sein wollen
sure = sicher
available = verfügbar, frei

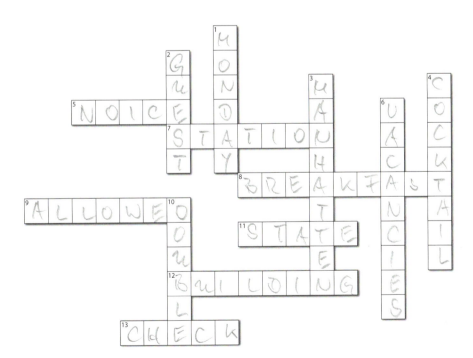

Unit 4E

Focus on words

1. *A* **vacancy** ist „eine Vakanz", übrigens auch im beruflichen Sinn von „freie / offene / unbesetzte Stelle". In unserem Dialog aber ist *a* **vacancy** „ein freies Zimmer". Entsprechend steht an *B&Bs* meist schon an der Tür oder im Fenster ein Schild: entweder **VACANCIES** (= Zimmer frei) oder **NO VACANCIES** (= belegt).

2. *A* **single** ist in unserem Text ein Einzelzimmer (abgeleitet vom Adjektiv *single* = „einzeln"), kann aber auch „eine Einzelfahrkarte" sein: *Two* **singles** *to Glasgow* (= Zwei Einzelfahrkarten nach Glasgow). Eine „Rückfahrkarte" wäre im BE *a return ticket* oder einfach *a return*: *Two* **returns** *to Dartford*. Statt *return ticket* sagen die Amerikaner **round-trip ticket**. – Der/Die deutsche „Single" ist auch englisch *a* **single**, **singlehood** ist „das Singledasein" und *a* **single** *mother* ist „eine alleinerziehende Mutter".

3. *Let me just* **check** (= lassen Sie mich nur gerade mal nachsehen): *Check* ist hier in seiner Grundbedeutung „überprüfen / kontrollieren / checken" gebraucht, aber dieses Verb hat in den letzten Jahrzehnten seinen Anwendungsbereich enorm erweitert:

You **check in** at the airport.	*Sie checken (sich) am Flughafen ein.*
You **check (in)** your bag.	*Sie geben Ihre Reisetasche auf.*
You **check into** your hotel.	*Sie melden sich im Hotel an.*
You **check out of** your hotel.	*Sie reisen ab.*
You **check** a website	*Sie schauen auf einer Website nach.*
You **check** the news.	*Sie sehen, was es an Nachrichten gibt.*

Ganz besonders aktuell ist **check out** im Sinn „in Augenschein nehmen, um zu sehen, ob er/sie/es einem gefällt": *Let's* **check out** *the new restaurant* (= Lass uns doch mal sehen, wie das neue Restaurant ist).

4. *Do you* **allow** *children / dogs?* („Lassen Sie Kinder / Hunde zu? / Nehmen Sie auch ...?"): Statt *allow* hier auch *take*. Die Grundbedeutung von *allow* ist „erlauben / gestatten / zulassen": *Smoking is not* **allowed** *here* (= das Rauchen ist hier nicht gestattet), **NO DOGS ALLOWED / DOGS NOT ALLOWED** (= Hunde müssen draußen bleiben).

5. **Children** (= Kinder) ist eine unregelmäßige (also nicht mit *-s* gebildete) Mehrzahlform; die Einzahl ist **child** (*i* wie in *while*). (→ 9D3)

6. *I'm* **afraid** heißt eigentlich „ich habe Angst": *I'm* **afraid** *of the dog* (= ich habe Angst vor dem Hund). Sehr wichtig geworden ist *I'm afraid* aber auch als Einleitung zu einer vom Sprecher bedauerten Aussage und entspricht dann dem deutschen „leider": *I'm* **afraid** *she isn't in* (= sie ist leider nicht da), *I'm* **afraid** *I have some bad news* (= ich habe leider eine schlechte Nachricht).

what are you afraid of? = wovor hast du Angst?

7. *If it's well-behaved*: *It* bezieht sich hier auf einen Hund. Wenn es sich um einen „persönlich bekannten" Hund bzw. eine Hündin handelt (→Toby in 1A), würde man entsprechend *he* oder *she* sagen: *He's / She's a very nice dog*.

8. *1,300 miles*: Mit dem Komma werden in Zahlen die Tausender kenntlich gemacht, es entspricht also dem deutschen Punkt: „1.300 Meilen". *1 mile = 1.6 kilometres* (= 1,6 km – dem englischen Dezimalpunkt entspricht also das deutsche Dezimalkomma).

Unit 4F

Focus on culture

1. Einzelheiten, die man mit dem B&B oder Hotel vielleicht klären möchte:
   a *How much do you charge for ...?* (= Was berechnen Sie für ...?)
   b *Do you offer senior discounts?* (= Bieten Sie Ermäßigungen für Senioren an?)
   c *What's your cancellation policy?* (= Wie sind Ihre Stornierungsbedingungen?)
   d *Can I pay by credit card?* (= Kann ich mit Kreditkarte bezahlen?)
   e *Where do I park my car?* (= Wo parke ich mein Auto?)
   f *What time do you serve breakfast?* (= Um welche Zeit gibt es Frühstück?)
   g *Do you offer a vegetarian / an organic breakfast?* (= Bieten Sie ein vegetarisches Frühstück / ein Bio-Frühstück an?)
   h *Is the house suitable for wheelchair users?* (= Ist das Haus geeignet für Rollstuhlfahrer?)
   i *What time is check-in / check-out?* (= Wann kann man anreisen / muss man abreisen?)
   j *Is there a(n) TV / phone / DVD player / ... in the room?* (= Ist in dem Zimmer ein Fernseher / DVD-Abspielgerät / ...?)
   k *Does the room have Internet access* (= Internetzugang)?
   l Mitunter wird Ihnen gesagt: *The room is en suite* (gesprochen: „on swieht"). Auf diese eigenartige Weise wird ausgedrückt: *The room has a private bathroom.*

2. *How many states are there in the United States?*
Ja, wie viele Bundesstaaten sind es? Fragen Sie in Ihrem Bekanntenkreis und Sie werden viele verschiedene Antworten bekommen: so zwischen 48 und 52. Die 48 ergibt sogar einen gewissen Sinn – *it makes sense. Why?* Nun, wenn Sie sich eine politische Karte der USA (*a political map of the USA*) anschauen, so sehen Sie da 48 Staaten „an einem Stück", die man deshalb auch *the 48 contiguous states* nennt (*contiguous*, mit Betonung auf der zweiten Silbe, ist ein seltenes, schwieriges Wort, das „aneinandergrenzend / sich berührend" bedeutet). Zu diesen 48 Staaten kamen 1959 Alaska und Hawaii als „nicht an die 48 grenzend" hinzu. Es sind also 50 Bundesstaaten: *There are 50 states in the United States* oder, wie man auch sagt: *in the Union.* Bei *New York* ist zwischen *New York City* und *New York State* zu unterscheiden, wobei die Stadt im Staat liegt und deshalb so bezeichnet wird: *New York, New York*; oder *New York, NY.*

3. *New York Jets*
Bekanntes Profiteam im *American Football*, der – vollkommen anders als „unser" Fußball – mit einem ovalen Ball äußerst körperbetont und daher mit Schutzausrüstung gespielt wird. *Football* ist die beliebteste Sportart (*the most popular sport*) der USA.

1/19

charge = berechnen
offer = anbieten
discount = Rabatt
cancellation = Streichung
policy = (Geschäfts-)Politik
organic = Bio(-)
suitable = geeignet
wheelchair = Rollstuhl
phone = Telefon

make sense = einleuchten
map = Landkarte, (Stadt-)Plan
contiguous = aneinandergrenzend

Unit 4G

1/20

Test yourself

Für diesen Test benötigen Sie die Tonaufnahme. Dort hören Sie einen Telefondialog, in dem es um eine Zimmerreservierung bei einem Hotel (*reserving a room at a hotel*) geht. Versuchen Sie die wesentlichen Angaben zu verstehen und kreuzen Sie die Antworten im nachstehenden Test entsprechend an.

Zwei Vokabelhilfen:
hairdryer (*dryer* reimt sich mit „Flyer")   Haartrockner / Föhn
DVD (gesprochen „diewie<u>die</u>")   (kurz für:) DVD-Player

Gedruckt finden Sie den Dialog auf Seite 192, aber beantworten Sie die Fragen am besten nach dem bloßen (gegebenenfalls mehrfachen) Hören.

reserve a room = ein Zimmer reservieren
want (to) = wollen
£18 = **18 pounds** = 18 Pfund
include = einschließen
bath(room) = Bad(ezimmer)

The man wants to book
☐ a double room   ☒ a single room   ☐ a twin room

He wants the room
☒ for Friday night   ☒ from Friday to Sunday   ☐ from now to Friday

The hotel has
☒ a double room   ☐ a single room   ☐ no vacancies

The hotel
☐ can't offer a room   ☒ offers a double room   ☐ offers a single room

The price per night of a single room is
☐ £18   ☒ £80   ☐ £118

The price includes
☒ a big breakfast   ☐ a small breakfast   ☐ no breakfast

The room has
☒ a private bathroom   ☐ a separate bathroom   ☐ no bathroom

The man
☒ doesn't want a DVD player   ☐ doesn't have a DVD player   ☐ wants a DVD player

Down under

Unit 5

- ❯ Verlaufsform oder einfache Form?
- ❯ Verlaufsform für künftige Handlungen
- ❯ Pronomen: besitzanzeigende Fürwörter
- ❯ *The fancy verb "fancy"*
- ❯ *Is it "is it?" or "isn't it?"?*
- ❯ *Work in York and love in a cove*
- ❯ *... and a challenge for those with a fear of heights!*

Unit 5A

Dialogue

1/21

■ = Colin
● = Ann

call = anrufen
busy = beschäftigt
keep busy = viel zu tun haben
off to India = (ab) nach Indien
the same = der-/die-/das-selbe
get married = heiraten

Diese Lektion beginnt mit einem Telefongespräch zwischen zwei Leuten in England und endet – irgendwie – *down under*, wie man umgangssprachlich Australien und/oder Neuseeland nennt. Eine E-Mail lockt uns nach Sydney, das sich seinen *nickname* (= Spitznamen) *the Harbour City* damit verdiente, dass es um einen Hafen herum gebaut wurde. *And what a harbour!* Es kommen hier vier Dinge zusammen, die alle schon als *one of the most beautiful in the world* bezeichnet worden sind: *the city, the harbour, the Sydney Harbour Bridge, and the Sydney Opera House. See you in Sydney!*

Chatting on the phone

■ Hello! ... Colin here.
● Colin, what a surprise! Nice of you to call. How are you doing?
■ Oh fine, thanks. And you? Keeping busy?
● Very much so. We've got the grandchildren here and they're keeping us on our toes.
■ I can imagine. Rebecca ... how old is she now? At least nine.
● Eleven actually, Abigail is eight, and Jessica is five.
■ Goodness, how time flies! Before you know it, they're grown up and off to Australia, Mexico or India with their boyfriends. – Speaking of grown children, where's the proud mother of your lively granddaughters?
● Off to Australia, with her partner.
■ The girls' father?
● The very same.
■ And what are they doing down under? Taking a weekend break? Sunset and dinner in Sydney harbour, then back to grey old England?
● They're getting married in Sydney.
■ Fancy travelling ten thousand miles to get married. But then, who wants to get married in the local church these days?

Plaudern am Telefon

■ Hallo! ... Hier ist Colin.
● Colin, was für eine Überraschung! Nett, dass du anrufst. Wie geht's dir denn so?
■ O gut, danke! Und dir? Immer noch viel zu tun?
● Ja, sehr. Wir haben die Enkelkinder hier, und die halten uns („auf unsern Zehen") auf Trab.
■ Das kann ich mir vorstellen. Rebecca ... wie alt ist sie jetzt? Mindestens neun.
● Sogar schon elf, Abigail ist acht, und Jessica ist fünf.
■ Meine Güte, wie die Zeit („fliegt") verfliegt! Eh man sich's versieht, sind sie erwachsen und auf dem Weg nach Australien, Mexiko oder Indien mit ihrem Freund. – Apropos erwachsene Kinder, wo ist die stolze Mutter eurer lebhaften Enkeltöchter?
● Nach Australien, mit ihrem Lebensgefährten.
■ Dem Vater der Mädchen?
● Genau dem.
■ Und was machen sie in Australien? Machen sie einen Wochenendurlaub? Sonnen-untergang und Abendessen im Hafen von Sydney, dann zurück ins graue alte England?
● Sie heiraten in Sydney.
■ Na so was – zehntausend Meilen reisen, um zu heiraten. Aber andererseits, wer will heute noch in der Kirche am Ort heiraten?

Unit 5B

Rules and practice

1 Verlaufsform oder einfache Form?

Der Dialog 5A enthält einige Beispiele für eine Verbform, die im Deutschen keine direkte Entsprechung hat, die **Verlaufsform**:

They **are keeping** us on our toes.	Sie („sind haltend") halten uns ganz schön auf Trab.
What **are** they **doing** down under?	Was („sind sie tuend") machen sie denn in Australien?
Are they **taking** a weekend break?	(„Sind sie nehmend") Machen sie einen Wochenendurlaub?

Mit der **Verlaufsform** betont man, dass die Handlung gerade abläuft, dass sie vorübergehender Natur ist.

Das Gegenteil der Verlaufsform ist die **einfache Form**. Bei der einfachen Form fällt die Betonung des Geradeablaufens, des „nur vorübergehend so Seins" weg. Sie berichtet unanschaulich, registriert einfach, dass etwas geschieht oder so ist. Sie ist auch die Zeitform, mit der man Gewohnheitshandlungen ausdrückt.

How time **flies** (*nicht:* is flying)!	Wie die Zeit verfliegt! (Allgemeine Lebenserfahrung)
They **have** (*nicht:* are having) three granddaughters.	Sie haben drei Enkelinnen. („Besitz")
I always **walk** (*nicht:* am always walking) through the park.	Ich gehe immer durch den Park. (Gewohnheitshandlung)

Mitunter besteht zwischen Verlaufsform und einfacher Form ein wesentlicher Bedeutungsunterschied:

What **are you doing**? – I'm watching a show.	Was machst du gerade? – Ich seh mir 'ne Show an.
What **do you do**? – I'm a doctor.	Was machen Sie beruflich? – Ich bin Arzt / Ärztin.

Verlaufsform betont das „Geradeablaufen"

Unit 5B

win – winning =
 gewinnen –
 gewinnend
at the moment =
 im Moment
is that you? =
 bist du es?
where ... from? =
 von wo ...?
hear = hören

✎ Setzen Sie nun in den folgenden Sätzen die jeweils angemessene Form ein.

a She (call) __calling__ her grandfather every weekend.

b "(you call) __you are calling__ from London? Goodness, what (you do) __do you do__ in London?"

c When the weather is fine, thousands of people (watch) __are watching__ the Changing of the Guard.

d "What (you watch) __do you watching__?" – "The New York Jets. They (win) __will win__."

e We (sometimes have) _____ a curry in an Indian restaurant.

f I (never take) _____ a taxi.

g I (read) _____ an interesting book at the moment. It's about Sydney.

h "Why (the dog bark) _____?" – "There's someone at the door."

i Yorkshire terriers (bark) _____ a lot.

j "Oh, is that you, Colin? Where (you call) _____ from?"

k (all the rooms have) _____ Internet access?

l "Hello, Colin, can you hear me? The children (make) _____ a lot of noise. We've got the grandchildren here while their parents (get) _____ married in Australia."

2 My, your, his etc.: Die besitzanzeigenden Pronomen

Der Gebrauch der besitzanzeigenden Pronomen (= Fürwörter) bietet keine besonderen Schwierigkeiten, abgesehen von den vier verschiedenen Entsprechungen für das deutsche „ihr / Ihr". Hier unterscheiden wir:

Bezug auf eine **weibliche Person** (*she* → **her**):

She's in Australia with **her** partner.	*Sie ist in Australien mit **ihrem** Partner.*

Bezug auf ein **Mehrzahlwort** (*they* → **their**):

The children are in **their** room.	*Die Kinder sind in **ihrem** Zimmer.*

Bezug auf eine **Sache** oder ein **nicht personifiziertes Tier** (*it* → **its**):

Every city has **its** problems.	*Jede Stadt hat **ihre** Probleme.*

Bezug auf eine im Deutschen mit „Sie" angeredete Person (*you* → **your**):

You say in **your** ad ...	*Sie sagen in **Ihrer** Anzeige ...*

Setzen Sie jeweils das naheliegendste Pronomen aus der folgenden Liste ein.

Unit 5B

my, your, his, her, its, our, their

love = lieben
guest = Gast
careful = sorgfältig
choice = (Aus-)Wahl
enemy = Feind

a Every mother loves _her_ children.
b Guests can enjoy _their_ drinks in the hotel bar.
c I like the hotel for _its_ old-world charm.
d The children are keeping us on _our_ feet.
e The Queen is very fond of _her_ dogs.
f We love the park with _its_ fine old trees.
g Where can I park _my_ car?
h A man cannot be too careful in the choice of _his_ enemies.
i You can't be too careful in the choice of _your_ hotel.

3 *Fancy travelling ten thousand miles to get married!*

1/22

Das Verb *fancy* heißt in der Grundbedeutung „sich (etwas) vorstellen", hat aber eine Reihe von umgangssprachlichen Verwendungen, die sich nicht immer direkt ins Deutsche übertragen lassen. Beispiele:

Fancy that!	Stell dir das vor! / Na so was! / Sieh mal an!
Fancy seeing you here!	Nein, dass ich dich hier treffe!
Fancy getting married in a helicopter!	Stell dir das nur vor – in einem Hubschrauber zu heiraten!
Fancy getting married in a helicopter?	Hätten Sie Lust, in einem Hubschrauber zu heiraten?
Fancy a weekend in London?	Hätten Sie Lust auf ein Wochenende in London?
Nobody fancies getting up in the middle of the night.	Niemand steht gern mitten in der Nacht auf.
I think she fancies older men.	Ich glaube, sie steht auf ältere Männer.

Schließlich können Sie *fancy* auch als Adjektiv benutzen, so etwa, wenn Sie von einem *fancy hotel* oder *fancy restaurant* reden und damit eines meinen, das ausgefallen, schick und natürlich teuer ist, was dann ebenfalls mit *fancy* ausgedrückt werden kann: *fancy prices* sind überhöhte Preise, die man als vernünftiger Mensch nicht bezahlt.

a fancy restaurant = ein ausgefallenes Restaurant

Unit 5C

sit = sitzen
while = während
work out =
 Fitnesstraining
 machen
across the water =
 über das Wasser
light = Licht
behind = hinter
climb = klettern
climb something =
 auf etw klettern
did = tat(en)
below = unter
cove =
 (kleine) Bucht
a fear of heights =
 Höhenangst

Reading text

Email from Sydney

Dear Mum and Dad,
I am sitting at my laptop while Steve is working out in the gym.
The hotel is just fantastic.
From our window, across the water, I can see the Opera House in the evening light. Right behind our hotel is the famous Harbour Bridge. Many people climb the bridge, and we did too. What a view! Far below you are the cars on the bridge and the ships in the water, all around you is Sydney with its coves and islands and tall buildings, and in the distance the mountains on one side and the open sea on the other. By the way, it's the largest steel-arch bridge in the world and you actually climb 134 metres into the sky! Not the best pastime for those with a fear of heights, is it?
Tomorrow we're flying back. 22 hours cramped in a small seat. But we'll survive.
Love,
Claire

E-Mail aus Sydney
Liebe Mama, lieber Papa,
ich sitze an meinem Laptop, während Steve im Fitnessraum sein Fitnesstraining macht. Das Hotel ist einfach fantastisch.
Von unserm Fenster aus, über das Wasser, kann ich das Opernhaus im Abendlicht sehen. Direkt hinter unserm Hotel ist die berühmte Hafenbrücke. Viele Leute erklettern die Brücke, und wir taten das auch. Was für ein Ausblick! Weit unter einem sind die Autos auf der Brücke und die Schiffe im Wasser, ganz um einen herum ist Sydney mit seinen Buchten und Inseln und hohen Gebäuden, und in der Ferne die Berge auf einer Seite und das offene Meer auf der anderen. Übrigens ist sie die größte Stahlbogenbrücke der Welt und man klettert tatsächlich 134 Meter in die Luft / in den Himmel. Nicht der beste Zeitvertreib für Leute mit Höhenangst, nicht wahr / was?
Morgen fliegen wir zurück. 22 Stunden eingezwängt in einem kleinen Sitz. Aber wir werden (es) überleben.
Alles Liebe / Herzliche Grüße
Claire

Rules and practice

Unit 5D

1 Noch einmal: die Verlaufsform (→ 5B1)

Unser Text (5C) enthält zwei weitere Beispiele für den Gebrauch der Verlaufsform, den wir bereits kennengelernt haben, nämlich Betonung des „gerade stattfindenden Ablaufs" einer Handlung:

I **am sitting** at my laptop while Steve **is working out** in the gym.   *Ich sitze hier an meinem Laptop, während Steve im Fitnessraum trainiert.*

In einem weiteren Beispiel jedoch bezeichnet die Verlaufsform nicht eine gerade ablaufende, sondern eine für die Zukunft geplante Handlung:

Tomorrow we **are flying back**.   *Morgen fliegen wir zurück.*

tomorrow = morgen

Dieser Gebrauch der Verlaufsform ist möglich, wenn der Zukunftsbezug durch eine Zeitbestimmung der Zukunft erkennbar gemacht wird, hier durch *tomorrow*.

✎ Üben Sie diese Konstruktion nun mit Sätzen nach folgendem Muster:

visit / the museum / on Friday → They are visiting the museum on Friday.

a go / swimming / this afternoon _____
b watch / TV / tonight _____
c go / to the British Museum / tomorrow _____
d take / a break / this weekend _____
e get / married / next month _____
f serve / breakfast / in half an hour _____

take a break = ausspannen
next month = nächsten Monat
in half an hour = in einer halben Stunde

2 Setzen Sie die fehlenden Wörter ein.

a I am sitting __at__ my laptop __while__ Steve is working out in the gym.
b The Opera House is __across__ the water __across from__ our hotel.
c The famous Sydney Harbour Bridge is right __behind__ our hotel.
d Many people __climbed__ the bridge, and we __did__ too.
e The __view__ from the bridge is one of the most beautiful __in__ the world.
f Sydney with __its__ coves and islands and tall buildings is all __around__ you.
g The cars __on__ the bridge and the ships in the water are far __below__ you.
h The __top__ of the bridge is 134 __metres__ above the water.
i If you have a fear of heights, __don't__ climb the bridge!

Unit 5D

3 Is it? = „nicht wahr?" / „was?" (→ 1D4)

In 1D4 haben wir bereits das Frageanhängsel *isn't it?* kennengelernt und es mit „nicht wahr?" übersetzt. Wir haben aber auch gleich festgestellt, dass das englische Frageanhängsel nicht immer gleich bleibt, sondern sich nach dem richtet, was vorne steht:

The view is fantastic, isn't **it**?	Die Aussicht ist fantastisch, nicht wahr / nech?
Joe is fantastic, isn't **he**?	Joe ist fantastisch, nicht wahr / nech?
Anna is fantastic, isn't **she**?	Anna ist fantastisch, nicht wahr / nech?

Jetzt lernen wir, dass das Frageanhängsel auch *is it/he/she?* sein kann, nämlich dann, wenn das vorangehende *is* verneint ist:

(**It's**) **Not** the best pastime for those with a fear of heights, **is it**?	Nicht der beste Zeitvertreib für Leute mit Höhenangst, was / nech?
The view **isn't** very good, **is it**?	Die Aussicht ist nicht sehr gut, was / nech?
Joe **isn't** very good, **is he**?	Joe ist nicht sehr gut, was / nech?
Anna **isn't** very good, **is she**?	Anna ist nicht sehr gut, was / nech?

over there = da drüben
real = wirklich
difference = Unterschied

  Setzen Sie das passende Frageanhängsel (*is[n't] it/he/she?*) ein.

a Steve is in the gym, _isn't he_
b That isn't the famous Harbour Bridge, _is it_
c Claire isn't in her room, _is she_
d That's the open sea over there, _isn't it_
e Bridge climbing is a wonderful pastime, _isn't it_
f Jessica is five, _isn't she_
g Uncle Fred is a goat farmer, _isn't he_
h Paul isn't the girl's real father, _is he_
i There isn't much difference between them, _is there_

1/24

4 Hör-Sprech-Übung. Üben Sie die Frageanhängsel jetzt nochmal mündlich. Das ist Stress, denn Sie müssen blitzschnell entscheiden: *isn't* oder *is*; *he, she, it* oder *there*?

Sie hören zum Beispiel:	Manhattan is an island.
Sie sagen:	Manhattan is an island, isn't it?
Sie hören die richtige Antwort:	Manhattan is an island, isn't it?
Sie wiederholen die Antwort:	Manhattan is an island, isn't it?

Unit 5D

5 Wie drückt man das auf Englisch aus?

a Steve macht gerade sein Fitnesstraining.
b Das Hotel ist einfach toll.
c Von unserm Fenster aus können wir das Opernhaus sehen.
d Direkt hinter unserem Hotel ist die berühmte Sydney-Hafen-Brücke.
e Der Blick von der Brücke ist fantastisch.
f Man sieht die wunderschöne Stadt mit ihren vielen kleinen Buchten.
g Die Sydney-Hafen-Brücke ist die größte Stahlbogenbrücke der Welt.
h Morgen fliegen wir zurück.
i Der Flug von Sydney nach London dauert 22 Stunden.

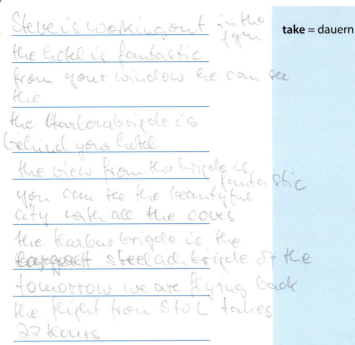

take = dauern

6 Aussprache. Hier wieder einige Wortgruppen zum Üben der Aussprache. Hören Sie genau hin und sprechen Sie mit.

1/25

give *but* gym
walk *but* work
love *but* cove
over *but* cover
eight *but* height

climb *like* time (Das *b* in *climb* ist stumm!)
now *and* how *but* show *and* know
down *and* town *but* grown
Susy *but* busy
come *but* Commons

Small Crossword

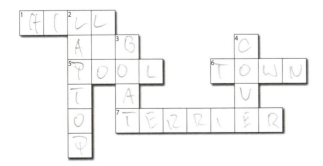

ACROSS
1 A small mountain.
5 A small lake.
6 A small city.
7 A small dog.

DOWN
2 A small computer.
3 A small ship.
4 A small bay.

63

Unit 5E Focus on words

1. **Cove** ist eine Bucht, aber eine kleine! Eine größere, „normale" Bucht heißt **bay**. Berühmt z. B. die **San Francisco Bay**. Aber auch in Sydney gibt es außer *coves* auch *bays*. Sehen Sie sich das mal auf einer Karte von Sydney (*a map of Sydney*) im Internet an.

2. **Island** (gesprochen ohne *s!*) ist das normale Wort für „Insel". In Namen dagegen kommt auch das sonst nur noch literarisch gebräuchliche Wort *isle* (gesprochen: „a-il") vor: *the British Isles* (= die Britischen Inseln), *the Isle of Wight* (= die Insel Wight).

3. Bei **„See"** gilt es aufzupassen: „die See" ist **the sea**, „der (Binnen-)See" ist **the lake**. Für *the sea* sagen wir im Deutschen oft „das Meer". The **Baltic Sea** ist „die Ostsee"; **Lake Constance** (ohne *the!*) ist „der Bodensee".

4. **Boyfriend** ist der Freund, mit dem man eine erotische Beziehung hat; umgekehrt spricht man von **girlfriend**. Die Bezeichnungen *boyfriend* und *girlfriend* sind an kein Lebensalter gebunden: *His girlfriend* (= seine Freundin) und *her boyfriend* (= ihr Freund) können also durchaus bejahrt sein.
Friend allein dagegen impliziert keine romantische oder sexuelle Beziehung und wird mit Bezug auf beide Geschlechter gebraucht: *my friend Colin* (= mein Freund Colin), *my friend Ann* (= meine Freundin Ann).
„Mein Lebensgefährte / meine Lebensgefährtin" wäre in diesem Zusammenhang *my* **partner**, „mein (Ehe-)Mann" ist *my* **husband**, „meine (Ehe-)Frau" *my* **wife**.

5. „Großelterliche Beziehung" wird immer mit **grand-** ausgedrückt:

grandparents, grandfather, grandmother	*Großeltern, Großvater, Großmutter*
grandchild, grandson, granddaughter	*Enkel(kind), Enkel(sohn), Enkelin*
great-grandparents, great-grandfather	*Urgroßeltern, Urgroßvater*
great-granddaughter	*Urenkelin*

6. **Get married** heißt wörtlich „geheiratet / verheiratet werden", ist aber ein gängiger Ausdruck für „heiraten", wenn die Person, die man heiratet, nicht genannt ist. Dagegen nicht *get married*, sondern **marry** z. B. in *will she marry him?* (= wird sie ihn heiraten?).

7. **Tall** heißt eigentlich „groß (gewachsen)": *he's very tall* (= er ist sehr groß), *a very tall woman* (= eine sehr große / hochgewachsene Frau). *Tall buildings* sind „hohe Häuser / Hochhäuser". Auch hier sagt man mitunter **high** *buildings*, aber bei präziser Verwendung von *high* meint man damit eher „hoch gelegen", sodass man unterscheiden könnte zwischen *the world's* **highest** *hotel* (= das am höchsten gelegene Hotel der Welt) und *the world's* **tallest** *hotel* (= das Hotel mit den meisten Stockwerken).

8. **Mountain** bezeichnet einen hohen Berg, während **hill** ein kleinerer Berg bzw. ein Hügel ist: *Mount Everest is the highest* **mountain** *in the world*. **Mountains** sind also hohe Berge bzw. ein Gebirge: *a holiday in the* **mountains** (= ein Urlaub in den Bergen / im Gebirge). Ach ja, und im Englischen *you make a mountain out of a molehill* (= macht man einen Berg aus einem Maulwurfshaufen), während man im Deutschen aus einer Mücke einen Elefanten macht

Unit 5F

Focus on culture

1. They're getting married in Sydney

The Australian wedding industry (= Hochzeitsbranche) *is well organized* (= gut organisiert), und *wedding planners* (= Hochzeitsplanerinnen) übernehmen die Vorbereitung bis in die letzte Einzelheit, sodass *the happy couple* (= das glückliche Paar) nur noch *their "I do"* (= sein Ja) und *their wedding rings* (= Eheringe) auszutauschen braucht. Besonderheit: Man kann praktisch überall heiraten – vor oder im *Sydney Opera House*, *on the beach* (= am Strand), *on a clifftop* (= auf einem Felsvorsprung über dem Meer) und sogar *on the Sydney Harbour Bridge*.

2. Sydney Opera House

The most famous (= berühmteste) *building in Australia and one of the wonders* (= Wunder) *of the modern world*. Von 1959 bis 1973 gebaut, umfasst der auf einer Halbinsel malerisch gelegene Gesamtkomplex *five theatres with a total of 5,532 seats* (= fünf Theater mit insgesamt 5532 Sitzplätzen). Seit 2007 *a UNESCO World Heritage Site* (= Weltkulturerbe-Stätte).

3. Sydney Harbour Bridge

Die von 1924 bis 1932 gebaute Brücke ist neben dem *Sydney Opera House* eines der beiden Wahrzeichen Sydneys. Die von erfahrenen *climb leaders* geführten Besteigungen (*guided climbs*) sind absolut sicher, setzen allerdings körperliche Fitness voraus. Auf *acrophobics* (= unter Höhenangst Leidende) wird besondere Rücksicht genommen. Die 3½ Stunden dauernde Besteigung ist *an unforgettable experience* (= ein unvergessliches Erlebnis) – auch für Senioren, *the oldest climber was 100 years old! Visit the website* http://www.bridgeclimb.com. Dort können Sie unter *Panoramic view from the bridge* den Rundblick simulieren, den *climbers* vom Bogenscheitel der Brücke aus genießen.

Unit 5G

do a quiz = einen Quiz machen
Australian = australisch, Australier(in)
what time is it? = wie viel Uhr ist es?
11am = 11 Uhr vormittags
11pm = 23 Uhr
which of the following = welche von den folgenden
begin = beginnen
head of state = Staatsoberhaupt
prime minister = Premierminister
governor-general = Generalgouverneur
north = Norden
south = Süden
west = Westen
east = Osten
official language = Amtssprache
Aboriginal = die Ureinwohner Australiens betreffend
French = Französisch

Test yourself

Do you like to do quizzes?
Nein? Dann überspringen Sie diese Seite einfach.
Ja? Dann viel Glück! *Good luck!*
Wenn Sie alle 9 richtig haben, gönnen Sie sich eine Flasche *Australian Shiraz* (= Shiraz ist ein besonders in Australien erzeugter Rotwein)!

1. How old was Sydney in 1988?
   - [ ] 100 years.
   - [ ] 200 years.
   - [ ] 300 years.
   - [ ] 400 years.

2. It's 11am German time on Saturday 10 January. What time is it in Sydney, Australia?
   - [ ] 1am on Friday 9 January.
   - [ ] 3am on Friday 9 January.
   - [ ] 9pm on Saturday 10 January.
   - [ ] 11pm on Saturday 10 January.

3. What's the capital of Australia?
   - [ ] Adelaide.
   - [ ] Canberra.
   - [x] Melbourne.
   - [ ] Sydney.

4. Which of the following is not an Australian city?
   - [ ] Brisbane.
   - [ ] Darwin.
   - [x] Montreal.
   - [ ] Perth.

5. What's the population of Australia?
   - [ ] About 22 million.
   - [ ] About 55 million.
   - [ ] About 88 million.
   - [ ] About 111 million.

6. When does summer begin in Australia?
   - [x] In December.
   - [ ] In June.
   - [ ] In March.
   - [ ] In September.

7. Who's Australia's head of state?
   - [ ] The Australian Prime Minister.
   - [x] The British Queen.
   - [ ] The Governor-General of Australia.
   - [ ] The US President.

8. Where do most Australians live?
   - [ ] In the northeast.
   - [ ] In the northwest.
   - [ ] In the southeast.
   - [ ] In the southwest.

9. What's the official language of Australia?
   - [ ] Aboriginal.
   - [ ] Australian.
   - [x] English.
   - [ ] French.

Travellers

Unit 6

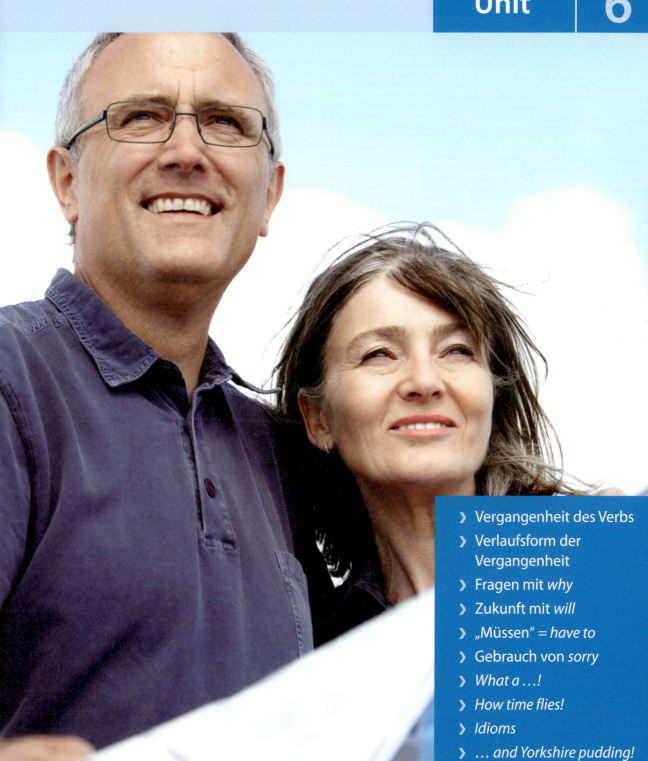

- Vergangenheit des Verbs
- Verlaufsform der Vergangenheit
- Fragen mit *why*
- Zukunft mit *will*
- „Müssen" = *have to*
- Gebrauch von *sorry*
- *What a …!*
- *How time flies!*
- *Idioms*
- *… and Yorkshire pudding!*

Unit 6A — Dialogue

1/26

■ = Sheila
● = John

look = aussehen
enjoy = genießen
didn't want to go = wollte nicht fahren
in the first place = erst gar nicht
insist (on) = bestehen (auf)
go – went = gehen – ging
wrong = falsch
nightmare = Albtraum
terrible = furchtbar, schrecklich
appalling = entsetzlich
cover = bedecken

Missverstehen Sie den folgenden Dialog bitte nicht; er soll nicht the *Englishman abroad* (= den Engländer im Ausland) darstellen, sondern freundlich die falschen Erwartungen ironisieren, die jedem von uns den Urlaubsgenuss trüben können.
Der *reading text* (6C) veranschaulicht die alte Erkenntnis, dass das, was wir sehen, unsere innere Einstellung widerspiegelt.
Beim Lesen der beiden Texte kommen uns zwei Sprichwörter (*proverbs*) in den Sinn – ein englisches und ein deutsches, jeweils ohne genaue Entsprechung in der anderen Sprache: *When in Rome, do as the Romans do.* (= Wenn du in Rom bist, mach's, wie die Römer es machen.) Und, natürlich: Wie man in den Wald hineinruft, so schallt es heraus.

A less than perfect holiday

■ Hello, John, how are you?
● Fine, thanks. And you?
■ Oh, I'm very well, thank you. But you don't look too happy. Didn't you enjoy your holiday?
● No I can't say I did. I didn't want to go in the first place, but Edith insisted.
■ What went wrong?
● Well, to begin with, the pilots were on strike, so we waited endlessly at airports.
■ Oh dear!
● And when we finally arrived, there were no taxis and we had to walk to the hotel.
■ Poor Edith!
● Why "poor Edith"? I had to carry our two heavy bags …
■ Oh I'm sorry, John – what a nightmare!
● Everything was a nightmare. The hotel staff didn't speak English, breakfast was terrible and the restaurant food was appalling …
■ No fish and chips, roast beef, or Yorkshire pudding?
● No English food at all, everything covered in garlic …
■ How absolutely disgusting!

Ein weniger als perfekter Urlaub

■ Hallo, John, wie geht es dir?
● Danke, gut. Und dir?
■ Oh, danke, mir geht es sehr gut. Aber du siehst nicht allzu glücklich aus. Hast du denn keinen schönen Urlaub gehabt?
● Nein, kann ich nicht behaupten. Ich wollte ja gar nicht fahren, aber Edith bestand darauf.
■ Was ist denn schiefgegangen?
● Nun, zunächst mal streikten die Piloten, sodass wir endlos an Flughäfen warteten.
■ Ach du meine Güte!
● Und als wir schließlich ankamen, waren keine Taxis da, und wir mussten zum Hotel laufen.
■ Arme Edith!
● Warum „arme Edith"? Ich musste unsere beiden schweren Taschen tragen …
■ Oh, das tut mir leid, John, was für ein Albtraum!
● Alles war ein Albtraum. Das Hotelpersonal sprach kein Englisch, das Frühstück war furchtbar und das Restaurantessen war entsetzlich …
■ Kein Fisch mit Pommes (frites), Roastbeef oder Yorkshire Pudding?
● Überhaupt kein englisches Essen, alles voller Knoblauch …
■ Wie (absolut) widerlich!

Unit 6B

Rules and practice

1 Die Vergangenheitsform des Verbs (Präteritum, *past tense*)

arrive	**arrived**	*ankommen*	*ankam / kam an*
insist	**insisted**	*darauf bestehen*	*bestand darauf*
go	**went**	*gehen / fahren*	*ging / fuhr*
am / is	**was**	*bin / ist*	*war*
are	**were**	*sind*	*waren*
have / has	**had**	*haben / hat*	*hatte*
do / does	**did**	*tun / tut*	*tat*

Wir sehen hier, wie im Englischen die Vergangenheitsform gebildet wird:

1. Bei regelmäßigen Verben (wie *arrive*, *insist*) durch Anhängen von *-ed*, wobei ein stummes End-*e* (wie in *arrive*) entfällt.

2. Bei unregelmäßigen Verben (wie *go*) wird die Vergangenheitsform „individuell" gebildet, d. h. man muss sie (leider!) von Verb zu Verb extra lernen. Im Zweifel können Sie die unregelmäßigen Verben in der Tabelle auf Seite 219 nachschlagen, wobei die Vergangenheit die jeweils 2. Form ist:
   go – **went** – gone   *gehen* – **ging** – *gegangen*

3. Besonders zu beachten sind die „Sonderverben":
   Be: Die Vergangenheit von *am* und *is* ist *was*; die Vergangenheit von *are* ist *were*.
   Have/has: Had ist die einzige Vergangenheitsform.
   Do/does: Did ist die einzige Vergangenheitsform.

✎ Setzen Sie in die Vergangenheit.

a She looks happy.   *She looked*

b She enjoys her holiday.   *" enjoyed*

c She wants to go for a walk.   *" wanted*

Unit 6B

wait for = warten auf
quiet = ruhig, still

d She loves the lake. — *loved*
e She goes swimming every morning. — *went*
f She always waits for me. — *waited*
g There are some ducks in the lake. — *were*
h She has some food for the ducks. — *had*
i The hotel is very nice but it doesn't allow dogs. — *was*
j It's very quiet. — *it was quiet* ~~quietest~~

2 Setzen Sie in die Vergangenheit.

however = jedoch
far = weit

a Carol wants to book a double room for three nights. — *wanted*
b The Lovejoy B&B doesn't allow children. — *didn't*
c That's all right with Carol because she doesn't like children's noise. — *was   "*
d Carol's Yorkshire terrier, however, is welcome as long as it doesn't bark too much and doesn't attack other dogs. — *was   didn't*
e But there's a small problem. — *was*
f Carol wants a room in Manhattan, New York, but the Lovejoy B&B is in Manhattan, Kansas. — *wanted   was*
g It's a little too far from Grand Central Station. — *was.*

3 „Müssen" wird häufig durch *have to* ausgedrückt

Must (= muss) ist ein „Spezialverb" wie zum Beispiel auch *can* und *will*. Diesen Verben ist gemeinsam, dass sie keine *-s*-Form und keine *-ing*-Form haben und auch nicht mit *do* umschrieben werden. *Can* und *will* haben jeweils noch eine zweite Form: *could* (= könnte / konnte) bzw. *would* (= würde). Von *must* gibt es nur eine Form. Will man „müssen" in der Vergangenheit ausdrücken, so benutzt man *had to*, und „müssen" in der Zukunft ist *will have to*:

could = könnte, konnte
would = würde
have to = müssen
had to = musste

We **had to** walk to the hotel.	Wir **mussten** zum Hotel laufen.
I **had to** carry our two heavy bags.	Ich **musste** unsere zwei schweren Taschen tragen.
I'm afraid we'll **have to** walk.	Ich fürchte, wir werden laufen müssen.

4 Hör-Sprech-Übung. Sie hören einen Satz mit dem Verb in der Vergangenheitsform. Wiederholen Sie den Satz, indem Sie jeweils *had to* (= musste) hinzufügen. Beachten Sie, dass Sie dabei das Verb aus der Vergangenheitsform (z. B. *waited*) in die Grundform (z. B. *wait*) umwandeln müssen, d. h. *we waited* (= wir warteten) wird *we had to wait* (= wir mussten warten).

Unit 6B
1/27

Sie hören zum Beispiel: ....We watched a lot of TV.
Sie sagen: ....We had to watch a lot of TV.
Sie hören die richtige Antwort: ....We had to watch a lot of TV.
Sie wiederholen die Antwort: ....We had to watch a lot of TV.

5 Übersetzen Sie.

a John genoss seinen Urlaub nicht. — *John didn't enjoy his holidays*
b Die Piloten streikten und er musste endlos auf Flughäfen warten. — *the pilots were on strike and he had to wait endlessly*
c Als er ankam, waren keine Taxis da. — *When he arrived there were no taxis*
d Er musste zu Fuß zum Hotel gehen. — *he had to walk*
e Er musste zwei schwere Taschen tragen. — *he had to carry the heavy bags*
f Das Hotelpersonal sprach kein Englisch. — *the staff didn't speak English*
g Das Frühstück war furchtbar. — *the breakfast was terrible*
h Das Restaurantessen war entsetzlich. — *the rest. food was appalling*

6 Stellen Sie Fragen mit *why*.

They had to wait. → Why did they have to wait?
They didn't climb the bridge. → Why didn't they climb the bridge?

a They called the police. — *Why did they call*
b They went to a B&B. — *Why did they go*
c They wanted to get married in Australia. — *Why did they want*
d They went to Soho. — *Why did they go*
e They didn't take a taxi. — *Why didn't they take*
f They didn't enjoy their holiday. — *Why didn't they enjoy*
g They didn't want to go. — *Why didn't they want*
h There were no taxis. — *Why were there no*
i They weren't happy. — *Why weren't they*

didn't want to go =
wollten nicht fahren
weren't =
were not =
waren nicht

Unit 6C

1/28

inside = innen (drin)
ask = fragen
reply = **answer** = antworten
frown = die Stirn runzeln
most unpleasant = höchst unangenehm / unsympathisch
a few hours = ein paar Stunden
later = später
come – came = kommen – kam
what are they like? = wie sind sie?
smile = lächeln
pleasant = angenehm, nett

Reading text

You see what is inside you

Aesop, the famous Greek storyteller, was sitting by the road one day when a traveller asked him, "What sort of people live in Athens?"
Aesop replied, "Tell me where you come from and what sort of people live there, and I will tell you what sort of people you will find in Athens."
Frowning, the man answered, "I am from Argos and the people there are most unpleasant."
"I am sorry to tell you," said Aesop, "that you will find the people of Athens much the same."
A few hours later another traveller came down the road, and he too stopped and asked Aesop, "Tell me, my friend, what are the people of Athens like?"
Again Aesop replied, "Tell me where you come from and what people are like there and I will tell you what people are like in Athens."
Smiling, the man answered, "I come from Argos, and the people there are very pleasant."
"I am happy to tell you," said Aesop, "that you will find the people of Athens much the same."

Du siehst, was in dir ist
Äsop, der berühmte griechische Geschichtenerzähler, saß eines Tages an der Straße, als ein Reisender ihn fragte: „Was für (eine Art von) Menschen leben in Athen?"
Äsop erwiderte: „Sag mir, wo du herkommst und was für Menschen dort wohnen, und ich werde dir sagen, was für Menschen du in Athen finden wirst."
Die Stirn runzelnd antwortete der Mann: „Ich bin aus Argos, und die Menschen dort sind höchst unsympathisch."
„Ich muss dir leider sagen", sagte Äsop, „dass du die Menschen von Athen („sehr dieselben") sehr ähnlich finden wirst."
Ein paar Stunden später kam ein anderer Reisender die Straße herunter, und auch er hielt an und fragte Äsop: „Sag mir, mein Freund, wie sind die Menschen von Athen denn so?"
Wieder antwortete Äsop: „Sag mir, wo du herkommst und wie die Menschen dort sind, und ich werde dir sagen, wie die Menschen in Athen sind."
Lächelnd antwortete der Mann: „Ich komme aus Argos, und die Menschen dort sind sehr nett."
„Ich freue mich, dir sagen zu können", sagte Äsop, „dass du die Menschen von Athen sehr ähnlich finden wirst."

Rules and practice

Unit 6D

1 Noch einmal: die Vergangenheitsform

answer	answered	antworten	antwortete
ask	asked	fragen	fragte
insist	insisted	darauf bestehen	bestand darauf
arrive	arrived	ankommen	ankam / kam an
reply	replied	erwidern	erwiderte
stop	stopped	anhalten	anhielt / hielt an
say	said	sagen	sagte
come	came	kommen	kam

1. Die Vergangenheitsformen *answered*, *asked* und *insisted* zeigen uns, wie die Endung *-ed* unterschiedlich ausgesprochen wird:
   bei *answered* als weiches „d";
   bei *asked* als hartes „t";
   bei *insisted* als zusätzliche Silbe „id" (das „i" kurz gesprochen).

2. Weiter zeigen uns die Beispiele die zu beachtenden Schreibregeln:
   Stummes End-*e* entfällt: *arrive – arrived*, *arrange – arranged*, *like – liked*.
   -y wird (außer nach *a, e, o*) zu *-i-*: *reply – replied*, *carry – carried*, aber *stay – stayed*.
   Mitlaute werden nach kurzem, betontem *a, e, i, o, u* verdoppelt: *stop – stopped*.

3. Beachten Sie außerdem die zwei neuen unregelmäßigen Verben *say – said* (Aussprache: „ßäd") und *come – came*.

✎ Setzen Sie in die Gegenwart.

a John didn't want to go on holiday but his wife insisted. _____

b A lot of things went wrong. _____

c The pilots were on strike, so they waited endlessly at airports. _____

d When they finally arrived, there were no taxis and they had to walk to the hotel. _____

e John had to carry their two heavy bags. _____

f Everything was a nightmare. _____

g The hotel staff didn't speak English. _____

h When John came home, he was hungry for roast beef and fish and chips. _____

Unit 6D

1/29

enjoy = genießen
carry = tragen
listen = zuhören
call = anrufen
suppose = vermuten
survive = überleben
ask = fragen
want (to) = wollen

2 Aussprache. Üben Sie die drei verschiedenen Aussprachen der *-ed*-Endung.

a **Weiches „d":** enjoy – enjoyed, answer – answered, carry – carried, reply – replied, allow – allowed, listen – listened, call – called, travel – travelled, arrange – arranged, suppose – supposed, climb – climbed, arrive – arrived, survive – survived, live – lived.
b **Hartes „t":** ask – asked, walk – walked, look – looked, like – liked, bark – barked, attack – attacked, watch – watched, stop – stopped, help – helped.
c **Silbisch „id":** wait – waited, want – wanted, insist – insisted.

3 Die Verlaufsform der Vergangenheit

Aesop **was sitting** by the road one day when a traveller **asked** him …
Aesop saß eines Tages an der Straße, als ihn ein Reisender fragte …

Mit der Verlaufsform haben wir uns schon in 5B1 beschäftigt. Dort ging es um die Verlaufsform der Gegenwart: *They* **are keeping** *us on our feet, What* **are** *you* **doing**? etc. Jetzt sehen wir, dass die Verlaufsform auch in der Vergangenheit gebraucht werden kann: *Aesop* **was sitting** …, *we* **were waiting** …
Hier haben wir einen gewissermaßen „klassischen" Gebrauch der Verlaufsform: Sie ermöglicht das Gegeneinanderstellen zweier Handlungen von unterschiedlicher Dauer – einer länger dauernden Handlung (*was sitting by the road*), in die eine kurze Handlung gleichsam „hineinplatzt" (*a traveller asked him*). Die längere Handlung steht in der Verlaufsform, die kurze in der einfachen Form:

Aesop was sitting   a traveller asked him

Setzen Sie die Vergangenheitsform des eingeklammerten Verbs ein: Verlaufsform oder einfache Form?

a Your SMS (arrive) _____ while we (wait) _____ for our taxi.
b When we (walk) _____ along the river, a big dog (attack) _____ us.
c When we (be) _____ in Australia we also (climb) _____ the Sydney Harbour Bridge.
d I (sit) _____ at my laptop while Steve (work) _____ out in the gym.
e While we (listen) _____ to a lunchtime concert in the Church of St-Martin-in-the-Fields, he (ask) _____ me, "Will you marry me?"
f We (enjoy) _____ our drinks when this unpleasant man (come) _____ in.
g We (wait) _____ at the bus stop when a car (stop) _____ and the driver (ask) _____ where we (go) _____.

Unit 6D

4 Setzen Sie die eingeklammerten Verben in die Vergangenheit.

a Aesop (is) _____ sitting by the road one day.

b A traveller (wants) _____ to know what sort of people (live) _____ in Athens.

c Aesop (asks) _____ him where he (comes) _____ from.

d The man (answers) _____ that he (is) _____ from Argos and that the people there (are) _____ most unpleasant.

e Aesop (says) _____ that he (will) _____ find the people of Athens much the same.

5 Setzen Sie die fett gedruckten Verben unter Gebrauch von *will* (= werde[n]) in die Zukunft. Benutzen Sie nach Möglichkeit die Kurzform -*'ll*.

Zukunftsform *will*

a The pilots **were** on strike, so we **waited** endlessly at airports. _____

b There **were** no taxis and we **had** to walk to the hotel. _____

c I **had** to carry our two heavy bags. _____

d There **was** no English food at all. _____

e Everything **was** covered in garlic. _____

f It **was** a nightmare. _____

g But we **survived**. _____

6 Ersetzen Sie die fett gedruckten Wörter durch andere mit etwa gleicher Bedeutung.

synonyms = Synonyme = Wörter mit gleicher oder fast gleicher Bedeutung

a Aesop **replied** … (_____)

b The people there are very **pleasant**. (_____)

c The hotel is **fantastic**. (_____)

d It's not the best pastime for **those** (_____) with a fear of heights.

e I'm **fine, thanks.** (_____)

f You don't look **too** (_____) happy.

g Breakfast was **terrible** (_____)

h The grandchildren are keeping us **on our toes**. (_____)

i What are they doing **down under**? (_____)

75

Unit 6E

bad = schlecht
complain = klagen
mustn't („t" ist stumm) = darf nicht
grumble = murren, klagen

tell = sagen

late = spät
step on = treten auf
toe = Zeh(e)

die = sterben
hear = hören

bad = schlecht
news = Nachricht(en)

surprise = Überraschung
fool = Dummkopf, Idiot

fly – flies = fliegen – fliegt

Focus on words

1. *How are you?* In 6A lauten die Antworten *Fine, thanks* und *I'm very well, thank you*. Denkbare konventionelle Antworten wären auch *OK, Not bad, Can't complain*, vielleicht auch *Mustn't grumble*, aber nicht viel mehr! Dies ist ein der Gesprächseröffnung dienender Austausch von Floskeln, bei dem man keine eingehenderen Informationen über seinen Gesundheitszustand gibt.

2. Gebrauch von *sorry*: Wir hatten bereits *I'm afraid* als Einleitung zu einer vom Sprecher bedauerten Aussage (→4E6). Nun haben wir in dieser Lektion zweimal *I'm sorry*:

Oh I'm **sorry**, John!	Oh, das tut mir leid, John!
I am **sorry** to tell you ...	Es tut mir leid, dir/Ihnen sagen zu müssen ...

Mit *I'm sorry* entschuldigt man sich für etwas:

I'm **sorry** I'm late.	Entschuldige, dass ich zu spät komme.
"Oh, you stepped on my toe!"	„Oh, du bist mir auf den Zeh getreten!"
– "Oh, (I'm) **sorry**!"	– „Ach, (das) tut mir leid!"

Mit *I'm sorry* drückt man sein Mitgefühl aus:

"Our dog died last week." – "(Oh,) I'm **sorry** to hear that."	„Unser Hund ist vorige Woche gestorben." – „Oh, das tut mir (aber) leid."

I'm sorry benutzt man auch, wenn man etwas Bedauerliches mitzuteilen hat; es ist dann eine stärkere Alternative zu *I'm afraid* (→4E6):

I'm **sorry** I have some bad news.	Leider habe ich eine schlechte Nachricht.

Sorry kann man sagen, wenn man etwas nicht verstanden hat:

Sorry, what did you say your name was?	Entschuldigung, wie war nochmal Ihr Name?

3. Ausrufe mit *What a ... !*:

What a surprise!	Was für eine Überraschung!
What a view!	Was für ein Ausblick!
Oh, **what a** fool I am!	Ach, was für ein Idiot ich doch bin!

4. Ausrufe mit *How ... !*:

How time flies!	Wie (doch) die Zeit verfliegt / vergeht!
How absolutely disgusting!	Wie (absolut) widerlich / ekelhaft!

5. *Bag* kann jede Art von Tasche, Beutel oder Tüte sein. Die früher auf Reisen benutzten *suitcases* (= Koffer) sind heute zumeist von praktischen Reisetaschen (= *travelling bags, holdalls*) abgelöst worden. Häufig spricht man auch hier nur noch von *bags* (*How many bags do you have?*), und *my bags* ist einfach „mein Gepäck".

Unit 6F

Focus on culture

1. Fish and chips, roast beef, Yorkshire pudding:
Roast beef and Yorkshire pudding sind Bestandteile von *England's traditional Sunday lunch*, wobei sich *roast* mit *most* reimt (nicht mit *lost*) und *pudding* mit einem kurzen „u" wie im Deutschen ausgesprochen wird, im Übrigen aber nicht das Leiseste mit einem deutschen Pudding gemein hat. Rezepte (*recipes*, „ressipihs" gesprochen) finden Sie massenhaft im Internet.
Fish 'n' chips hingegen ist *a traditional British fast food or takeaway food*, wobei die *chips* (mit kulturbedingten Abstrichen) deutschen Pommes frites entsprechen und die Amerikaner sie als *French fries* bezeichnen, solange sie sich nicht über die Franzosen ärgern (wie 2003 im Zusammenhang mit dem Irakkrieg – damals wurden die *French fries* von *patriotic Americans* in *freedom fries* umbenannt).

2. Athens (= Athen):
Nichtenglische geografische Namen werden oft ins Englische übersetzt und lauten dann anders als in der Ursprungssprache und im Deutschen.
Wichtige europäische Länder- und Städtenamen, die stärker vom Deutschen abweichen:

recipe = (Koch-)Rezept
prescription = (Arzt-)Rezept
takeaway (food) = Essen zum Mitnehmen
freedom = (die) Freiheit

1/30

Austria	(= Österreich)	Slovakia	(= Rumänien)
Belgium	(= Belgien)	Spain	(= Spanien)
Bulgaria	(= Bulgarien)	Sweden	(= Schweden)
Czech Republic	(= Tschechien)	Switzerland	(= die Schweiz)
Denmark	(= Dänemark)	Turkey	(= die Türkei)
Estonia	(= Estland)		
France	(= Frankreich)	Athens	(= Athen)
Germany	(= Deutschland)	Brussels	(= Brüssel)
Greece	(= Griechenland)	Cologne	(= Köln)
Hungary	(= Ungarn)	Lisbon	(= Lissabon)
Italy	(= Italien)	Milan	(= Mailand)
Latvia	(= Lettland)	Moscow	(= Moskau)
Lithuania	(= Litauen)	Munich	(= München)
the Netherlands	(= die Niederlande)	Naples	(= Neapel)
Norway	(= Norwegen)	Prague	(= Prag)
Poland	(= Polen)	Rome	(= Rom)
Romania	(= Russland)	Vienna	(= Wien)
Russia	(= die Slowakei)	Warsaw	(= Warschau)

Unit 6G — Test yourself

1/31

Now for the fun part – nun zum angenehmen Teil

Idioms sind sprachlich das Salz in der Suppe, sie sind anschaulich, manchmal witzig und oft ohne Gegenstück in einer anderen Sprache. Ein *idiom* ist ein sprachliches Bild; man sieht das Bild vor seinem geistigen Auge und weiß intuitiv: „Aha, das ist gemeint!"
Im Deutschen kommt man vom Regen in die Traufe, im Englischen dagegen *out of the frying pan into the fire* (= aus der Bratpfanne ins Feuer).
Im Deutschen deckt man den Brunnen erst zu, wenn das Kind hineingefallen ist, im Englischen *you lock the stable door after the horse has bolted* (= man verschließt die Stalltür, nachdem das Pferd auf und davon ist). Wer sich in einem Dilemma, einer Zwangslage befindet, sieht sich auf Englisch ironisch-bildhaft *between a rock and a hard place*.
Manchmal benutzen beide Sprachen das gleiche Bild, etwa wenn man im Deutschen das Kind mit dem Bade ausschüttet und im Englischen *you throw the baby out with the bathwater*.
In der folgenden Liste finden Sie nun links 10 englische *idioms*, denen rechts – in anderer Reihenfolge – die 10 deutschen Entsprechungen gegenübergestellt sind. Ordnen Sie die englischen und deutschen Sätze einander zu.
Die Sätze enthalten einige noch nicht eingeführte Wörter, weshalb wir die englischen Sätze in die Tonaufnahme aufgenommen und im Schlüssel (→ S. 195) für Sie wörtlich übersetzt haben.

frying pan = Bratpfanne
fire = Feuer
lock = abschließen
stable = (Pferde-)Stall
after = nachdem
horse = Pferd
bolt (Ausspr.: „boult") = durchgehen
rock = Felsen
a hard place = eine harte Stelle
throw = werfen

beat = schlagen
bush (kurzes „u") = Busch
leg = Bein
stand on = stehen auf
against = gegen
which side = welche Seite
bread = Brot
melt = schmelzen
have = **eat** = essen
devil = Teufel
come up = nach oben kommen
driver's seat = Fahrersitz
past ... = über ... hinaus
sell-by date = Haltbarkeitsdatum

a She didn't beat around the bush.
b She hasn't got a leg to stand on against us.
c She knows which side her bread is buttered.
d She looks as if butter wouldn't melt in her mouth.
e She runs rings around him.
f She'll have me for breakfast if I do that.
g She's between the devil and the deep blue sea.
h She's come up in the world.
i She's in the driver's seat.
j She's past her sell-by date.

1 *Sie hat die Zügel in der Hand.*
2 *Sie hat es weit gebracht.*
3 *Sie hat ihre besten Tage hinter sich.*
4 *Sie hat nichts gegen uns in der Hand.*
5 *Sie ist in einer Zwickmühle.*
6 *Sie redete nicht um den heißen Brei herum.*
7 *Sie sieht aus, als ob sie kein Wässerchen trüben könnte.*
8 *Sie sieht schon, wo sie bleibt.*
9 *Sie steckt ihn vollkommen in die Tasche.*
10 *Wenn ich das mache, nimmt sie mich auseinander.*

a	b	c	d	e	f	g	h	i	j

Runners

Unit 7

> Zukunftsformen des Verbs
> *Ago*
> Unregelmäßige Verben
> *Is it "is it?" or "isn't it?"?*
> Wörter auf *-ment*
> *Fit as a fiddle etc.*
> *... and a visit to Boston!*

Unit 7A Dialogue

1/32

■ = Alan
● = Mary

retire =
  in Rente gehen
go in to work =
  zur Arbeit gehen
not … any more =
  nicht mehr …
miss = vermissen
the people I work
  with = die
  Kollegen
probably =
  wahrscheinlich
won't = will not =
  werde nicht
get up early =
  früh aufstehen
at least =
  wenigstens,
  mindestens
be into sth →7E1
ten years ago =
  vor zehn Jahren
(un)usual =
  (un)gewöhnlich

A healthy mind in a healthy body (= ein gesunder Geist in einem gesunden Körper): für viele Menschen verheißt das Langstreckenlaufen (= *long-distance running*) beides und schenkt einem das Glück (= *happiness*) gleich noch dazu – Grund genug dafür, dass wir uns hier ein wenig auf Englisch mit dem Thema beschäftigen und auch die Stadt eines berühmten Marathons aufsuchen.

Going into retirement

■ You're retiring, aren't you?

● Yes, the twenty-seventh will be my last working day. It'll be strange, not having to go in to work any more.

■ Will you miss it?

● Well, the job is a lot of fun, of course – the office, the people I work with, most of them anyway. Will I miss it? I probably will. What I won't miss is getting up early every morning.

■ I can imagine. So you'll be taking it easy.

● Well, for a time at least, I'll relax, do some reading, go out with friends, improve my running.

■ You're into running?

● Yes, didn't you know? I took up jogging about ten years ago. I was a bit overweight then and completely unfit. At first I could only jog for a couple of minutes, then I managed a mile, three miles, eventually ten miles. Now I'm going to train for the marathon.

■ You want to run the marathon?

● Yes, nothing unusual about that. A lot of runners are over sixty.

(Übergang in den) Ruhestand

■ Du gehst in den Ruhestand, nicht wahr?

● Ja, der Siebenundzwanzigste wird mein letzter Arbeitstag sein. Es wird seltsam sein, nicht mehr zur Arbeit gehen zu müssen.

■ Wird sie dir fehlen?

● Tja, der Beruf / die Arbeit macht natürlich viel Spaß – das Büro, die Leute, mit denen man arbeitet, die meisten von ihnen jedenfalls. Werde ich es vermissen? Wahrscheinlich werde ich es. Was ich nicht vermissen werde, ist, jeden Morgen früh aufzustehen.

■ Das kann ich mir vorstellen. Du wirst es also ruhig angehen lassen.

● Tja, wenigstens eine Zeit lang werde ich mich entspannen, ein bisschen lesen, mit Freunden ausgehen, mein Laufen verbessern.

■ Du läufst?

● Ja, wusstest du das nicht? Ich habe vor zehn Jahren mit dem Joggen angefangen. Ich war damals ein bisschen übergewichtig und überhaupt nicht fit. Zuerst konnte ich nur ein paar Minuten joggen, dann schaffte ich eine Meile, drei Meilen, schließlich zehn Meilen. Jetzt werde ich für den Marathon trainieren.

■ Du willst den Marathon laufen?

● Ja, da ist nichts Ungewöhnliches dran. Viele Läufer sind über sechzig.

Unit 7B

Rules and practice

1 Wie man die Zukunft ausdrückt

Der Dialog (7A) zeigt uns vier Möglichkeiten, die Zukünftigkeit einer Handlung auszudrücken:

a. Will

The twenty-seventh **will** be my last working day.	*Der Siebenundzwanzigste wird mein letzter Arbeitstag sein.*
It**'ll** (= It **will**) be strange.	*Es wird seltsam sein.*
What I **won't** (= **will not**) miss is …	*Was ich nicht vermissen werde, ist …*

b. Am/are/is going to

Now I**'m** (= I **am**) **going to** train for the marathon.	*Jetzt werde ich für den Marathon trainieren.*

c. Verlaufsform (*am/is/are* + *-ing*)

You**'re** (= You **are**) **retiring**, aren't you?	*Du gehst doch in den Ruhestand, nech?*

d. Will + be + -ing

So you**'ll** (= you **will**) **be taking** it easy.	*Du wirst es jetzt also langsam angehen lassen.*

Welche Form benutzen Sie im konkreten Fall?

a. *Will* ist die **neutralste und bei weitem am häufigsten** gebrauchte Zukunftsform, weshalb Sie sich im Zweifel für diese Form entscheiden sollten. Selbst in den Fällen, wo eine der anderen Formen idiomatischer, „kraftvoller" wäre, wird man die *will*-Zukunftsform doch immer verstehen. Besonders angebracht ist *will*, wenn die Handlung nicht sicher vorgesehen bzw. zu erwarten ist (*I think I'll …, Maybe / Perhaps she'll …*) oder wenn sie spontan, d. h. ohne Vorbedacht, erfolgt. – Die verneinte Form *will not* wird häufig zu *won't* zusammengezogen.

perhaps = vielleicht
maybe = vielleicht

Unit 7B

tomorrow = morgen

b. Mit *am/are/is going to* betont man, dass man die **Absicht** hat, etwas zu tun. *Now I'm going to train for the marathon* (= Jetzt habe ich die Absicht / habe ich vor / habe ich mir vorgenommen, für den Marathon zu trainieren).

c. Mit der **Verlaufsform** betont man, dass die Handlung **geplant** ist.
Die Verlaufsform kann man logischerweise nur benutzen, wenn der Zukunftsbezug entweder durch eine Zeitbestimmung der Zukunft deutlich gemacht ist oder aus dem Zusammenhang hervorgeht.
Zeitbestimmung: *Tomorrow we're flying back.*
Zusammenhang: *You're retiring, aren't you?*

d. *Will* + *be* + *-ing*: Mit dieser Form (*will* + Verlaufsform) betont man, dass die Handlung **für die Zukunft vorgesehen** ist, dass sie aufgrund des normalen Laufs der Ereignisse **zu erwarten** ist.

✎ Setzen Sie eine passende Zukunftsform ein: *will, am/is/are going to, am/is/are + -ing* oder *will + be + -ing*. (Mitunter sind mehrere Formen möglich, wobei dann „Untertöne" wie „Absicht", „Planung", „Erwartung" mitschwingen, die wir Ihnen im Schlüssel erklären. Benutzen Sie im Zweifel *will*!)

do some reading = etwas lesen
go to bed = ins Bett gehen
go in to work = arbeiten gehen
get up early = früh aufstehen
take up jogging = mit Joggen anfangen
climb = erklettern, besteigen
tonight = heute Abend

a I (miss) _____ you.
b I (tell) _____ you what you can do.
c I think I (take) _____ it easy today.
d I (take) _____ it easy today.
e I think I (do) _____ some reading before I go to bed.
f I (not have) _____ to go in to work tomorrow.
g I (not miss) _____ getting up early every morning.
h I think I (have) _____ to improve my running.
i Maybe I (take) _____ up jogging.
j Next year I (run) _____ the marathon.
k We (fly) _____ to London tomorrow.
l She (retire) _____ at the end of October.
m We (be) _____ in London next week.
n Tomorrow we (climb) _____ the Sydney Harbour Bridge.
o I (not climb) _____ Mount Everest.
p I'm afraid you (have) _____ to walk to the hotel.
q We (have) _____ the grandchildren over at the weekend. I'm sure they (keep) _____ us on our toes.
r What (you do) _____ tonight?

2 *Ten years ago* = vor zehn Jahren

Unit 7B

Beachten Sie, dass *ago* im Gegensatz zum deutschen „vor" nachgestellt wird:

| I took up jogging **about ten years ago**. | Ich habe **vor etwa zehn Jahren** mit dem Joggen angefangen. |

about ten years ago = vor etwa zehn Jahren

Noch etwas anderes fällt Ihnen vielleicht auf: Im Deutschen sagen wir hier „ich habe angefangen", im Englischen dagegen *I took up* (= „ich fing an" / wörtlich „ich nahm auf"). Die Form mit *have* (also das Perfekt / *present perfect tense*) kann man nämlich im Englischen nicht benutzen, wenn die Handlung durch eine **Zeitbestimmung der Vergangenheit** (hier: *about ten years ago*) „datiert" ist. (→ 8B1, 11B1)

✏ Benutzen Sie statt des deutschen Perfekts (z. B. „hat besucht", „sind angekommen") im Englischen die Vergangenheitsform (z. B. *visited, arrived*).

a Sie sind vor zwei Stunden angekommen. _____
b John hat vor etwa drei Tagen angerufen. _____
c Wir haben hier vor Jahren gelebt. _____
d Er hat uns vor etwa sechs Monaten besucht. *he had visit at 6 mt ago*
e Vor ein paar Tagen hat er einen Yorkshireterrier angegriffen. *a few days ago*
f Vor zwei Jahren haben wir einen hohen Berg in Malaysia bestiegen. *2 years ago*  *climed a big mountain*

arrive = ankommen
call = anrufen
month = Monat
attack = angreifen
mountain = Berg

3 *You're retiring, aren't you?*

Bisher haben wir Frageanhängsel mit *is* kennengelernt: *isn't it?, is it?* etc. Wir wissen, dass die Form des Frageanhängsels abhängig ist von Person und Verb im vorderen Teil des Satzes. Hier nun ist es *you* und *are*: **You are** retiring, **aren't you?** (= Du gehst doch in den Ruhestand, nicht wahr?) Hätten vorne statt der Hilfsverben *is* oder *are* die Hilfsverben *can* oder *will* gestanden, so wären auch diese im Frageanhängsel wiederholt worden:

You can manage three miles,	**can't you?**	Drei Meilen schaffst du doch, oder?
You can't manage ten miles,	**can you?**	Drei Meilen schaffst du nicht, oder?
You'll miss the office,	**won't you?**	Das Büro wird dir fehlen, was?
You won't miss the office,	**will you?**	Das Büro wird dir nicht fehlen was?

manage three miles = drei Meilen schaffen
you'll = you will
won't = will not

4 Hör-Sprech-Übung. In dieser Übung hören Sie Sätze von der CD, die Sie durch Hinzufügung des passenden Frageanhängsels zu Fragen machen sollen.

1/33

Sie hören zum Beispiel: …………………………….It's strange.
Sie sagen: …………………………….It's strange, isn't it?

strange = seltsam

Unit 7C

Reading text

A marathon veteran

Let's call him Gary. He had run the Boston Marathon 34 times. At 65, and training for his 35th marathon, he felt fit as a fiddle. Then, during a training race, he suddenly felt a pain in his chest. He didn't stop running, and he ran again the next day. The pain was still there and it didn't go away. Gary waited another two days and then went to see his doctor, who sent him straight to the emergency room of the nearest hospital. Tests showed that he had suffered a heart attack and had to have a stent. After the surgery he followed doctor's orders for a few weeks. Then he became restless. A month after his heart attack he was back running, and another four months later he ran his 35th Boston Marathon. As one of 953 runners in the 60 to 69 age group he finished the race in four hours and 16 minutes, ten minutes faster than the previous year.

Ein Marathon-Veteran

Wir wollen ihn Gary nennen. Er war 34-mal den Boston-Marathon gelaufen. Mit 65, beim Training für seinen 35. Marathon, fühlte er sich topfit. Dann, während eines Trainingslaufes, fühlte er plötzlich Schmerzen in der Brust. Er hörte nicht auf zu laufen, und er lief am nächsten Tag wieder. Die Schmerzen waren immer noch da und sie gingen nicht weg. Gary wartete noch weitere zwei Tage und ging dann zum Arzt, der ihn direkt in die Notaufnahme des nächsten Krankenhauses schickte. Untersuchungen ergaben, dass er einen Herzinfarkt erlitten hatte und einen Stent bekommen musste. Nach dem Eingriff befolgte er ein paar Wochen lang die Anweisungen des Arztes. Dann wurde er unruhig. Einen Monat nach seinem Herzinfarkt lief er wieder, und nach weiteren vier Monaten lief er seinen 35. Boston-Marathon. Als einer von 953 Läufern in der Altersgruppe 60 bis 69 beendete er den Lauf in vier Stunden und 16 Minuten, zehn Minuten schneller als im vorhergehenden Jahr.

---

let's = let us = lass(t) uns
had run = war gelaufen
34 times = 34-mal
fiddle = Fiedel
suddenly = plötzlich
stop running = aufhören zu laufen
run – ran = laufen – lief
the pain = die Schmerzen
go to see = aufsuchen
had to have = musste haben
became = wurde

Rules and practice

Unit 7D

1 Versuchen Sie, aus der Erinnerung die fehlenden Wörter einzusetzen.

a Gary had __run__ (maked) the Boston Marathon 34 times.
b At 65 he was __in training__ for his 35th Marathon. (repairing)
c He __felt__ fit as a fiddle.
d But __during__ a training race he suddenly felt a pain in his chest.
e He didn't stop __running__, and he ran again the next day.
f The pain was still there and it __didn't__ go away.
g After another two days Gary __went__ to see his doctor.
h The doctor __send__ him straight to the emergency room of the nearest hospital.
i Tests showed that he had __suffered__ a heart attack. (he had a/a)
j He had to __have__ a stent.
k After the surgery he __followed__ doctor's orders for a few weeks.
l Then he __became__ restless.
m A month after his heart attack he was back __running__.
n Another four months later he _____ his 35th Boston Marathon.
o He __finished__ the race in four hours and 16 minutes.

2 Neue unregelmäßige Verben (→ 6B1)

Um ein Verb in allen denkbaren Verbindungen benutzen zu können, benötigen wir drei Formen, hier am Beispiel *work* dargestellt:
1. Grundform: *work* (= arbeiten). Von der Grundform abgeleitet wird die *-s*-Form *works* (= arbeitet) und die *-ing*-Form *working* (= arbeitend, Arbeiten).
2. Vergangenheitsform: *worked* (= arbeitete).
3. „3. Form" (*-ed*-Partizip): *worked* (= gearbeitet).

Bei regelmäßigen Verben wie *work* wird die 2. und 3. Form also mit *-ed* gebildet. Bei unregelmäßigen Verben sehen diese beiden Formen ganz unterschiedlich aus (→ S. 219 Tabelle der unregelmäßigen Verben).
Begegnet sind uns bisher die unregelmäßigen Verben *come*, *eat*, *go*, *say* und *see*. In dieser *unit* kommen die folgenden hinzu:

become – became – become	werden – wurde – geworden
feel – felt – felt	(sich) fühlen – (sich) fühlte – (sich) gefühlt
run – ran – run	laufen – lief – gelaufen
send – sent – sent	schicken – schickte – geschickt
show – showed – shown	zeigen – zeigte – gezeigt

Unit 7D

call = nennen
a few days ago =
  vor ein paar
  Tagen
last year =
  voriges Jahr
yesterday =
  gestern

✎ Setzen Sie die passende Form des Verbs ein.

a His name is Frederick, but we have always (call) _called_ him Fred.
b I (finish) _finished_ my last marathon in four hours and three minutes.
c We can see from the tests that he has (suffer) _suffered_ a heart attack.
d When she felt a pain in her chest she (stop) _stopped_ running.
e The doctors think that he (have) _will have_ to have a stent.
f She (say) _said_ she doesn't like him.
g I (send) _sent_ him an email a few days ago.
h Gary (run) _ran_ the Boston Marathon last year.
i I (go) _went_ to see my doctor yesterday.
j She has (become) _become_ very restless.
k Has he (show) _shown_ you his new laptop?
l I have never (feel) _felt_ better.

3 *He had run* = „er war gelaufen"

Dem englischen *he had run* entspricht ein deutsches „er **war** gelaufen". Dieses Perfekt wird im Englischen **immer mit *had*** gebildet, nicht – wie die entsprechende deutsche Zeitform – manchmal mit „war". Vergleichen Sie:

Englisch: *had*	Deutsch: „hatte"
He **had suffered** a heart attack.	Er **hatte** einen Herzinfarkt **erlitten**.
He **had**n't **stopped** running.	Er **hatte** nicht **aufgehört** zu laufen.
He **had waited** another two days.	Er **hatte** weitere zwei Tage **gewartet**.

Englisch: *had*	Deutsch: „war"
He **had run** the marathon 34 times.	Er **war** den Marathon 34-mal **gelaufen**.
He **had gone** to the doctor.	Er **war** zum Arzt **gegangen**.
He **had followed** doctor's orders.	Er **war** den Anweisungen des Arztes **gefolgt**.

retire = in den
  Ruhestand
  gehen
a little =
  ein bisschen
relax =
  sich entspannen
German =
  Deutsch
improve =
  verbessern

 Übersetzen Sie.

a Sie war am Ende des Jahres in den Ruhestand gegangen. _She had retired at the end of the year_
b Sie hatte sich ein bisschen entspannt. _She had relaxed a little bit_
c Sie war mit Freunden ausgegangen. _She had gone out with friends_
d Sie hatte ihr Deutsch verbessert. _She had improved her German_

Unit 7D

e Sie war viel gejoggt. — *She had jog a lot*
f Sie hatte Berge bestiegen. — *She had climed the mount.*
g Sie hatte für den Marathon trainiert. — *She had trained*
h Sie war den Marathon gelaufen. — *She had running*

jog a lot = viel joggen

4 Fragen mit regelmäßigen und unregelmäßigen Verben. Fragen Sie nach den fett gedruckten Wörtern.

She missed **the office**. – What …? → What did she miss?

a She ran the Boston Marathon **34 times**. – How often … _____?
b She felt **fit as a fiddle**. – How … _____?
c She ran again **the next day**. – When … _____?
d She waited **two days**. – How long … _____?
e She went to see **her doctor**. – Who … _____?
f He sent her **to the hospital**. – Where … _____?
g The tests showed that she **had suffered a heart attack**. – What … _____?
h She retired **four months later**. – When … _____?

34 times = 34-mal
how often? = wie oft?
again = wieder
how long? = wie lange?
who = (auch:) wen

5 Noch einmal die Zukunft (→7B1). Beachten Sie bei der Übersetzung der folgenden Sätze: Alle handeln von Dingen, die man sich vorgenommen hat, die man beabsichtigt. Jetzt wissen Sie, welche Zukunftsform Sie am besten benutzen, nicht wahr?

a Ich werde dich Gary nennen. _____
b Ich werde nicht aufhören zu rennen. _____
c Ich werde morgen wieder laufen. _____
d Ich werde für den Marathon trainieren. _____
e Ich werde den Boston Marathon laufen. _____
f Dieses Jahr werde ich schneller als letztes Jahr sein. _____
g Ich werde „fit wie eine Fiedel" sein. _____
h Ich werde nicht in den Ruhestand gehen. _____
i Ich werde heiraten. _____

call = nennen
stop = aufhören
fast = schnell
get married = heiraten

Unit 7E — Focus on words

movie = Film

1. *You're into running?* (≈ Du machst Laufen als Hobby?): Eine direkte Übersetzung für *be into something* gibt es nicht. „Sich für etwas interessieren und es aktiv betreiben" wäre eine Definition für diesen modernen idiomatischen Ausdruck. *I'm into movies* wäre etwa „ich interessiere mich sehr für Filme" und für *she's into yoga* sagt man auf Deutsch so etwas wie „sie macht Yoga" oder vielleicht auch „sie steht auf Yoga".

2. *Unfit, unusual:* Im Gegensatz zum Deutschen („un̲glücklich") wird die verneinende Vorsilbe un- im Englischen nicht betont. Die Betonung entspricht der des unverneinten Worts: un*ha̲ppy*, un*plea̲sant*, un*i̲nteresting*, un*attra̲ctive*, un*we̲lcome*

3. *Next – nearest:* Beides heißt „nächste". Mit *next* bezeichnet man die **Reihenfolge**, mit *nearest* die **räumliche Entfernung**:

The **next** stop is Crawley.	*Der nächste Halt ist Crawley.*
The **nearest** hospital is in Crawley.	*Das nächste Krankenhaus ist in Crawley.*

stop = Halt(estelle)

1/35

4. *Retire* (= in den Ruhestand gehen) – *retirement* (= Ruhestand): Weitere nützliche Verben, die durch Anhängen von *-ment* zu Substantiven (= Hauptwörtern) werden:

arrange	*arrangieren / vereinbaren*	arrangement	*Vereinbarung*
enjoy	*genießen / Freude haben an*	enjoyment	*Spaß / Freude*
govern	*regieren*	government	*Regierung*
improve	*verbessern*	improvement	*Verbesserung*
manage	*leiten / bewältigen*	management	*Leitung / Führung*
disappoint	*enttäuschen*	disappointment	*Enttäuschung*
pay	*(be)zahlen*	payment	*(Be-)Zahlung*
punish	*bestrafen*	punishment	*Bestrafung*
ship	*liefern*	shipment	*Lieferung*

1/36

5. *He felt fit as a fiddle:* Einer der vielen schönen idiomatischen Vergleiche, die es im Englischen gibt. Andere Beispiele:

bold as brass	„kühn wie Messing" / frech wie Oskar / rotzfrech
busy as a bee	fleißig wie eine Biene / bienenfleißig
cold as ice	kalt wie Eis / eiskalt
drunk as a skunk	„betrunken wie ein Stinktier" / stockbesoffen
dry as dust	trocken wie Staub / staubtrocken
flat as a pancake	„flach wie ein Eierkuchen" / flach wie ein Brett
good as gold	gut wie Gold
hot as hell	heiß wie die Hölle / höllisch heiß
mad as a hatter	verrückt wie ein Hutmacher / total verrückt
meek as a lamb (b *ist stumm*)	sanft wie ein Lamm / lammfromm
proud as a peacock	stolz wie ein Pfau
thick as a brick	„dumm wie ein Ziegelstein" / dumm wie Bohnenstroh
timid as a mouse (*scharfes* s!)	schüchtern wie eine Maus
white as a sheet	weiß wie ein Laken

as = wie
bold = kühn
busy = fleißig
drunk = betrunken
dry = trocken
flat = flach
hot = heiß
mad = verrückt
proud = stolz
timid = schüchtern

Unit 7F

Focus on culture

1. The Boston Marathon

The world's oldest annual (= *jährlich*) marathon, begun in 1897 and, with about 20,000 runners each year, one of the best-known marathons in the world. It takes place on Patriots' Day, the third (3rd) Monday in April.

2. Boston

Boston, in the northeastern United States, is the capital of the state of Massachusetts and, with a population of about 600,000, the state's largest city. Boston was the scene of the so-called Boston Tea Party, 1773, in which American colonists protested against the British tax on tea. A group of colonists, dressed as Indians, boarded three tea ships and threw 342 large boxes of tea into the harbour. In 1775, the American Revolution began, and in 1783 the United States became an independent nation.

1/37

begun = begonnen (→ S. 219)
best-known = bekanntest
take place = stattfinden
third = dritte

largest = größte
scene = Schauplatz
so-called = sogenannt
tax = Steuer
dressed as = verkleidet als
board = besteigen
threw = warfen
began = begann
became = wurde(n)
independent = unabhängig

Unit 7G   Test yourself

Definitions Crossword

heavy = schwer
surgery = eine Operation
ill = krank
cake = Kuchen
frying pan = Bratpfanne
look = aussehen
a bit = ein bisschen
like = wie
young = jung
sheep = Schaf
animal = Tier
lie on = liegen auf
at night = nachts
violin (Betonung auf „-in") = Geige
run slowly = langsam laufen
devil = Teufel
put your feet up = die Füße hochlegen

ACROSS

1 1.6 kilometres.
3 A person who has worked in a job for a very long time.
7 Too heavy.
11 A place where you go for surgery or when you are very ill.
12 A cake that you make in a frying pan.
13 An expensive metal.
14 A metal that looks a bit like gold.
15 People who run.
17 A young sheep.
18 A room where people work.
19 A grey little animal that is very quick.

DOWN

1 A race of about 42 kilometres or 26 miles.
2 60 minutes.
4 What you lie on in your bed at night.
5 A violin.
6 Run slowly as fitness training.
8 In the end.
9 Make (something) better.
10 The place where the devil lives.
14 Having a lot to do.
15 Stop working because too old.
16 Take it easy, put your feet up.

90

Memory

Unit 8

- Das *present perfect* (die „*have*-Form" des Verbs)
- Unregelmäßige Verben
- *Was / were going to*
- Gebrauch der *-ly*-Wörter
- Gebrauch der *-ing*-Form
- *Some – any*
- *Used to*
- *Should – shouldn't*
- Relativsatz ohne Relativpronomen
- *... and your English is bloody damn good!*

Unit 8A — Dialogue

1/38

■ = Ken
● = Paul

used to be = pflegte zu sein
become = werden, geworden
terrible = schrecklich
remember sth = sich etw merken
interrupt = unterbrechen
happen = passieren
go ahead! = schieß los!
already = bereits, schon
anywhere = irgendwohin
think about = nachdenken über

I used to be so good at remembering names, but today … (= früher konnte ich mir so gut Namen merken, aber heute …) Ums (scheinbar) schlechte Gedächtnis geht es in dieser Lektion. Wir treffen zwei Männer, die äußerst zerstreut zu sein scheinen, aber, wie sich erweist, es gar nicht sind.

Memory isn't everything

■ My memory really isn't what it used to be. The other day …
● You're not alone. I've become terrible with names myself, just can't remember them. But what were you going to say?
■ What do you mean? Was I going to say something?
● Well, you said, "The other day …"
■ I've no idea what I was going to say. Did you interrupt me?
● Yes I think I did. Sorry! But I can tell you what happened to ME the other day.
■ Yes, go ahead. I'm not going to interrupt YOU.
● You've interrupted me already. I was going to tell you something and now I've forgotten what it was.
■ You wanted to tell me what happened to you the other day.
● Damn it! YOU said, "The other day …," and then you stopped talking.
■ Because YOU interrupted me.
● I don't think this is getting us anywhere.
■ You're right. One shouldn't talk while playing chess. I was thinking about my next move all the time. – Check!

● I knew you were up to something. But you haven't got me yet. Just let me think …

Gedächtnis ist nicht alles

■ Mein Gedächtnis ist wirklich nicht, was es einmal war. Neulich …
● Du bist nicht allein. / Da bist du nicht allein. Ich bin selbst „furchtbar geworden" mit Namen, kann sie mir einfach nicht merken. Aber was wolltest du sagen?
■ Was meinst du (damit)? Wollte ich etwas sagen?
● Nun, du sagtest: „Neulich …"
■ Ich habe keine Ahnung, was ich sagen wollte. Hast du mich unterbrochen?
● Ja, ich glaube(, das habe ich). Tut mir leid. Aber ich kann dir sagen, was MIR neulich passiert ist.
■ Ja, tue das. Ich werde DICH nicht unterbrechen.
● Du hast mich bereits unterbrochen. Ich wollte dir etwas erzählen, und jetzt habe ich vergessen, was es war.
■ Du wolltest mir erzählen, was dir neulich passiert ist.
● Verdammt (noch mal)! DU sagtest: „Neulich …", und dann hörtest du auf zu reden.
■ Weil DU mich unterbrachst.
● Ich glaube, dies führt zu nichts.
■ Du hast recht. Man sollte nicht reden, während man Schach spielt. Ich habe die ganze Zeit über meinen nächsten Zug nachgedacht. – Schach!

● Ich wusste, dass du etwas im Schilde führtest. Aber du hast mich noch nicht. Lass mich nur nachdenken …

Unit 8B

Rules and practice

1 Das *present perfect* (→ 7B2)

Lassen Sie sich durch den Begriff *present perfect* nicht irritieren. Hauptsache, Sie kennen die Form, um die es hier geht – wir nennen sie manchmal auch einfach die *have*-Form des Verbs:

| You **have interrupted** me. | Du **hast** mich **unterbrochen**. |
| He **has suffered** a heart attack. | Er **hat** einen Herzinfarkt **erlitten**. |

Zur Bildung des *present perfect* benötigen wir außer *have/has* die 3. Form des Verbs:

| 1. Form: | interrupt | 2. Form: | interrupted | 3. Form: | **interrupted** |
| | *unterbrechen* | | *unterbrach* | | ***unterbrochen*** |

Wir erinnern uns (→ 7D2): Bei regelmäßigen Verben (wie z. B. *interrupt*) werden die 2. und 3. Form gleich gebildet, nämlich durch Anhängen von *-ed*.

✎ Übersetzen Sie nun die folgenden Sätze. Sie haben alle die gleiche Struktur:

Subjekt („sie" etc.) + *have(n't) / has* + 3. Form (*-ed*) des Verbs + Objekt („dich" etc.)

a Wir haben dich vermisst. _____
b Er hat das Spiel beendet. _____
c Sie hat ihr Englisch verbessert. _____
d Sie haben ein Doppelzimmer gebucht. _____
e Sie haben meine E-Mail nicht beantwortet. _____

miss = vermissen
game = Spiel
finish = beenden
improve = verbessern
answer = beantworten

2 Die folgenden Sätze haben im Prinzip die gleiche Struktur wie die in 1a–e. Wiederum Subjekt + *have/has* + Verb, aber danach kein Objekt, sondern eine andere Art von „Zusatz". – Übersetzen Sie.

Unit 8B

too long = zu lange
enough = genug
stop talking = aufhören zu reden
always = immer

a Er hat zu lange gewartet. _____
b Ihr habt genug trainiert. _____
c Sie haben aufgehört zu reden. _____
d Ich habe immer mit jungen Leuten gearbeitet. _____

3 Wir haben das *present perfect* als „*have*-Form" bezeichnet, weil dieses Perfekt immer mit *have* gebildet wird (→ 7D3). Im Englischen, aber nicht im Deutschen! Im Deutschen bilden wir diese Form manchmal mit „sein": „ist angekommen", „ist gegangen". Im Englischen müssen Sie umdenken: „hat angekommen", „hat passiert", „hat in den Ruhestand gegangen". – Übersetzen Sie.

arrive = ankommen
happen = passieren
retire = in den Ruhestand gehen

a Der Brief ist angekommen. _____
b Was ist passiert? _____
c Sie ist in den Ruhestand gegangen. _____

4 Neue unregelmäßige Verben (→ 7D2)

Neue unregelmäßige Verben (→ Tabelle S. 219)

become – became – **become**	werden – wurde – **geworden**
forget – forgot – **forgotten**	vergessen – vergaß – **vergessen**
get – got – **got**	kriegen – kriegte – **gekriegt**
run – ran – **run**	laufen – lief – **gelaufen**

✏️ Übersetzen Sie die folgenden Sätze mit unregelmäßigen Verben. Wortstellung: Subjekt + *have/has* + Verb + Rest.

terrible = schrecklich
34 times = 34-mal

a Ich habe vergessen, was es war. _____
b Ihr Service ist schrecklich geworden. _____
c Er ist den Marathon 34-mal gelaufen. _____
d Du hast mich noch nicht (gekriegt). _____

5 *Was / were going to*

Wir haben *am/are/is going to* als eine Zukunftsform kennengelernt, mit der besonders die **Absicht**, etwas zu tun, betont wird:

I**'m going to** train for the marathon.	*Ich werde für den Marathon trainieren.*
I**'m not going to** interrupt you.	*Ich werde dich nicht unterbrechen.*

In 8A finden wir nun mehrere Beispiele für den Gebrauch der *going to*-Konstruktion in der Vergangenheit:

Unit 8B

What **were** you **going to** say?	*Was wolltest du sagen?*
Was I **going to** say something?	*Wollte ich etwas sagen?*
I **was going to** tell you something.	*Ich wollte dir etwas sagen.*

Wie die Übersetzungen deutlich machen, bezeichnet *was/were going to* hier eine Absicht, die nicht oder noch nicht ausgeführt wurde. Eine solche nicht ausgeführte Absicht drücken wir im Deutschen meist mit der Vergangenheitsform von „wollen" aus. Entsprechend können wir im Englischen auch die Vergangenheitsform von *want to* benutzen.

 Ersetzen Sie bitte in den folgenden Sätzen die *going to*-Konstruktion durch eine solche mit *want to*.

I was going to tell you something. → I wanted to tell you something.
What were you going to say? → What did you want to say?

a I was going to get up early tomorrow. — *I want to get up*
b She was going to go to the doctor yesterday. — *She want to go*
c He was going to run the marathon but didn't. — *he wanted to run*
d She was going to retire at the end of the year. — *She wanted to retire*
e Were you going to play with the dogs? — *did you want to play*
f Were you going to walk to the hotel? — *did you want to walk*

get up early = früh aufstehen
tomorrow = morgen
yesterday = gestern
at the end = am Ende

6 Used to

Mit *used to* drückt man aus, dass etwas in der Vergangenheit häufig oder immer geschah oder der Fall war. Für das Verständnis hilfreich ist die wörtliche deutsche Übersetzung „pflegte zu":

My memory isn't what it **used to** be.	*Mein Gedächtnis ist nicht, was es **zu** sein **pflegte**.*

Häufig übersetzt man *used to* mit „früher", „(ein)mal" oder „immer":

My memory **used to** be better.	*Früher war mein Gedächtnis besser.*
There **used to** be trees here.	*Früher waren hier mal Bäume.*
She **used to** be so happy here.	*Sie war doch immer so glücklich hier.*

used to = gewöhnt sein
be = sein

7 Hör-Sprech-Übung. Sie sprechen über ein Ehepaar, das Sie früher einmal kannten. Von der CD hören Sie Aktivitäten, die Sie diesen Eheleuten jeweils in einem Satz mit *used to* zuordnen.

1/39

Sie hören zum Beispiel: ....go to the theatre a lot
Sie sagen: ....They used to go to the theatre a lot.

do sth a lot = etw häufig tun

Unit 8C

1/40

Reading text

What's your name again?

A lot of people have difficulty remembering names, especially as they grow older. You run into someone you know in the street, in the supermarket or at a social event, there's a moment of panic ("What on earth was her name?") and your mind goes blank. Of course, you can avoid addressing the person by name ("Oh, hello, how nice to see you!"), but that might seem impolite. What to do? Well, the best policy is probably to be frank and say with a smile: "I'm sorry, I know we've met before but I've forgotten your name. What was it again?"

Tricks for remembering names:
- When someone tells you their name, repeat it immediately and use it several times in your conversation.
- Writing the name down will also help you remember it.
- Remembering the meaning of a name may be helpful, but it can lead to embarrassing mistakes. You meet a man named Frost and you think of "cold and white". The next time you meet Mr Frost you might address him as Mr Snow.

Wie war doch noch Ihr Name?

Viele Leute haben Schwierigkeiten, sich Namen zu merken, besonders wenn sie älter werden. Sie treffen jemand, den Sie kennen, auf der Straße, im Supermarkt oder bei einem gesellschaftlichen Anlass, es gibt einen Augenblick der Panik („Wie in aller Welt hieß sie noch?") und Ihr Verstand („wird leer") setzt aus. Natürlich können Sie es vermeiden, den Betreffenden mit Namen anzureden („Ah, hallo, wie schön, Sie zu sehen!"), aber das könnte unhöflich erscheinen.

Was kann/soll man da machen? Nun, die beste („Politik") Verfahrensweise ist es wahrscheinlich, offen zu sein und mit einem Lächeln zu sagen: „Es tut mir leid, ich weiß, dass wir uns schon mal begegnet sind, aber ich habe Ihren Namen vergessen. Wie war er doch gleich?"

Tricks für das Merken von Namen:
- Wenn Ihnen jemand seinen Namen sagt, wiederholen Sie ihn sofort und benutzen Sie ihn mehrmals in Ihrem Gespräch.
- Den Namen auf(zu)schreiben wird Ihnen auch helfen, ihn zu behalten.
- Sich die Bedeutung eines Namens zu merken, kann hilfreich sein, aber es kann zu peinlichen Fehlern führen. Sie treffen einen Mann namens Frost und Sie denken an „kalt und weiß". Wenn Sie Mr Frost das nächste Mal treffen, könnten (könnte es passieren, dass) Sie ihn mit Mr Snow anreden.

---

again = wieder
difficulty = Schwierigkeit(en)
remember names = sich Namen merken
especially = besonders
grow older = älter werden
run into someone = (zufällig) jemand treffen
mind = Verstand, Kopf
blank = leer
go blank = „Mattscheibe haben"
avoid doing sth = es vermeiden, etw zu tun
address = ansprechen
frank = offen, ehrlich
repeat = wiederholen
immediately = sofort
write down = aufschreiben
may be = kann sein
might be = könnte sein
a man named Frost = ein Mann namens Frost
snow = Schnee

Rules and practice

Unit 8D

1 Gebrauch der -ly-Wörter (Adverbien) (1)

-ly-Wörter (Adverbien) dienen unter anderem der näheren Bestimmung von Verben. Im Gegensatz zum Deutschen steht das -ly-Wort sehr häufig **vor** dem Verb:

I **eventually** managed ten miles.   Ich schaffte **schließlich** zehn Meilen.

Setzen Sie die folgenden -ly-Adverbien an passender Stelle in den Sätzen ein.

finally, immediately, probably, really, suddenly

a When they arrived, there were no taxis. _____
b She will miss the people she worked with. _____
c He felt a pain in his chest. _____
d His doctor sent him to the emergency room. _____
e I don't want a new computer. _____

feel – felt = fühlen – fühlte
send – sent = schicken – schickte
don't want a new PC = will keinen neuen PC

2 Gebrauch der -ly-Wörter (Adverbien) (2). – Setzen Sie die -ly-Adverbien nach Gefühl ein: nach Verb oder vor Nichtverb.

absolutely, completely, endlessly, especially, exclusively, really

a We had to wait at the airport. _____
b The food was disgusting. _____
c My memory isn't what it used to be. _____
d There's an indoor pool for our guests. _____
e I was a bit overweight and unfit. _____
f A lot of people have difficulty remembering names as they grow older. _____

3 Gebrauch der -ing-Form des Verbs

Ihnen ist sicher schon aufgefallen, wie häufig die -ing-Form vorkommt und wie wenig wir dazu bisher gesagt haben – mit einer großen Ausnahme: ihrer Verwendung in der Verlaufsform in Gegenwart, Vergangenheit und Zukunft (→ 5B1, 5D1, 6D3, 7B1c). In vielen Fällen hat die -ing-Form aber nichts mit der Verlaufsform zu tun, und mit einigen dieser Fälle wollen wir uns jetzt beschäftigen.

Unit 8D

a. -ing-Form zur Satzverkürzung

Hier entspricht -ing etwa dem deutschen „-end" („spielend", „überblickend").

One shouldn't talk while (one is) **playing** chess.	Man sollte nicht reden, während man Schach spielt.
The hotel is on a hill **overlooking** a lake.	Das Hotel ist auf einem Berg mit Blick auf einen See.

b. -ing-Form nach einer Form von go

You can go **swimming** in the lake.	Man kann im See schwimmen gehen.

c. -ing-Form nach Präpositionen

Präpositionen sind Wörter wie *for*, *of* oder *in* und drücken in der Regel ein Verhältnis zu einem nachfolgenden Substantiv oder Pronomen aus (z. B. *for our guests, for them*). Folgt auf die Präposition ein Verb, so muss dieses in der *-ing*-Form stehen:

Tricks for **remembering** names	Tricks für das Merken von Namen

d. -ing-Form als Subjekt

Hier wird das Verb durch das Anhängen von *-ing* praktisch zu einem Substantiv. Dem entspricht im Deutschen die großgeschriebene Grundform des Verbs.

Smoking is not allowed here.	(Das) Rauchen ist hier nicht erlaubt.

e. -ing-Form als Objekt oder sonstige Ergänzung nach einem Verb

I took up **jogging** about ten years ago.	Ich habe vor etwa zehn Jahren mit Joggen angefangen.
What I won't miss is **getting up** early every morning.	Was ich nicht vermissen werde, ist jeden Morgen früh aufzustehen.

 Setzen Sie die folgenden Verben ein – in der *-ing*-Form oder in der Grundform.

eat, get, read, remember, shop, speak, train, watch, write

a _____ of restaurants, it's lunchtime and I'm hungry.

b At 65, and _____ for his 35th marathon, he felt fit as a fiddle.

c We can go _____ on Fifth Avenue.

d She's fond of _____ reality TV shows.

e If you write a name down, you will _____ it better.

f _____ a name down will help you remember it.

g _____ the meaning of a name may be helpful.

fit as a fiddle = topfit

h Fancy _____ married in Sydney, ten thousand miles away.

i You should never _____ junk food.

j You should avoid _____ junk food.

k I think I'll do some _____ before I go to bed.

4   Hier fehlt doch etwas!

Zweimal hatten wir bisher eine Konstruktion, die sehr häufig vorkommt, vom Deutschen her aber schwer zu durchschauen ist:

| 1. You run into someone **you know**. | *Sie treffen jemand, **den** Sie kennen.* |
| 2. The people **I work with** are very nice. | *Die Leute, **mit denen** ich zusammenarbeite, sind sehr nett.* |

Den fett gedruckten Satzteil nennt man einen Relativsatz (→ 9D4). Ein Relativsatz ist eine nähere Bestimmung zu einem Substantiv (hier: *the people*) bzw. Pronomen (hier: *someone*). Mit anderen Worten:
1. *Someone* wird durch *you know* näher bestimmt; es ist nicht einfach irgendjemand, sondern „jemand, den Sie kennen".
2. *The people* wird durch *I work with* näher bestimmt; es sind nicht einfach irgendwelche Leute, sondern „die Leute, mit denen ich zusammenarbeite", also die Kollegen.

Aber wir sehen: Im Deutschen ist der Relativsatz mit einem (oben unterstrichenen) Bezugswort (Relativpronomen) versehen, das im Englischen fehlt: 1. „den", 2. „denen". Auch im Englischen könnten wir das Bezugswort (Relativpronomen) einsetzen; es wäre, da es sich auf Personen bezieht, *who*:
1. You run into someone *who you know*.
2. The people *who I work with* are very nice.
Es ist aber sehr unüblich, in Relativsätzen dieses Typs das Relativpronomen zu setzen, weshalb wir jetzt Relativsätze ohne Relativpronomen üben.

✎ Relativsätze ohne Relativpronomen. – Übersetzen Sie.

a das Zimmer, das wir buchten   _____

b die Geschichten, die er erzählt   _____

c das Essen, das wir hier bekommen   _____

d die Taschen, die ich tragen musste   _____

e das Haus, in dem sie leben   _____

Unit 8D

book a room = ein Zimmer buchen
tell a story = eine Geschichte erzählen
food = Essen
carry a bag = eine Tasche tragen

Unit 8E — Focus on words

bejahend: **some**
verneinend: **any**
fragend: **any**

1. Some – any: Bejahend steht *some* (= einige / etwas); **verneinend** oder **fragend** steht *any*; das Gleiche gilt für die Zusammensetzungen *something/anything*, *someone / anyone* und *somewhere/anywhere*:

There were **some** ducks on the lake.	*Es waren (einige) Enten auf dem See.*
Were there **any** ducks on the lake?	*Waren Enten auf dem See?*
There weren't **any** ducks on the lake.	*Es waren keine Enten auf dem See.*
She knows **something** about it.	*Sie weiß etwas davon.*
She doesn't know **anything** about it.	*Sie weiß nichts davon.*
There's **someone** in the house.	*Es ist jemand im Haus.*
Is there **anyone*** in the house?	*Ist jemand im Haus?*
The dog is **somewhere** in the house.	*Der Hund ist irgendwo im Haus.*
The dog isn't **anywhere** in the house.	*Der Hund ist nirgendwo im Haus.*

*Sagt man hier *someone*, so deutet man damit an, dass man schon vermutet, dass jemand im Haus ist, und das bestätigt haben möchte. Entsprechendes gilt für *Was I going to say something?* in 8A.

2. Every, everything, everyone

every = jede(r, s)
everything = alles
everyone = jeder, alle

every man, **every** woman, **every** child	*jeder Mann, jede Frau, jedes Kind*
Everything is expensive.	*Alles ist teuer.*
Everyone knows it.	*Jeder weiß es. / Alle wissen es.*

3. Should – shouldn't: Oscar Wilde (1854–1900) legt einem seiner Bühnencharaktere den schönen Satz in den Mund:

never = nie
diary = Tagebuch
sensational = sensationell
train = Zug

I never travel without my diary. One **should** always have something sensational to read in the train.	*Ich reise nie ohne mein Tagebuch. Man **sollte** im Zug immer etwas Sensationelles zu lesen haben.*

Die Verneinung *shouldn't* finden Sie in unserem Dialog:

One **shouldn't** talk while playing chess.	*Man **sollte nicht** reden, während man Schach spielt. / Man **sollte** beim Schachspielen **nicht** reden.*

4. May – might: *May* und *might* heißen „kann" und „könnte", wobei „können" hier nicht Fähigkeit, sondern Möglichkeit ausdrückt. *It may happen* = „es kann passieren" / „es ist möglich, dass es passiert"; *it might happen* = „es könnte passieren". Bei *might* ist die Wahrscheinlichkeit geringer als bei *may*:

Remembering the meaning of a name **may** be helpful.	*Sich die Bedeutung eines Namens zu merken **kann** hilfreich sein.*
It **might** seem impolite.	*Es **könnte** unhöflich erscheinen.*
The next time you **might** address him as Mr Snow.	*Beim nächsten Mal **könnten** Sie ihn als Mr Snow anreden.*

Unit 8F

Focus on culture

1/41

1. *Chess*: *Playing chess is fun and a good way to keep your brain fit and avoid Alzheimer's disease. It is a game for two players using a chessboard on which they move their pieces trying to get the other player's king into a position where he cannot move* (*checkmate* = schachmatt). *Apart from the king, each player has 15 pieces: the queen, two bishops* (= Läufer), *two knights* (= Springer), *two rooks* (= Türme), *and eight pawns* (= Bauern). Beachten Sie aber, dass die meisten der Figurennamen außerhalb des Schachspiels ganz andere Bedeutungen haben: *bishop* (= Bischof), *knight* (= Ritter), *rook* (= Saatkrähe), *pawn* (= Pfand).

brain = Gehirn
avoid = vermeiden
disease = Krankheit
chessboard = Schachbrett
move = (sich) bewegen
piece = Spielfigur
try = versuchen

2. *Remember – remembrance:* Ein wichtiger britischer Feiertag ist *Remembrance Sunday* (≈ Volkstrauertag), an dem der in den beiden Weltkriegen Gefallenen gedacht wird. An diesem *Sunday closest to 11 November* finden überall im Land Gedenkveranstaltungen statt, die größte im Beisein der *Queen* am *Cenotaph* (= Mahnmal / Ehrenmal) im Londoner *Whitehall*. An diesem Tag stecken sich viele Briten rote Papierblumen an (*poppies* = Mohnblumen – sie blühten auf den Schlachtfeldern in Belgien und Frankreich), weshalb der Tag volkstümlich auch *Poppy Day* heißt.

remember = sich erinnern
close to = nahe bei

3. Kraftausdrücke (= *swear words*) sind Geschmackssache – *a matter of taste*. In 8A haben wir *damn it!* (= verdammt noch mal!), was ein eher milder Fluch ist. Beachten Sie zur Aussprache: das *n* in *damn* wird nicht gesprochen.
Sehr viel stärker wird Ärger mit *fuck it!* zum Ausdruck gebracht, oder es werden Aussagen durch *fucking* bzw. *the fuck* verstärkt: *I couldn't remember his fucking name. I was in a fucking panic. What the fuck was his (fucking) name?* Diese vulgärsprachlichen Verstärker gelten als tabu, sind aber in der Umgangssprache häufig zu hören, wobei in der Regel keinerlei sexuelle Vorstellung mitschwingt.
Weniger drastisch als *fucking*, aber immer noch recht derb ist *bloody* (→ 2E3, 9G) – im britischen Englisch das häufigste *swear word*: *Don't be such a bloody fool.* (= Sei doch nicht so ein verdammter Idiot!), *It's bloody cold in here.* (= Es ist verdammt kalt hier drin.), *You know bloody well what I mean.* (= Du weißt verdammt gut, was ich meine.) Häufig wird *bloody* auch zur Verstärkung einer positiven, anerkennenden Äußerung gebraucht: *She's a bloody nice girl.* (= Sie ist ein verdammt nettes Mädchen.), *Their latest album is bloody (damn) good.* (= Ihr neuestes Album ist verdammt gut.)
Als Ausländer(in) sollte man auf den Gebrauch dieser *swear words* verzichten, da man ihre Wirkung auf englischsprachige Gesprächspartner(innen) schlecht einschätzen kann.

swear word = Kraftausdruck
a matter of taste = eine Geschmackssache
damn: das „n" ist stumm!
fuck him! = scheiß auf ihn!
fucking = Scheiß-
what the fuck = was zum Teufel
bloody = verdammt, Scheiß-

Unit 8G — Test yourself

1/42

Listening comprehension exercise (= Hörverstehensübung)

In der Tonaufnahme finden Sie an dieser Stelle ein Gespräch zwischen einem Mann und einer Frau. Hören Sie den kleinen Dialog bitte so oft, bis Sie die folgenden Fragen alle beantworten können. (Das Gespräch ist auch im Schlüssel abgedruckt, auf S. 197.)

a What's the woman's name? — Jessica
b Where's she from? — Berlin
c What's the man's name? — Martin
d Where's he from? — Sherfield
e When did they first meet? — after the marathon
f And where was their first meeting? — bar of the Westhotel
g What does the woman say about small hotels? — she likes small
h What does the man say about small hotels? — he like small hotels too

meet someone = jemand treffen
(first) meet someone = jemand kennenlernen
meeting = Begegnung
meet – met = treffen – traf
by London standards = nach Londoner Maßstäben

Food

Unit 9

- Essen im Restaurant
- Vorschläge formulieren
- *Would(n't)* = würde (nicht)
- *Could* = konnte / könnte
- Hilfsverben als Stellvertreter
- Steigerung und Vergleich
- Unregelmäßige Plurale
- Relativsätze
- *… and a delicious temptation!*

Unit 9A Dialogue

2/1

■ = David
● = Katie

like = wie
shall we? = sollen wir? / wollen wir?
let's = **let us** = lass(t) uns
would you like to have = würdest du gern haben
salmon: stummes „l"
they do have = sie haben wirklich
I'd love = **I would love** = ich würde gernhaben
it would put pounds on me = er würde Pfunde „auf mich tun"
you must be joking = du „musst sein spaßend"

At a restaurant

■ This looks like a nice place, don't you think?
● It does indeed. Shall we sit outside?

■ Better not, if you ask me. Too hot and too many wasps.
● Fair enough. Let's go inside then.
■ The table over there, in the corner?
● Yes, lovely.
■ Waiter, um, can we have the menu, please? – Ah, here we are. Thank you very much. – Now, let's see ... What would you like to have?
● Hmm, I think I'll go for the table d'hôte menu. That's three courses, isn't it?
■ Yes, starter, main course, and dessert.

● Mm-hmm, I think I'll have the prawn cocktail as a starter ...
■ Yes ...?
● ... and the salmon for the main course ... and, hmm, they do have some tempting desserts ...
I'd love the cheesecake, but it would put pounds on me.

■ Why don't you try the Dundee pudding, it's with fruits ...

● ... and topped with almonds, it says here, and whisky syrup and creamy custard. Sounds delicious. – And you? What are you going to have?
■ I think I'll just have a mixed salad.

● Oh David, you must be joking.

■ No, not joking – dieting!

In einem Restaurant

■ Dies sieht wie ein nettes Lokal aus, meinst du nicht?
● Das tut es in der Tat. Wollen wir uns draußen hinsetzen?
■ Besser nicht, wenn du mich fragst. Zu heiß und zu viele Wespen.
● Na gut. Gehen wir nach drinnen.
■ Der Tisch da drüben, in der Ecke?
● Ja, prima.
■ Herr Ober, ähm, können wir bitte die Speisekarte haben? – Ah, da ist sie. Vielen Dank! – So, nun wollen wir mal sehen ... Was hättest du denn gern?
● Hm, ich glaube, ich nehme das Tagesmenü. Das sind drei Gänge, nech?
■ Ja, Vorspeise, Hauptgericht und Dessert.

● Mm-hm, ich glaube, ich nehme den Krabbencocktail als Vorspeise ...
■ Ja ...?
● ... und den Lachs als Hauptgericht ... und, hm, die haben aber auch verführerische Desserts ...
Am liebsten nähm ich den Cheesecake, aber da würde ich Pfunde zunehmen.

■ Warum probierst du nicht den Dundee-Pudding, der ist mit Früchten ...

● ... und mit Mandeln drauf, heißt es hier, und Whiskysirup und sahniger Vanillesoße. Klingt köstlich. – Und du? Was nimmst du?
■ Ich glaube, ich nehme nur einen gemischten Salat.

● Aber David, das soll wohl ein Witz sein?

■ Nein, kein Witz – ich mache Diät.

Unit 9B

Rules and practice

1 Der Dialog zeigt uns mehrere Möglichkeiten, einen Vorschlag zu machen bzw. nach den Wünschen des Gesprächspartners zu fragen:

Shall we sit outside?	*Wollen wir uns nach draußen setzen?*
Let's (= Let us) go inside then.	*Dann lass(t) uns reingehen.*
Why don't you try the Dundee pudding?	*Warum probierst du nicht (mal) den Dundee pudding?*

shall we ...?
shall I ...?
let's ...
why don't you ...?
why don't we ...?
do you want me to ...?

Mit *shall I* kann man nach dem Wunsch der angesprochenen Person fragen:

Shall I wait? — *Soll ich warten?*

Diese Frage kann man mit etwa gleicher Bedeutung auch so formulieren:

Do you want me to wait? — *Willst du, dass ich warte?*

 Formulieren Sie den fett gedruckten Satzteil entsprechend der Aussageabsicht um.

Shall we try the Dundee pudding? → Why don't we try / Let's try the Dundee pudding.
Shall I give you my email address? → Do you want me to give you my email address?

a **Shall we** take the bus? _____
b **Let's** play some chess. _____
c **Why don't we** relax a bit? _____
d **Shall I** stop here? _____
e **Do you want me to** get you a taxi? _____
f **Let's** get married. _____
g **Shall I** arrange theatre tickets? _____

try = probieren
relax = sich ausruhen
stop = anhalten
get a taxi = ein Taxi besorgen

Unit 9B

would / -'d = würde

2 *Would* heißt „würde" und wird oft auf die Kurzform *'d* reduziert:

It **would** put pounds on me.	„Er würde Pfunde auf mich tun." / Ich würde Pfunde zulegen.
What **would** you like to have?	Was würdest du gern haben? / Was hättest du gern?
I'd (= I **would**) love the cheesecake.	„Ich würde den Käsekuchen lieben." / Ich hätte liebend gern den Käsekuchen.

In Verbindung mit einem weiteren Verb entspricht *would* dem deutschen Konjunktiv:

I would be	I'd be	ich würde sein	ich wäre
I would have	I'd have	ich würde haben	ich hätte
I would go	I'd go	ich würde gehen	ich ginge
I would take	I'd take	ich würde nehmen	ich nähme etc.

✎ Übersetzen Sie diese ganz einfachen Fügungen mit *would* = „würde". Denken Sie an die Wortstellung: Subjekt – Verbgruppe (*would* + Verb) – Ergänzung/Objekt.

take = nehmen
wait = warten
try = probieren
frank = offen
mistake = Fehler
ticket = (Eintritts-)Karte
get = besorgen
actually = eigentlich
need = brauchen

a Ich würde diesen Tisch nehmen. _____

b Ich würde zwei Tage warten. _____

c Ich würde den Dundee-Pudding probieren. _____

d Ich würde offen sein / wäre offen. _____

e Es würde ein Fehler sein / wäre ein Fehler. _____

f Wir würden ein großes Problem haben / hätten ein großes Problem. _____

g Sie würde Karten für das Konzert besorgen. _____

h Wir würden eigentlich zwei Zimmer brauchen. _____

3 Die folgenden Sätze sind alle verneint, d. h. statt *would* benutzen Sie jeweils *wouldn't*. Übersetzen Sie.

expensive = teuer
interested = interessiert
unusual = ungewöhnlich
go swimming = schwimmen gehen
have to = müssen
happy = glücklich

a Es wäre nicht teuer. _____

b Ich wäre nicht interessiert. _____

c Das wäre nichts Ungewöhnliches. _____

d Er würde mir nicht helfen. _____

e Ich würde hier nicht schwimmen gehen. _____

f Ich würde das nicht sagen. _____

g Du würdest nicht ins Büro gehen müssen. _____

h Sie wäre dort nicht glücklich. _____

4 Hilfsverben als „Hauptverb-Stellvertreter"

Unit 9B

Hilfsverben sind z. B. *can, will, would, should, do (does, did), be (am, is, are, was, were)* und *have (has)*. In den folgenden Beispielen wird durch den Gebrauch eines Hilfsverbs eine Wiederholung des Hauptverbs vermieden.

It looks nice. – It **does** indeed.	= It looks nice indeed.
Many people climb the bridge and we **did** too.	= … and we climbed the bridge too.
Did you interrupt me? – Yes I think I **did**.	= Yes I think I interrupted you.
Didn't you enjoy your holiday? – No I can't say I **did**.	= No I can't say I enjoyed my holiday.
Will I miss it? – I probably **will**.	= I probably will miss it.
Isn't this park just beautiful? – Yes it **is**.	= Yes it is beautiful.

climb = besteigen
interrupt = unterbrechen
enjoy = genießen
probably = wahrscheinlich

Fügen Sie in den folgenden Sätzen das passende Stellvertreter-Hilfsverb ein.

a Are they sitting outside? – Yes they _____.

b It's too hot here. – Yes it _____.

c The salmon looks good. – Yes it _____.

d Do you remember her name? – Yes I _____.

e Hasn't she retired? – Yes she _____.

f Didn't she retire last November? – Yes she _____.

g Won't you miss going to the office? – Yes I probably _____.

h Won't you miss going to the office? – No I suppose I _____.

i Can you see the lake from your window? – No I _____.

j Would the tickets be expensive? – No _____.

k Do you remember the girl's name? – No _____.

l Didn't they give you something to eat? – No _____.

m Weren't there any taxis? – No _____.

sit outside = draußen sitzen
salmon („l" ist stumm) = Lachs
remember = sich erinnern an
retire = in den Ruhestand gehen

5 Hör-Sprech-Übung. In dieser Übung hören Sie Sätze von der CD, die Sie mit *indeed* bestätigen sollen.

2/2

Sie hören zum Beispiel: ....This building looks strange.
Sie sagen: ....It does indeed.
Sie hören die richtige Antwort: ....It does indeed.
Sie wiederholen die Antwort: ....It does indeed.

strange = eigenartig
indeed = tatsächlich, wirklich, in der Tat
tempting = verführerisch

Unit 9C Reading text

2/3

the other day = neulich
have lunch = (zu) Mittag essen
niece (Aussprache „nieß")
more ... than = mehr ... als
more attractive than = attraktiver als
a year ago = vor einem Jahr
chubby = rundlich
then = damalig
needless = unnötig
more – less = mehr – weniger
no = kein(e)
pizza (langes „i")
twice a week = zweimal die Woche
even if = auch wenn
as flat as = so flach wie

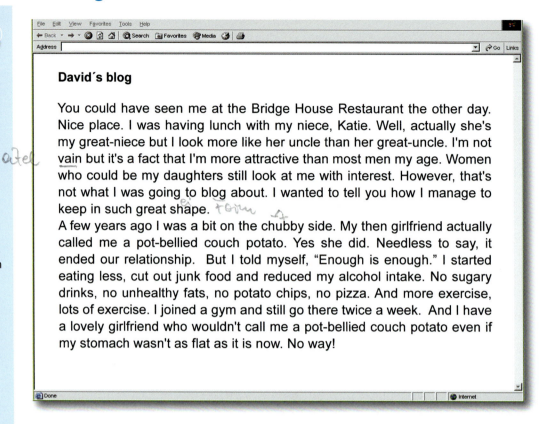

Davids blog

Ihr hättet mich neulich im Bridge House Restaurant sehen können. Nettes Lokal. Ich aß zu Mittag mit meiner Nichte Katie. Nun / Also eigentlich ist sie meine Großnichte, aber ich sehe mehr wie ihr Onkel aus als (wie) ihr Großonkel. Ich bin nicht eitel, aber es ist (nun mal) eine Tatsache, dass ich attraktiver bin als die meisten Männer meines Alters. Frauen, die meine Töchter sein könnten, sehen mich immer noch mit Interesse an. Aber das ist nicht das, worüber ich bloggen / ein Blog schreiben wollte. Ich wollte euch erzählen, wie ich es schaffe, so toll in Form zu bleiben.

Vor ein paar Jahren war ich ein bisschen rundlich. Meine damalige Freundin nannte mich (doch) tatsächlich eine spitzbäuchige Couchkartoffel. Ja, (das tat sie) tatsächlich! Das beendete natürlich unsere Beziehung. Aber ich sagte mir: „Genug ist genug." Ich begann weniger zu essen, verzichtete auf Junkfood und reduzierte meinen Alkoholkonsum. Keine zuckrigen Getränke, keine ungesunden Fette, keine Pommes frites, keine Pizza. Und mehr Bewegung, viel Bewegung. Ich meldete mich bei einem Fitnesscenter an und gehe immer noch zweimal die Woche hin. Und ich habe eine reizende / nette Freundin, die mich nicht eine spitzbäuchige Couchkartoffel nennen würde, selbst wenn mein Bauch nicht so flach wäre, wie er jetzt ist. Auf keinen Fall! / Ausgeschlossen!

Unit 9D

Rules and practice

1 Could

In Aussagen über die Vergangenheit entspricht *could* dem deutschen „**konnte**":

| At first I **could** only jog for a couple of minutes, then I managed a mile. | Zuerst konnte ich nur ein paar Minuten joggen, dann schaffte ich eine Meile. |

In Aussagen über die Gegenwart entspricht *could* dem deutschen „**könnte**":

| Women who **could** be my daughters still look at me with interest. | Frauen, die meine Töchter sein könnten, sehen mich immer noch mit Interesse an. |

Eine interessante Form ist *could have* + 3. Form des Verbs:

| You **could have seen** me at the Bridge House Restaurant the other day. | Ihr („könntet haben gesehen mich") hättet mich neulich im Bridge House Restaurant sehen können. |

✎ Zur Übung der Form *could have* + 3. Form des Verbs übersetzen Sie bitte die folgenden Sätze.

a Ihr hättet anfangen können. _____
b Du hättest mich fragen können. _____
c Wir hätten das vermeiden können. _____
d Das hätte hier nicht passieren können. _____
e Wir hätten Schach spielen können. _____
f Ich hätte schneller laufen können. _____

2 Steigerung und Vergleich

ten minutes **faster than** the previous Jahr	zehn Minuten schneller als im Vorjahr
more attractive than most men	attraktiver als die meisten Männer
less than perfect	weniger als perfekt

---

could =
  konnte / könnte
could have seen =
  hätte sehen können

start = anfangen
ask = fragen
avoid =
  vermeiden
happen =
  passieren
play chess =
  Schach spielen
run faster =
  schneller laufen

faster than =
  schneller als
more attractive than =
  attraktiver als
less than =
  weniger als

Unit 9D

Beachten Sie:

1. Adjektive (= Eigenschaftswörter) werden gesteigert entweder
   a) durch **Anhängen von -(e)r** (wie im Deutschen) oder
   b) durch **Voranstellen von** *more*.
   Mit *-er* werden kürzere Wörter (wie *fast*), mit *more* längere Wörter (wie *attractive*) gesteigert. In Zweifelsfällen benutzen Sie *more*!

2. Als Schreibregel ist zu beachten, dass bei Wörtern wie *flat*, *hot* und *big* der Endkonsonant verdoppelt wird: *flatter*, *hotter*, *bigger*.
   Ein *-e* am Ende entfällt: *nice – nicer*, *large – larger*.

flat – flatter =
 flach – flacher
hot – hotter =
 heiß – heißer
big – bigger =
 groß – größer
large – larger =
 groß – größer

3. Unregelmäßig gesteigert werden nur wenige Wörter:

good – **better**	gut – besser
much – **more**	viel – mehr
many – **more**	viele – mehr
little – **less**	wenig – weniger
bad – **worse**	schlecht – schlechter
(wor- wie in *word*, dann scharfes *s*)	

[handwritten: good / better than / the best]

4. Dem deutschen „als" entspricht hier *than* – nicht *as* oder *when*, die Sie aus anderen Zusammenhängen kennen.

✏️ Bilden Sie Sätze nach folgendem Muster.

London / large / Paris → London is larger than Paris.

vain = eitel
pancake =
 Pfannkuchen
overweight =
 übergewichtig
expensive = teuer
Snow White =
 Schneewittchen
beautiful = schön
stepmother =
 Stiefmutter
nothing = nichts

a London / old / New York   *is older than*
b she / nice / her sister   *is nicer than*
c my boyfriend / vain / me   *is vainer than*
d Kansas / flat / a pancake
e many people / overweight / me
f London / expensive / Berlin
g Snow White / beautiful / her stepmother
h nothing / good / love

3 Unregelmäßige Plurale

Plurale (= Mehrzahlformen) sind unregelmäßig, wenn sie nicht mit *-s* gebildet werden. Drei Wörter mit unregelmäßiger Mehrzahlform sind besonders wichtig:

man	**men** (reimt sich auf engl. *ten*)	Mann – Männer
woman (Aussprache: „wumm...")	**women** (Aussprache: „wimm...")	Frau – Frauen
child (Aussprache: „tschaild")	**children** (Aussprache: „tschill...")	Kind – Kinder

4 Relativsätze und Relativpronomen

Unit 9D

Durch einen Relativsatz (→ 8D4) wird ein **Wort** (oder eine **Wortgruppe**) näher bestimmt:

| **Women** who could be my daughters still look at me with interest. | *Frauen, die meine Töchter sein könnten, sehen mich immer noch mit Interesse an.* |

Personen: **who**
Sachen: **which / that**

Hier ist *who could be my daughters* der Relativsatz und *women* das näher bestimmte Wort.

Im vorstehenden Beispiel ist *who* das **Relativpronomen** (= bezügliches Fürwort).
Who wird mit Bezug auf **Personen** gebraucht; mit Bezug auf **Sachen** dagegen benutzt man *which* oder *that*:

| **A small computer** which you can carry is a laptop. | *Ein kleiner Computer, den man tragen kann, ist ein Laptop.* |
| **A small computer** that you can carry is a laptop. | *Ein kleiner Computer, den man tragen kann, ist ein Laptop.* |

✎ Setzen Sie *who* oder *which / that* ein.

a A storyteller is someone _who_ tells stories.
b A traveller is a person _who_ travels.
c A pancake is a cake _that_ you make in a frying pan.
d A mouse is a grey little animal _which_ is very quick.
e A couch potato is someone _who_ watches TV a lot.
f The marathon is a famous race _that/which_ is about 26 miles long.
g A pilot is someone _who_ flies an aircraft.
h Sydney is a city _that_ never sleeps.
i Boston was the scene of the so-called Boston Tea Party, 1773, in _which_ American colonists protested against the British tax on tea.
j I have a lovely girlfriend _who_ wouldn't call me a pot-bellied couch potato even if my stomach wasn't as flat as it is now.

someone = jemand
frying pan = Bratpfanne
mouse (scharfes „s") = Maus
grey = grau
animal = Tier
quick = schnell
watch TV = fernsehen
1 mile = 1,6 km
pilot („ai" wie in „mile")
fly an aircraft = ein Flugzeug fliegen
scene (langes „i") = Schauplatz
tax on tea = Steuer auf Tee

5 Hör-Sprech-Übung.
In dieser Übung hören Sie Sätze mit *didn't* von der CD, auf die Sie mit *could have* + 3. Form des Verbs antworten sollen.

2/4

Sie hören zum Beispiel:	We didn't book online. *(Wir buchten nicht online/haben nicht online gebucht.)*
Sie sagen:	But we could have booked online. *(Aber wir hätten online buchen können.)*
Sie hören die richtige Antwort:	But we could have booked online.
Sie wiederholen die Antwort:	But we could have booked online.

book online = online buchen

Unit 9E

Focus on words

like = mögen, gernhaben

dessert = Nachtisch
desert = Wüste

lettuce = Kopfsalat

munch = mampfen
in front of = vor (örtlich)

food (langes „u", weiches „d")

1. *The menu* (= die Speisekarte): Das (Tages-)Menü wäre the **set menu** oder the **set meal** oder (vornehm französisch ausgedrückt) **the table d'hôte**.

2. *What would you like? – What do you like?* Das Erstere heißt „Was würden Sie gern haben?" / „Was hätten Sie gern?", das Letztere dagegen „Was haben Sie gern?"

3. *Go for the table d'hôte menu* (= das Tagesmenü nehmen): Statt des hübsch idiomatischen **go for** geht auch **have** oder **take the table d'hôte menu**.

4. *Dessert* (= „Nachtisch"; Betonung auf der zweiten Silbe) ist zu unterscheiden von **desert** (Betonung auf der ersten Silbe), das „Wüste" heißt.

5. *Salmon* (= Lachs): Das „l" ist stumm!

6. *Almonds* (= Mandeln): Die ersten beiden Buchstaben *al-* werden als langes „ah" (also ohne das „l") gesprochen.

7. *Salad* bezeichnet nur den zubereiteten Salat, das Gericht, die Speise: **mixed salad** (= gemischter Salat), **fruit salad** (= Obstsalat), **potato salad** (= Kartoffelsalat) etc. Die Pflanze „Kopfsalat" hingegen heißt **lettuce** (Aussprache „lettiss").

8. *Most men* (= die meisten Männer): in diesem Fall kein *the* vor *most*!

9. *Chubby* = rundlich, mollig, pummelig, also ein bisschen dick.

10. *Couch potato* bedeutet wörtlich „Couchkartoffel". Der Anfang der 1980er-Jahre geprägte Begriff bezeichnet anschaulich einen wenig aktiven Menschen, der einen erheblichen Teil seiner Zeit *potato chips* mampfend vor dem Fernseher verbringt (= *munching potato chips in front of the TV*).

11. *Myself*: *I told myself* (= ich sagte mir). Entsprechend die anderen *-self*-Pronomen:

you	told	**yourself**	du sagtest *dir* / Sie sagten *sich*
he	told	**himself**	er sagte *sich*
she	told	**herself**	sie sagte *sich*
it	told	**itself**	es / sie / er sagte *sich*
we	told	**ourselves**	wir sagten *uns*
you	told	**yourselves**	ihr sagtet *euch* / Sie sagten *sich*
they	told	**themselves**	sie sagten *sich*

12. *Cut out*: *I cut out junk food* (= ich verzichtete auf Junkfood, also minderwertige Kost). Etwa gleichbedeutend wäre *I gave up junk food*, und *give up* (= aufgeben) wird auch oft im Zusammenhang mit dem Rauchen benutzt: *I gave up smoking* (= ich gab das Rauchen auf).

13. *Pizza:* Beachten Sie, dass das „i" im Gegensatz zur deutschen Aussprache lang ist.

14. *Gym* kommt von **gymnasium**, das „Turnhalle" bedeutet. *Gym* heißt ursprünglich ebenfalls „Turnhalle", wird aber heute vor allem auch in der Bedeutung „Fitnesscenter" / „Fitnessstudio" benutzt. *Join* ist „beitreten"; *join a gym* (= sich bei einem Fitnesscenter anmelden).

Unit 9F

Focus on culture

1. Cheesecake

Die Übersetzung „Käsekuchen" wird in keiner Weise dem gerecht, was jemand *the greatest temptation since Adam and Eve* (= die größte Versuchung seit Adam und Eva) genannt hat. Vergessen Sie alles, was Sie sich unter einem mitteleuropäischen Käsekuchen vorstellen! Wer einmal ein Stück *New York Cheesecake* gegessen hat, weiß a), was es im Paradies zu essen gibt, und b), was Sünde (= *sin*) ist. Wir könnten den Rest dieses Buches mit *cheesecake recipes* („<u>ress</u>ipihs" = Rezepte) füllen, wollen das aber im Interesse Ihres Englischlernens unterlassen. Nur so viel:
American cheesecakes are the real thing. Seit die Amerikaner 1872 *cream cheese* (≈ Doppelrahmfrischkäse) erfanden, haben sie auf dem Gebiet der *cheesecakes* die Nase vorn (= *they're ahead of the pack*). Sie backen den *cheesecake* zu einem Kuchen, während die Engländer ihren *cheesecake* kalt anrühren und auf einer *biscuit* („<u>biss</u>kitt") *base* (= Keksgrundlage) als *dessert* servieren. Beide Varianten schmecken wunderbar, aber die besten amerikanischen *cheesecakes* sind *out of this world*, also geradezu jenseitig köstlich, wie aus einer anderen Welt. Das Internet hält unter den Schlagwörtern *cheesecake recipe* Tausende von Rezepten für Sie bereit.

temptation = Versuchung
since = seit
sin = Sünde
recipe = Rezept
the real thing = das (einzig) Wahre
biscuit = Keks
base (scharfes „s") = Grundlage
out of this world = fantastisch gut

2. Pound

Von Deutschsprachigen wird oft übersehen, dass das britische Gewichtsmaß *pound* nicht mit dem deutschen „Pfund" identisch ist:

1 pound = 453.59 grams
1 Pfund = 500 grams = 1.102 pounds

Beachten Sie auch, dass dem deutschen **Dezimalkomma** im Englischen der **Dezimalpunkt** entspricht:

453.59 (= four hundred and fifty-three point five nine) = deutsch 453,59

Dagegen entspricht dem deutschen **Punkt** als **Tausendertrennzeichen** im Englischen das **Komma**:

The last time I looked the world's population was 6,700,897,578.

Als ich das letzte Mal nachschaute, betrug die Weltbevölkerung 6.700.897.578.

1 pound = 0,45 Kg
1 Pfund = **1.102 pounds**
1 gram = 1 Gramm
population = Bevölkerung

Unit 9G — Test yourself

2/5

fit of the blues = Anfall von Melancholie
I'm fed up = ich bin es leid
rubbish = Mist, Quatsch
Man(chester) United (Football Club)
lose = verlieren
Portsmouth (Football Club)
hate = hassen
Tuesday = Dienstag
veg(etable) = Gemüse
bread = Brot
meat = Fleisch
repetitive = monoton
quite enough = vollkommen genug
lie – lying = liegen
boring = langweilig
hardly ever = kaum je(mals)
locals = Einheimische
college = Hochschule
enrol = sich anmelden
language course = Sprachkurs

household = Haushalt
regularly = regelmäßig

Lesen und hören Sie den folgenden Text. Sie brauchen nicht jedes Wort zu verstehen, vielmehr geht es darum, *that you get the drift of the text*, dass Sie also erkennen, worauf der Sprecher hinauswill, *what's his message* (= Botschaft, Mitteilung).
Auffallend in dem Text ist der häufige Gebrauch des umgangssprachlichen Verstärkers *bloody* (→ 2E3, 8F3). Mit diesem Kraftausdruck, den er immer wieder vor ein Wort setzt, betont der Sprecher seine Verärgerung, seine Frustration. Er ist stocksauer. Bei „feineren Gemütern" eckt man durch den Gebrauch von *bloody* an, weshalb Sie dieses Wort im Zweifel lieber nicht benutzen sollten. Sie können den Text leicht für jedermann (und jedefrau) akzeptabel machen, indem Sie sämtliche *bloody* (bzw. einmal *bloody well*) herausnehmen. Sie haben dann einen ganz normalen Text.

A fit of the blues

I'm bloody fed up, that's what I am. I mean, to sit here on the bloody sofa like a bloody couch potato watching all this rubbish on the TV. And Man United losing to bloody Portsmouth – even football isn't much fun any more. And do you know what I hate? I hate shopping in the bloody supermarket. I have to go twice a week, usually Tuesdays and Fridays, and it's always the bloody same. I mean fruits and veg, bread, pasta, milk, cheese and meat and what have you. Always the bloody same, that's the problem. Life is so bloody repetitive. OK, I walk our dog four times a day, twenty minutes each walk. It's good for the dog, it's good for me, but it isn't enough. No it bloody well isn't. What else could I do, could we do? Travel more? No, two holidays a year are quite enough. Lying on the beach in the sunshine all day, eating too much, drinking too bloody much, it's boring and unhealthy. And we hardly ever talk to the locals, can't bloody talk to them because we don't speak their bloody language. Hey, that's an idea! Why don't we go to the college and enrol for a bloody language course!

enrol

Kreuzen Sie die zutreffende Antwort an.

(*true* = zutreffend, *false* = nicht zutreffend, *doesn't say* = nicht aus dem Text zu ersehen)

The speaker watches a lot of television.	X True.	False.	Doesn't say.
The speaker often watches football.	X True.	False.	Doesn't say.
He's a Portsmouth fan.	True.	X False.	Doesn't say.
He likes to do the household shopping.	True.	X False.	Doesn't say.
He regularly walks his dog.	X True.	False.	Doesn't say.
He would like to go on holiday more often.	True.	X False.	Doesn't say.
He would like to learn a foreign language.	X True.	False.	Doesn't say.

Golf

Unit 10

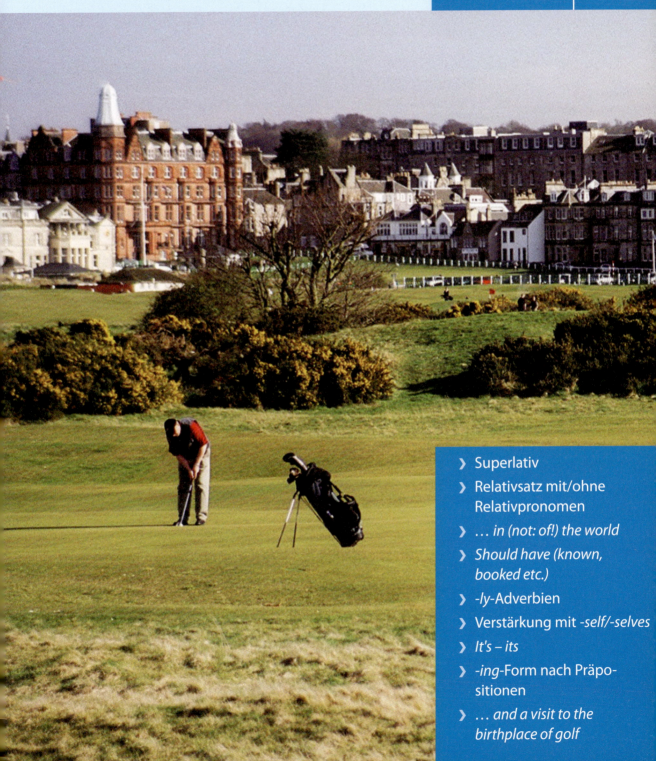

- Superlativ
- Relativsatz mit/ohne Relativpronomen
- … in (not: of!) the world
- Should have (known, booked etc.)
- -ly-Adverbien
- Verstärkung mit -self/-selves
- It's – its
- -ing-Form nach Präpositionen
- … and a visit to the birthplace of golf

Unit 10A Dialogue

2/6

■ = Julia
● = Alex

A golfing holiday

■ Hi Alex, back from your holiday?
● Yes – back from heaven.
■ Heaven? What do you mean? Did you go to Bali? Someone once called it the nearest thing to heaven on earth.
● No, we went to Scotland, St Andrews to be exact.
■ St Andrews in Scotland? I've heard the name but I couldn't say what it's about. Not sunny beaches or palm trees, to be sure.
● Well, it was sunny as a matter of fact, but you don't go to St Andrews for the weather. Does golf ring a bell?
■ Ah, I should have known – when you talk of heaven you mean golf. But let me guess: St Andrews has a nice golf course that's easy to play because it's got a high wall around it so lousy players like you can't hit the ball out of bounds.
● Did I ever tell you that you're the nastiest friend I have? And the worst thing is you don't know a thing about golf, or you'd know that the Old Course at St Andrews is the oldest golf course in the world.

■ I'm impressed.
● You should be. Playing at St Andrews is one of the most wonderful experiences a golfer can have.

Ein Golfurlaub

■ Hallo Alex, zurück aus dem Urlaub?
● Ja – zurück vom Himmel.
■ Himmel? Was meinst du damit? Seid ihr in Bali gewesen? Jemand hat es mal als Nächstes zum Himmel auf Erden bezeichnet.
● Nein, wir waren in Schottland, genau gesagt St Andrews.
■ St Andrews in Schottland? Den Namen habe ich gehört, aber ich könnte nicht sagen, was er bedeutet. Jedenfalls nicht sonnige Strände oder Palmenbäume.
● Nun, sonnig war es schon, aber nach St Andrews fährt man nicht wegen des Wetters. Sagt dir Golf etwas?
■ Ach, das hätte ich wissen müssen – wenn du vom Himmel redest, meinst du Golf. Aber lass mich raten: St Andrews hat einen hübschen Golfplatz, der leicht zu spielen ist, weil er eine hohe Mauer (drum herum) hat, damit / sodass miserable Spieler wie du den Ball nicht ins Aus schlagen können.
● Hab ich dir schon mal gesagt, dass du die gemeinste Freundin bist, die ich habe? Und das Schlimmste ist, dass du keine Ahnung von Golf hast, sonst wüsstest du, dass der Old Course (= „Alte [Golf-]Platz") in St Andrews der älteste Golfplatz der Welt ist.

■ Ich bin beeindruckt.
● Das solltest du auch sein. In St Andrews zu spielen, ist eines der schönsten Erlebnisse, die ein Golfer haben kann.

---

back = zurück
heaven = Himmel
someone = jemand
once = einmal
earth = Erde
go – went = fahren – fuhren
to be exact = genau gesagt
heard = gehört
ring a bell = eine Glocke läuten
guess = raten
it's (= it has) **got** = es/er hat
so (that) = damit
lousy = miserabel
hit = schlagen
ever = je(mals)
nasty = gemein, fies
worst = schlimmste
you'd = you would
course = (Golf-)Platz
impress = beeindrucken
experience = Erlebnis

Unit 10B

Rules and practice

1 Wiederholung des Dialogs aus 10A. Versuchen Sie die fehlenden Wörter einzusetzen.

■ Hi Alex, _back_ from your holiday?

● Yes – back from _heaven_.

■ Heaven? What do you _mean_? Did you _go_ to Bali? Someone once _called_ it the nearest thing to heaven on _earth_.

● No, we _went_ to Scotland, St Andrews to be _exact_.

■ St Andrews in Scotland? I've _heard_ the name but I couldn't say what it's _about_. Not sunny beaches or palm trees, to be _sure_.

● Well, it was sunny as a matter of _fact_, but you don't go to St Andrews for the _weather_. Does golf ring a _bell_?

■ Ah, I should have _known_ – when you talk of heaven you _mean_ golf. But _let_ me guess: St Andrews has a nice golf course that's easy to _play_ because it's got a high wall _around_ it so lousy players like you can't _play_ the ball out of bounds.

● Did I _ever_ tell you that you're the nastiest friend I _have_? And the worst thing is you don't know a thing _about_ golf, or you'd know that the Old Course at St Andrews is the oldest golf course _in_ the world.

■ I'm impressed.

● You should _be_. Playing at St Andrews is one of the most wonderful _experience_ a golfer can have.

Unit 10B

2 Wie man Superlative bildet

Im Deutschen wird der Superlativ immer (also auch bei sehr langen Wörtern) mit „-st-" gebildet. Im Englischen hängt man bei kürzeren Wörtern -est an, während man bei längeren *most* voranstellt:

Superlativ = höchste Steigerungsform

| the **oldest** golf course | *der älteste Golfplatz* |
| the **most beautiful** park | *der schönste Park* |

Bei einsilbigen Wörtern wird ein Endbuchstabe wie -d, -t oder -g nach kurz gesprochenem *a, e, i, o* verdoppelt:

| big – **biggest** | *groß – größte* |
| mad – **maddest** | *verrückt – verrückteste* |

Bei zweisilbigen Wörtern auf -y wird das -y zu -i-:

| happy – **happiest** | *glücklich – glücklichste* |
| nasty – **nastiest** | *fies – fieseste* |

Stummes -e am Wortende entfällt:

| nice – **nicest** | *nett – netteste* |
| large – **largest** | *groß – größte* |

Unregelmäßige Superlative:

| good – **best**   better | *gut – beste* |
| bad – **worst**   worst | *schlimm – schlimmste* |

✏️ Übersetzen Sie nun entsprechend dem Muster und lassen Sie das eingeklammerte Relativpronomen (→9D4) **jeweils weg** (→8D4).

| *das älteste Buch, das ich habe* | the **oldest** book (that) I have |
| *der schönste Park, den ich kenne* | the **most beautiful** park (that) I know |

know = kennen
nice = nett
unpleasant = unangenehm
people = Leute
nasty = fies
expensive = teuer
heavy = schwer
bag = Tasche
quiet = ruhig
mistake = Fehler
wonderful = herrlich
experience = Erlebnis

a das netteste Restaurant, das ich kenne _____

b der attraktivste Mann, den ich kenne _____

c die unangenehmsten Leute, die ich kenne _____

d die fieseste Freundin, die ich habe _____

e die teuerste Stadt, die ich kenne _____

f die schwerste Tasche, die wir hatten _____

g das ruhigste Zimmer, das das Hotel hat _____

h der größte Fehler, den ich machte _____

i das herrlichste Erlebnis, das ich hatte _____

Unit 10B

3 Übersetzen Sie nun nach dem folgenden Muster (und beachten Sie: „der Welt" = *in the world*!).

| *der älteste Golfplatz der Welt* | the **oldest** golf course in the world |
| *der berühmteste Golfplatz der Welt* | the **most famous** golf course in the world |

a die längste Brücke der Welt — _longest in_
b der beste Golfspieler der Welt — _____
c die schlechteste Pizza der Welt — _____
d der köstlichste Käsekuchen der Welt — _the most delicious_
e eines der interessantesten Museen der Welt — _the most interesting_
f eines der teuersten Gemälde der Welt — _the most expensive painting_

bad – worst = schlecht – schlechteste
delicious = köstlich
interesting = interessant
painting = Gemälde

4 Hör-Sprech-Übung. In dieser Übung hören Sie Sätze mit *I didn't* von der CD, auf die Sie mit *I should have* + 3. Form des Verbs antworten sollen.

Sie hören zum Beispiel: ....I didn't book online.
(= *Ich habe nicht online gebucht.*)
Sie sagen: ....I should have booked online.
(= *Ich hätte online buchen sollen.*)
Sie hören die richtige Antwort: ....I should have booked online.
Sie wiederholen die Antwort: ....I should have booked online.

2/7

5 Relativsätze (→8D4, 9D4, 10B2). Setzen Sie die Relativpronomen *who* oder *which / that* ein. Wo kann man das Relativpronomen weglassen?

Personen

a John is the best friend _(who)_ I have.
b The town has a nice golf course _which_ is easy to play.   *oder that*
c Jack is a man _who_ knows a lot about golf.   *oder ohne*
d Playing at St Andrews is one of the most wonderful experiences _which_ a golfer can have.
e Most of the people _(who)_ I work with are very pleasant.
f I like hotels _which_ are in the middle of town so I can just walk around.
g There are some names _____ I just can't remember.
h Couch potatoes are people _who_ watch a lot of television.
i Imagine, I ran into someone _(who)_ I know when I was shopping on Oxford Street.
j Paris has an opera house _which_ doesn't look like an opera house at all.

easy = leicht
know = wissen, kennen
experience = Erlebnis
pleasant = nett
middle = Mitte
imagine! = stell dir vor!
not ... at all = überhaupt nicht

ich traf jemand

119

Unit 10C — Reading text

2/8

fighting fit = topfit
old-fashioned = altmodisch
be in evidence = sichtbar sein
of course = natürlich
different from = anders als
advice = Rat
stay = bleiben
avoid = vermeiden
honest = ehrlich
manage = es schaffen
because of = wegen
prevent = (ver)hindern
important = wichtig
get a room ready = ein Zimmer fertig machen
spare room = Gästezimmer

Subject: Back from holiday

Hi Martin

Just a few lines so you know we're back from our holiday – fighting fit and ready for action.

Thank you for telling us about St Andrews. We found the town itself delightfully old-fashioned, picturesque, and well-preserved. Golf is very much in evidence, of course, but so is the university. We were surprised to hear that it's the oldest in Scotland. What a tradition!

The Old Course is a dream, completely different from all the courses I've ever played. Beautiful views of the scenery, the town and the sea. I followed your advice and stayed on the left side of every fairway to avoid the bunkers. To be honest, I didn't manage to avoid them all!

Did you know that the Old Course could sink into the sea by 2050 because of climate change? Well, I'm sure they'll prevent that from happening but it shows how important it is to stop global warming.

Well, so much about our trip. Home is a great place too. When are you coming to see us again? Let us know when to get the spare room ready.

Love
Sylvia

Zurück aus dem Urlaub

Hallo Martin!

Nur ein paar Zeilen, damit du weißt, dass wir zurück aus dem Urlaub sind – topfit und einsatzbereit.

Danke, dass du uns über St Andrews erzählt hast. Wir fanden die Stadt selbst reizend altmodisch, malerisch und gut erhalten. Golf tritt natürlich stark in Erscheinung, aber auch die Universität. Wir waren überrascht zu hören, dass es die älteste in Schottland ist. Was für eine Tradition!

Der Old Course (= „Alte [Golf-]Platz) ist traumhaft, vollkommen anders als alle Golfplätze, die ich je gespielt habe. Wunderschöne Aussichten auf die Landschaft, die Stadt und das Meer. Ich folgte deinem Rat und blieb auf der linken Seite von jedem Fairway, um die Bunker (= aus einer sandbedeckten Mulde bestehendes Hindernis) zu vermeiden. Um ehrlich zu sein, ich habe es nicht geschafft, sie alle zu vermeiden!

Wusstest du, dass der Old Course bis 2050 ins Meer (ver)sinken könnte, wegen des Klimawandels? Nun, ich bin sicher, man wird verhindern, dass das passiert, aber es zeigt, wie wichtig es ist, die Erderwärmung zu stoppen.

So viel also über unsere Reise. Zu Hause ist es auch sehr schön. Wann kommst du / kommt ihr uns wieder besuchen? Lass(t) uns wissen / Teil(t) uns mit / Sag(t) uns Bescheid, wann wir das Gästezimmer vorbereiten sollen.

Alles Liebe / Herzliche Grüße
Sylvia

Unit 10D

Rules and practice

1 Benutzen Sie jeweils ein passendes *-ly*-Wort aus der Liste zur „Anreicherung" bzw. Verstärkung des Adjektivs.

absolutely, completely, delightfully, easily, extremely, pleasantly

a We were _absolutely_ surprised at the quality of the food.
b We stayed at a _delightfully_ old-fashioned hotel.
c The hotel is _absolutely / easily_ accessible from JFK, LaGuardia, and Newark airports.
d Her new laptop is _absolutely_ state of the art.
e New York is _completely / extremely_ different from Washington.
f The town's old buildings are _completely_ well-preserved.
g The food at this restaurant is _delightfully_ wonderful.

stay at a hotel = in einem Hotel wohnen
accessible = erreichbar
state of the art = auf dem neuesten Stand
well-preserved = gut erhalten

2 Fügen Sie zur Verstärkung das passende *-self/-selves*-Wort (= „selbst") hinzu.

herself, himself, itself, myself, ourselves, themselves, yourself, yourselves

a The town _____ is delightfully old-fashioned.
b The players _____ like the course very much.
c Linda _____ is from a little village between Preston and Blackburn in England.
d We need partners. We can't do everything _____.
e David told me that _____.
f I'm a bit on the chubby side _____ but I like it that way.
g St Andrews _____ is a very pleasant little town.
h And what are you going to have _____, Roy?
i Do you people never have these problems _____?

delightfully = in reizender Weise
village = Dorf
need = benötigen
told = sagte
chubby = rundlich
never = nie(mals)

Unit 10D

important = wichtig
come to see = besuchen
foreign language = Fremdsprache
manage = es schaffen

3 Übersetzen Sie. (Der fett gedruckte Satzteil gehört ans Ende.)

a Ich war überrascht, **das** zu hören. *I was surprised to hear that*
b Es ist wichtig, **die Erderwärmung** zu stoppen. *It is important to stop Global Warming*
c Wann kommt ihr **uns** besuchen? *When do you visite us*
d Sie würde gern **eine Fremdsprache** lernen. *She wouldlike a foreign lang-*
e Ich möchte **ein Doppelzimmer** reservieren. *I want to reserver double room*
f Er schaffte es, **diesen Fehler** zu vermeiden. *he manage to avoid this mist*
g Sie wollen **in Australien** heiraten. *they want to get married in Aust*

4 Setzen Sie die folgenden Präpositionen an passender Stelle in den Sätzen ein.

about, around, at, by, for, from, in, into, on, to

stay = bleiben
left = linke(r, s)
avoid = (ver)meiden
experience = Erlebnis
advice = Rat

a When is Sylvia coming back __from__ her holiday?
b Here's an interesting article __about__ global warming.
c An American cheesecake is very different __from__ a German cheesecake.
d Stay __on__ the left side if you want to avoid the bunkers.
e A lot of land will sink __into__ the sea in the next fifty years.
f The Old Course could sink into the sea __by__ 2050.
g You don't go to St Andrews __for__ the weather.
h The Old Course at St Andrews is the oldest golf course __in__ the world.
i Playing __at__ St Andrews is a wonderful experience.
j I must write __to__ Martin to thank him for his advice.
k The gorillas live in a big park with a high wall __around__ it.

2/9

global warming = die Erderwärmung
important = wichtig

5 Hör-Sprech-Übung. Sie hören eine Wortgruppe von der CD, die Sie in einen Satz mit *It's important to …* einbetten sollen.

Sie hören zum Beispiel: ....stop global warming
Sie sagen: ....It's important to stop global warming.
Sie hören die richtige Antwort: ....It's important to stop global warming.
Sie wiederholen die Antwort: ....It's important to stop global warming.

6 Unterschied zwischen *it's* und *its*

It's und *its* werden oft verwechselt, auch von Muttersprachlern. Ausgesprochen werden beide Wörter gleich, aber sie haben gänzlich verschiedene Bedeutungen:

Unit 10D

It's ist eine Zusammenziehung aus *it is* oder *it has*:

| **It's** (= it is) important. | Es ist wichtig. |
| **It's** (= it has) got a high wall around it. | Er (= der Golfplatz) hat eine hohe Mauer. |

Its ist wie *his* oder *their* ein „besitzanzeigendes Fürwort". Es wird mit Bezug auf „Nicht-Personen" benutzt:

| Scotland is proud of **its** traditions. | Schottland ist stolz auf seine Traditionen. |
| The university is proud of **its** traditions. | Die Universität ist stolz auf ihre Traditionen. |

✎ Setzen Sie *it's* oder *its* ein.

a _____ lunchtime and I'm hungry.

b _____ a very nice house, _____ old and _____ got charm and character, but it has _____ price.

c St Andrews is proud of _____ university.

d Melbourne is famous for _____ beautiful parks, fine restaurants and wide boulevards.

e _____ happened again.

f You can't play a game if you don't know _____ rules.

g Living in a big city has _____ problems.

proud of = stolz auf
famous = berühmt
rule = Regel

7 *-ing*-Form nach Präpositionen (→8D3c). Setzen Sie eine passende Präposition + *-ing*-Form des eingeklammerten Verbs ein.

Thank you (tell) us about St Andrews. → Thank you **for telling** us about St Andrews.

a Thank you (come) _____ to our party.

b I'm sure they'll prevent that (happen) _____.

c I'm fond (watch) _____ the pelicans on the lake.

d I'm not very good (remember) _____ names.

e There are some tricks (remember) _____ names.

f She talked (go) _____ to London.

g We were thinking (buy) _____ a house.

h I have no time (read) _____ during the day.

i I think your problems come (eat) _____ too much unhealthy fat.

prevent = verhindern
be fond of doing sth = etw gern tun
buy (Ausspr.: bai) = kaufen
during = während
unhealthy = ungesund

123

Unit 10E — Focus on words

1. **Back from your holiday?** (= Zurück aus dem Urlaub?): Die Amerikaner sagen *vacation*: *Back from your vacation?* (→ 1E1)

2. **Nützliche Redensarten mit** *to be*

to St Andrews **to be exact**	genau gesagt nach St Andrews
not sunny beaches, **to be sure**	sicherlich doch keine sonnigen Strände
to be honest, I didn't manage to avoid them all	um ehrlich zu sein, alle konnte ich nicht vermeiden

3. *I've heard the name but I couldn't say **what it's about**.* (= Ich habe den Namen gehört, aber ich könnte nicht sagen, was er bedeutet.) Entsprechend könnte man sagen:

St Andrews **is about** golf.	*St Andrews bedeutet Golf.*
Vienna **is about** music.	*Wien bedeutet Musik.*

4. *Does golf **ring a bell**?* (= „Läutet Golf eine Glocke?" / „Sagt dir Golf etwas?")

5. *It's got a high wall around it **so (that)** lousy players like you can't hit the ball out of bounds* (= Er hat eine hohe Mauer [„drum herum"], **damit** miserable Spieler wie du den Ball nicht ins Aus schlagen können.): *So (that)* heißt also „damit" oder „so-dass", wie auch in 10C: *Just a few lines **so** you know we're back from our holiday.* (= Nur ein paar Zeilen, damit du weißt, dass wir aus dem Urlaub zurück sind.)

6. *Hi Martin:* In der Anrede stattdessen auch *Hello Martin* oder einfach *Martin* (das Letztere mit nachfolgendem Komma oder Gedankenstrich).

7. *(A) well-preserved (old town)* (= eine gut erhaltene alte Stadt): Lässt sich auch in Bezug auf Menschen verwenden:

a **well-preserved** 50-year-old	*eine gut erhaltene Fünfzigerin*

8. *Golf is very much in evidence: Evidence* heißt in der Grundbedeutung „Beweis(material)", der Ausdruck *be in evidence* heißt „präsent / sichtbar sein": *police were nowhere in evidence* (= Polizei war nirgends zu sehen).

9. *What a tradition!* (= Was für eine Tradition!): Vgl. 6E3.

10. *The Old Course is **a dream*** (= der alte Platz ist ein Traum): Der Platz ist also wunderbar. Wäre er das Gegenteil, so könnte man sagen: *Our golf course is **a nightmare*** (= unser Golfplatz ist ein Albtraum).

11. *Let us know **when to get** the spare room ready* (= Sag uns Bescheid, wann wir das Gästezimmer vorbereiten sollen.) Entsprechende Beispiele mit *when to*:

Tell me **when to** go.	*Sag mir, wann ich gehen soll.*
Some people just don't know **when to** stop.	*Manche Leute wissen einfach nicht, wann sie aufhören sollten.*

Unit 10F

Focus on culture

2/10

1. **St Andrews**, with a town population of about 14,000 and a student population of about 6,000, is on the North Sea coast about 50 miles, or 80 kilometres, north of Edinburgh. St Andrews is known as the birthplace of golf and the home of an excellent 600-year-old university.
The **Old Course** at St Andrews is mentioned (= *wird erwähnt*) in documents dating to the 16th century (= *16. Jahrhundert*), so it is about 500 years old. Golf was played (= *wurde gespielt*) in Scotland as early as the 15th (possibly 14th) century.

2. **Scotland**, with a population of over five million, is one of the four countries (England, Scotland, Wales, Northern Ireland) that make up the UK (= United Kingdom of Great Britain and Northern Ireland).
Scotland's capital is the beautiful old city of **Edinburgh** with a population of about 450,000.

3. **Golf:** A game played on a large, parklike area called a golf course. Using golf clubs, the players hit a small hard ball into a series of (usually 18) small holes in the ground trying to use as few strokes as possible (= *so wenig Schläge wie möglich*).

Fairway nennt man die kurz gemähte Spielbahn zwischen *tee* (= Abschlag) und *green* (= die Grasfläche um ein Loch – *a hole*).
Rough (Aussprache: „raff") ist das die *fairways* umgebende selten gemähte hohe Gras.
Bunkers (im AE auch *sand traps* – „Sandfallen" – genannt) am Rand der *fairways* oder *greens* stellen zusätzliche Herausforderungen dar (= *present additional challenges*).
Golf club kann lustigerweise sowohl „Golfschläger" als auch „Golfklub" heißen.
Apropos „Golfschläger": Da ein(e) zünftige(r) *golfer* bis zu 14 *golf clubs* (jeder mit eigenem Namen!) mit sich führt, benötigt er/sie ein Beförderungsgerät, das im BE als *trolley* und im AE als *golf cart* bezeichnet wird.
Motorisierte (= *motorized*) *golf cars* dienen außer der Schläger- auch der Spielerbeförderung.
Ein *caddie* ist jemand, der einen Golfer begleitet (*who accompanies a golfer*), seine Schläger trägt (*carries his clubs*) und in schwierigen Situationen (*difficult situations*) vielleicht auch Ratschläge und moralische Unterstützung gibt (*gives advice and moral support*).

---

town = Stadt
about = ca.
coast = Küste
known = bekannt
birthplace = Geburtsort
excellent = ausgezeichnet
early = früh
country = Land
make up = bilden
capital = Hauptstadt

area = Gebiet
called = genannt
club = Klub, Knüppel
hit = schlagen
usually = normalerweise
hole = Loch
ground = (Erd-)Boden
as few as = so wenig(e) wie
use = brauchen
stroke = Schlag
possible = möglich

Unit 10G

proverb = Sprichwort

Test yourself

Find the proverb

Wenn Sie die englischen Übersetzungen der folgenden Ausdrücke einsetzen, ergibt sich senkrecht die Entsprechung des deutschen Sprichworts „Wie gewonnen, so zerronnen."

1. Gästezimmer
2. peinlich
3. altmodisch
4. alles
5. um ehrlich zu sein
6. Briefmarkensammlung
7. vermeiden
8. wie die Zeit verfliegt
9. um genau zu sein
10. (*umgangssprachlich:*) in Australien
11. lass mich raten
12. unangenehm
13. gut erhalten
14. ein lebhaftes Kind
15. einen Spaziergang machen
16. eine verführerische Nachspeise
17. (der) Himmel auf Erden

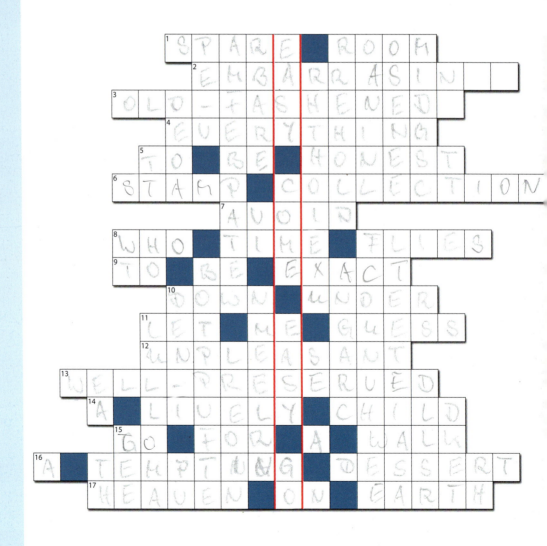

Fortune telling

Unit 11

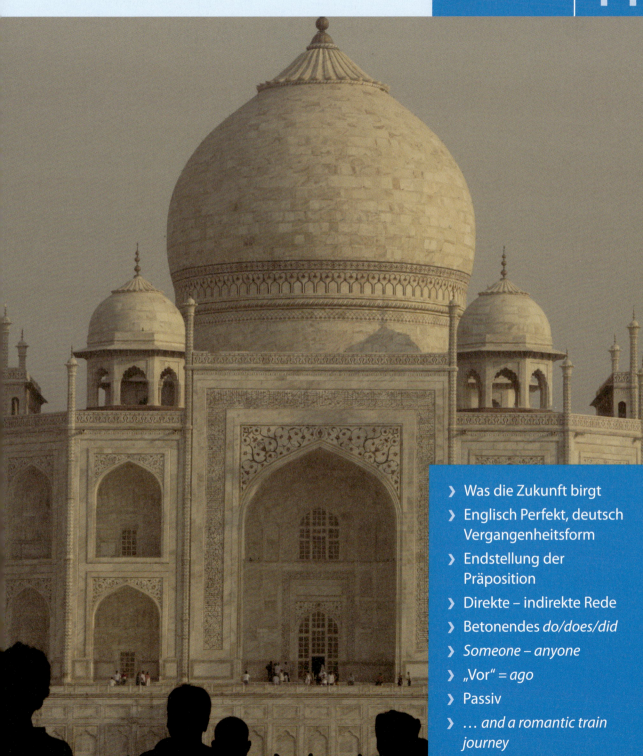

- Was die Zukunft birgt
- Englisch Perfekt, deutsch Vergangenheitsform
- Endstellung der Präposition
- Direkte – indirekte Rede
- Betonendes *do/does/did*
- *Someone – anyone*
- „Vor" = *ago*
- Passiv
- *… and a romantic train journey*

Unit 11A

2/11

■ = man
● = woman

go to see =
aufsuchen
see – saw =
besuchen –
besuchte
fortune teller =
Wahrsager(in)
what ... for? =
wozu?
I guess =
ich schätze
curious =
neugierig
what's in store for me = was mir bevorsteht
such as =
„solche wie"
I'd been = **I had been** = ich war/sei gewesen
in love = verliebt
many times =
viele Male
true = wahr
be true of =
zutreffen auf
might = könnte
meet = treffen, kennenlernen
come across =
begegnen
spend time =
Zeit verbringen
sound = klingen
somehow =
irgendwie
get to know =
kennenlernen
here we are =
hier ist es

Dialogue

A look at the crystal ball

■ I went to see a fortune teller yesterday.
● You saw a fortune teller? What did you do that for?
■ Um, I guess I was just curious about what was in store for me. And she did give me a few clues …
● Such as?
■ Well, she said I'd been in love many times …
● … which would be true of most men your age.
■ I know, but she also said I hadn't found my true love yet.
● Wow! And now you're thinking hard who she might be?
■ Well, yes … She said I'd meet her on a train journey.
● A train journey? Funny, I've never come across anyone interesting on a train.
■ Nor have I. But, then, we don't spend much time travelling in trains these days, do we?
● That's true, but ... have you ever heard of the Palace on Wheels?
■ No, I can't say I have. Sounds oriental, somehow.
● It's a luxury train in India, you know, the kind of train kings and maharajas used to travel in.
■ And you're on the train long enough to …
● Seven days. That should be long enough to see a lot of India and get to know a person really well. Let's look it up on the Internet, shall we: palaceonwheels dot net – here we are.

Ein Blick auf die Kristallkugel

■ Ich („besuchte") habe gestern eine Wahrsagerin besucht.
● Du warst bei einer Wahrsagerin? Warum hast du denn das gemacht?
■ Äh, ich war wohl einfach neugierig, was so auf mich zukommt. Und sie hat mir auch wirklich ein paar Hinweise gegeben …
● Wie etwa?
■ Nun, sie sagte, ich sei schon oft verliebt gewesen …
● … was wohl auf die meisten Männer deines Alters zutrifft.
■ Ich weiß, aber sie sagte auch, ich hätte meine wahre Liebe noch nicht gefunden.
● Mann! Und jetzt denkst du scharf darüber nach, wer sie sein könnte?
■ Na ja … Sie sagte, ich würde sie auf einer Zugreise treffen.
● Auf einer Zugreise? Komisch, ich bin noch nie jemand Interessantem im Zug begegnet.
■ Ich auch nicht. Aber wir verbringen ja heute auch nicht mehr viel Zeit mit Zugreisen, nech?
● Das stimmt, aber … hast du schon mal von dem Palast auf Rädern gehört?
■ Nein, kann ich nicht behaupten. Klingt irgendwie orientalisch.
● Das ist ein Luxuszug in Indien, weißt du, so ein Zug, in dem früher Könige und Maharadschas gereist sind.
■ Und man ist lange genug in dem Zug, um …
● Sieben Tage. Das dürfte lang genug sein, um viel von Indien zu sehen und einen Menschen wirklich gut kennenzulernen. Schaun wir das doch mal im Internet nach, ja: palaceonwheels Punkt net – hier haben wir's.

128

Rules and practice

Unit 11B

1 Deutsch Perfekt – englisch Vergangenheitsform (→ 7B2, 8B1)

Vergleichen Sie die Zeitformen im englischen und deutschen Satz:

> I **went to see** a fortune teller yesterday.   Ich **besuchte** gestern eine Wahrsagerin. /
> Ich **habe** gestern eine Wahrsagerin
> besucht.

Im Deutschen sagt man „Wir haben gestern Golf gespielt", nicht „Wir spielten gestern Golf." Das Letztere ist aber die korrekte englische Ausdrucksweise: *We played golf yesterday*. Durch die „Datierung" der Handlung mit einer Zeitbestimmung der Vergangenheit wie *yesterday* oder *three days ago* wird der Gebrauch des Perfekts (*have played*) ausgeschlossen; **es muss die Vergangenheitsform (*played*) benutzt werden.**

Übersetzen Sie die folgenden Sätze unter Beachtung dieser Regel.

a Sie ist gestern angekommen.   _____

b Paul hat gestern angerufen.   _____

c Ich habe ihn gestern im Krankenhaus
   besucht.   _____

d Gestern haben wir Schach gespielt. _____

e Ich habe gestern unsere Zimmer gebucht. _____

f Ich bin gestern meinen ersten Marathon
   gelaufen.   _____

arrive = ankommen
call = anrufen

2 Endstellung der Präposition

Sie haben wohl schon bemerkt, dass Präpositionen wie *for*, *from* oder *like* oft dort stehen, wo wir sie vom Deutschen her nicht erwarten würden, nämlich in Endposition:

> What did you do that **for**?   *Wozu hast du das getan?*
> Tell me where you come **from**.   *Sag mir, wo du herkommst.*
> What's the hotel **like**?   *Wie ist das Hotel (denn so)?*

Setzen Sie die (jeweils nachgestellte) Präposition ein. Wenn Sie nicht sicher sind, was die Sätze genau bedeuten, übersetzen Sie sie bitte. (Schlüssel → S. 201.)

a What are the people of Athens _____?

b Who were you having lunch _____?

c How many nights do you want to book
   _____?

d What are you waiting _____?

e What are you thinking _____?

f I've no idea what you're talking _____.

g Golf is something I know nothing
   _____.

I've no idea =
ich habe keine
Ahnung
nothing = nichts

Unit 11B

in love = verliebt
train journey = Zugreise

trip = Reise
is interested in = interessiert sich für
married = verheiratet
fear of heights = Höhenangst
church = Kirche

3 Indirekte Rede

In unserem Dialog berichtet der Mann, warum er zu der Wahrsagerin ging (*I was just curious about …*) und was die Wahrsagerin zu ihm gesagt hat (*she said …*). Wir nennen dieses Wiedergeben von wörtlich Gesagtem **indirekte Rede**. Im Deutschen sind wir bei der Formulierung von indirekter Rede mitunter etwas unsicher. Vergleichen Sie:

Direkte (= wörtliche Rede):	Sie sagte: „Ich bin verliebt."
Indirekte (= berichtete) Rede:	Sie sagte, sie **sei** / **wäre** / **ist** verliebt.

Im Englischen gibt es diese Unsicherheit hinsichtlich der korrekten Zeitform („sei", „wäre", „ist") nicht. Nach einem Einleitungssatz in der Vergangenheit (*she said*) „rutscht" vielmehr das Verb der direkten Rede um eine Stufe in die Vergangenheit:

Direkte Rede:	She said, "I **am** in love."
Indirekte Rede:	She said she **was** in love.
Direkte Rede:	She said, "You **have** been in love many times."
Indirekte Rede:	She said I **had** been in love many times.
Direkte Rede:	She said, "You **will** meet her on a train journey."
Indirekte Rede:	She said I **would** meet her on a train journey.

 Hier sind noch einige weitere Dinge, die die Wahrsagerin zu dem Mann gesagt haben könnte. Sie sind der Mann und berichten das Gesagte.

"You will go on a long trip." → She said I'd / I would go on a long trip.

a "You're interested in music."   She said I _____
b "You aren't married."   She said I _____
c "You have a fear of heights."   She said I _____
d "You like dogs."   She said I _____
e "You don't go to church."   She said I _____
f "You can't swim."   She said I _____
g "You will have five grandchildren."   She said I _____

4 Betonendes *do/does/did*

Außer zur Bildung der Frage (→4B2) und Verneinung (→4B3) kann *do/does/did* auch zur Betonung bzw. Verstärkung einer Aussage benutzt werden:

She **gave** me a few clues.	*Sie hat mir ein paar Hinweise gegeben.*
She **did give** me a few clues.	*Sie hat mir auch wirklich ein paar Hinweise gegeben.*

Unit 11B

5 Hör-Sprech-Übung. Sie hören einen Satz von der CD, den Sie unter Verwendung von *do/does/did* mit besonderem Nachdruck wiederholen.

Sie hören zum Beispiel: ....I love you.
Sie sagen: ....I do love you. (= Ich liebe dich doch!)
Sie hören die richtige Antwort: ....I do love you.
Sie wiederholen die Antwort: ....I do love you.

2/12

6 *Someone – anyone* (→8E1, 12E2)

Sehen Sie sich noch einmal die Erklärungen zu *some* und *any* an (→8E1). Überlegen Sie dann, warum in dem folgenden Satz *anyone* steht und nicht *someone*.

| I've never come across **anyone** interesting on a train. | Ich habe noch nie jemand Interessantes in einem Zug getroffen. |

Ja, *anyone* steht hier, weil die Aussage (durch *never*) verneint ist.

Bei fragendem Sinn würde ebenso *anyone* gebraucht:

| Have you ever come across **anyone** interesting on a train? | Hast du schon mal jemand Interessantes in einem Zug getroffen? |

Wird „jemand" weder verneint noch erfragt, so ist *someone* zu gebrauchen:

| I met **someone** interesting on the train today. | Ich habe heute jemand Interessantes im Zug getroffen. |

someone = jemand
anyone = jemand
not ... anyone = niemand

Setzen Sie *someone* oder *anyone* ein.

a Did __anyone__ call?
b A fortune teller is __someone__ who says they can tell you what will happen in the future.
c Has __anyone__ ever heard of the "Palace on Wheels"?
d I don't know __anyone__ in San Francisco.
e I think there's __someone__ in the garden.
f __Someone__ had to do it.
g There's _____ at the door.
h I don't think __anyone__ knows me here.
i Does __anyone__ there speak English?
j I'm not _____ who likes to go to parties.
   someone
   weil ich persönlich

call = anrufen
happen = geschehen
future = Zukunft
garden = Garten
had to = musste
door = Tür

Unit 11C

2/13

powerful = mächtig
favourite = Lieblings-
wife = (Ehe-)Frau
die = sterben
within = innerhalb
believe = glauben
after all = schließlich
dead = tot
devastated = zutiefst erschüttert
convince = überzeugen
order = befehlen
appear = erscheinen
predict = vorhersagen
dear = lieb
belief = Überzeugung
witch = Hexe
really = wirklich
or else = andernfalls
careful(ly) = sorgfältig, gründlich

Reading text

The fortune teller

Hundreds of years ago a powerful king went to see a fortune teller to hear what she had to say about the future. The old woman told him that his favourite wife, Sarabaya, would die within a year.
The king didn't believe the woman. After all, Sarabaya was young and healthy, why should she die?
A few months later Sarabaya was dead and the king was devastated. He also remembered what the fortune teller had told him and became convinced that she had used her magical powers to kill Sarabaya.
He ordered the woman to appear before him and said to her, "You predicted that my dear wife Sarabaya would die, and she has died. It is my belief that you are not a fortune teller but a witch. I believe you used your power to kill her. If, however, you are really a fortune teller, then tell me when you yourself will die, or else you will be killed."
The woman thought carefully, and then said, "I will die three days before you, Your Majesty."

Die Wahrsagerin
Vor hunderten von Jahren suchte ein mächtiger König eine Wahrsagerin auf, um zu hören, was sie über die Zukunft zu sagen hatte. Die alte Frau sagte ihm, dass seine Lieblingsfrau, Sarabaya, innerhalb eines Jahres sterben würde.
Der König glaubte der Frau nicht. Sarabaya war doch schließlich jung und gesund, warum sollte sie da sterben?
Ein paar Monate später war Sarabaya tot und der König war außer sich. Er erinnerte sich auch an das, was die Wahrsagerin ihm gesagt hatte, und kam zu der Überzeugung, dass sie ihre magischen Kräfte benutzt hatte, um Sarabaya zu töten.
Er ließ die Frau zu sich kommen und sagte zu ihr: „Du hast prophezeit, dass meine liebe Frau Sarabaya sterben würde, und sie ist gestorben. Ich bin der Überzeugung, dass du keine Wahrsagerin, sondern eine Hexe bist. Ich glaube, dass du deine Kraft benutzt hast, (um) sie zu töten. Falls du jedoch wirklich eine Wahrsagerin bist, so sage mir, wann du selbst sterben wirst, sonst wirst du getötet werden."
Die Frau dachte gründlich nach und sagte dann: „Ich werde drei Tage vor Euch sterben, Majestät."

Rules and practice

Unit 11D

1 Vorangestelltes „vor" = nachgestelltes *ago* (→ 7B2)

Sehen Sie sich noch einmal zwei Beispiele mit *ago* an:

I sent him an email **a few days ago**.	Ich habe ihm **vor ein paar Tagen** eine E-Mail geschickt.
Hundreds of years ago a powerful king went to see a fortune teller.	**Vor hunderten von Jahren** suchte ein mächtiger König eine Wahrsagerin auf.

 Verwandeln Sie die Sätze in solche mit *ago*. (Wenn Sie die genaue Zahl nicht ausrechnen wollen, sagen Sie einfach *about XX years ago*.)

The Second World War began in 1939 (nineteen thirty-nine).
(*2010 wäre die Antwort:*) The Second World War began 71 years ago / about 70 years ago.

a Elizabeth became Queen in 1952. _____
b John F. Kennedy was murdered in 1963. _____
c The Berlin Wall came down in 1989. _____
d Digital cameras first came on the market in the early 1990s (nineteen nineties). _____
e Tony Blair became Prime Minister in 1997. _____
f The Google search engine was founded in 1998. _____
g The Twin Towers were destroyed in 2001. _____
h The Millennium Bridge over the Thames opened in 2002. _____
i Germany got its first female chancellor in 2005. _____

second = zweite(r, s)
war = Krieg

murder = ermorden
wall = Mauer
come down = fallen
prime minister = Premierminister
search engine = Suchmaschine
found = gründen
twin towers = „Zwillingstürme"
destroy = zerstören
millennium = Jahrtausend
female = weiblich
male = männlich
chancellor = Kanzler(in)

2 Machen Sie aus indirekter Rede direkte Rede.

The old woman told him that his favourite wife would die within a year.
→ "Your favourite wife will die within a year."

a The king told the woman that he didn't believe her. _____
b The king said that Sarabaya was young and healthy. _____
c The king told the fortune teller that he remembered what she had told him. _____

Unit 11D

convinced = überzeugt
let her live = sie am Leben lassen

d He told her that he was convinced that she had used her magical powers to kill Sarabaya. _____

e He said that it was his belief that she was a witch. _____

f He said that she would be killed. _____

g He said he would let her live if she told him when she herself would die. _____

3 Das Passiv (→ 12B1)

Vereinzelt sind uns bereits Beispiele für die Passivkonstruktion begegnet:

Kennedy **was murdered** in 1963.	*Kennedy wurde 1963 ermordet.*
The Google search engine **was founded** in 1998.	*Die Google-Suchmaschine wurde 1998 gegründet.*
You **will be killed**.	*Du wirst getötet werden.*

murder = ermorden
found = gründen

In der Passivkonstruktion geht die Handlung nicht vom Subjekt aus, sondern wirkt auf das Subjekt ein: Das Subjekt Kennedy mordet nicht, sondern wird ermordet; die Suchmaschine gründet nicht, sondern wird gegründet; die Wahrsagerin wird nicht töten, sondern getötet werden. Vergleichen Sie dagegen die möglichen Aktivsätze:

a Lee Harvey Oswald **murdered** Kennedy in 1963.
b Larry Page and Sergey Brin **founded** Google in 1998.
c My men **will kill** you.

Sie sehen, dass sich Aktiv und Passiv vor allem hinsichtlich der Hervorhebung des Wesentlichen unterscheiden:
a Wenn Ihnen die Tatsache der Ermordung Kennedys, nicht aber der Täter wichtig ist, wählen Sie die Passivkonstruktion.
b Sie kennen Google, Sie wollen sagen, wie lange es Google schon gibt, Sie kennen die Namen der Gründer gar nicht (und sie sind Ihnen auch nicht wichtig), also wählen Sie das Passiv.
c Ebenso bei der Drohung des Königs: Der König droht der Wahrsagerin die Hinrichtung an; die Vollstrecker sind unwichtig, also Passiv.

✎ Vervollständigen Sie die folgenden Sätze entsprechend ihrer Aussage entweder in der Vergangenheit (*was/were* …) oder in der Zukunft (*will be* …).

traffic accident = Verkehrsunfall
publish = veröffentlichen
heart = Herz
transplant = verpflanzen
arrest = Festnahme

a Six people (kill) _____ in traffic accidents yesterday.

b The University of St Andrews (found) _____ between 1410 and 1413.

c The book (publish) _____ next month.

d More than 1,300 hearts (transplant) _____ last year.

e 114 arrests (make) _____ in the last two weeks.

f   What kinds of jobs (need) _____ in the future?
g   They (marry) _____ in Sydney in February 2007.
h   England (last invade) _____ in 1066.
i   I'm sure wind power (use) _____ more in the future.

Unit 11D

last = zuletzt
invade a country = in ein Land einfallen
wind power = Windkraft

4 Setzen Sie den Text in die Gegenwart. Beachten Sie: Die meisten der fett gedruckten Formen müssen Sie in die Gegenwartsform setzen, nicht aber die, welche sich – von der Gegenwart aus gesehen – auf die Vergangenheit beziehen. Diese müssen logischerweise in der Vergangenheitsform stehen.

A powerful king **went** _____ to see a fortune teller to hear what she **had** _____ to say about the future. The old woman **told** _telled_ him that his favourite wife, Sarabaya, **would** _will_ die within a year. The king **didn't** _doesn't_ believe the woman. After all, Sarabaya **was** _is_ young and healthy, why should she die?
A few months later Sarabaya **was** _is_ dead and the king **was** _is_ devastated. He also **remembered** _____ what the fortune teller **had told** _told_ him and **became** _became_ convinced that she **had used** _used_ her magical powers to kill Sarabaya.
He **ordered** _____ the woman to appear before him and **told** _tell_ her that it **was** _is_ his belief that she **was** _is_ not a fortune teller but a witch who **had used** _used_ her power to kill his wife. If, however, she **was** _is_ really a fortune teller, she should tell him when she herself **would** _will_ die, or else she **would** _will_ be killed.
The woman **thought** _think_ carefully, and then **said** _said_, "I will die three days before you, Your Majesty."

5 Hör-Sprech-Übung. In dieser Übung hören Sie einen mit *I don't know* eingeleiteten Fragewort-Satz, den Sie in eine direkte Frage umwandeln sollen.

2/14

Sie hören zum Beispiel: ....I don't know why the king visited a fortune teller.
Sie sagen: ....Why did the king visit a fortune teller?
Sie hören die richtige Antwort: ....Why did the king visit a fortune teller?
Sie wiederholen die Antwort: ....Why did the king visit a fortune teller?

Unit 11E

Focus on words

1. *Fortune* kann „Schicksal" heißen – daher *fortune teller* (= Wahrsager[in]), d. h. jemand, der einem sein Schicksal vorhersagt. *Fortune* ist aber auch „Glück" oder „Vermögen":

She had the good **fortune** to find an excellent teacher.	Sie hatte das **Glück**, einen ausgezeichneten Lehrer zu finden.
He lost a **fortune** at the casino.	Er verlor ein **Vermögen** im Spielkasino.

2. *Power* ist „Kraft / Macht": *magical powers* (= magische Kräfte / Zauberkraft), *wind power* (= Windkraft), *come to power* (= an die Macht kommen), *a powerful king* (= ein mächtiger König).

3. *See someone* heißt nicht nur „jemanden sehen", sondern auch „jemanden (z. B. einen Arzt oder Rechtsanwalt) konsultieren": *you should see a doctor about that* (= damit solltest du zum Arzt gehen). *Go to see* ist umgangssprachlicher als *visit* und heißt „besuchen / aufsuchen", wie in 11C: *the king went to see a fortune teller*; auch *visit* wäre hier möglich gewesen: *the king visited a fortune teller*.

4. *Love:* When you *fall in love* (= wenn man sich verliebt), *you are in love* (= ist man verliebt), und mitunter ist es *love at first sight* (= Liebe auf den ersten Blick). „Jemanden grüßen lassen" kann man ausdrücken mit den Worten *please give them my love* (= bitte grüß sie recht herzlich von mir), und ein herzlicher Briefschluss wäre *Love, Jack* oder *Much love, Kate*. *Make love to / with someone* dagegen bedeutet *having sex* oder *sleeping with that person*. *When there is no love lost* oder *very little love lost between people*, dann mögen sie sich nicht, *they dislike each other*.

5. *Trip – journey:* Sowohl *trip* als auch *journey* bezeichnet „Reise", und die selten gewordene „Schiffsreise" wäre *voyage*, welches Letztere heute auch eine „Weltraumreise" sein könnte: *a manned voyage to Mars* (= ein bemannter Flug zum Mars).

6. *Shall we?* = „ja?" Mit einem an einen *let's*-Satz angehängten *shall we?* wird ein Vorschlag höflich abgemildert, gewissermaßen das Einverständnis des Angesprochenen erbeten:

Let's look it up on the Internet, **shall we?**	Lass es uns im Internet nachsehen, ja? / Sehen wir doch mal im Internet nach!
Let's go inside, **shall we?**	Lass(t) uns reingehen, ja?

7. „Kennenlernen": „Jemanden kennenlernen" kann *(first) meet someone* sein: *we first met at a party* (= wir lernten uns auf einer Party kennen). Ein intensiveres Kennenlernen könnte man – wie in 11A – durch *get to know* ausdrücken: *Over the last month I've got to know her really well.* (= Im Laufe des letzten Monats habe ich sie wirklich gut kennengelernt.)

8. *Your Majesty:* Wichtige Information für ein Gespräch mit *the Queen*: Zu Beginn reden Sie sie mit *Your Majesty* an, im weiteren Verlauf des Gesprächs mit *ma'am* (langes a wie in *arm*). *And another piece of advice* (= noch ein Rat) *for your visit to Buckingham Palace: Don't speak to the Queen unless* (= es sei denn) *she speaks to you!*

Thank you ma'am!

Unit 11F

2/15

Focus on culture

1. The **Palace on Wheels** is a highly popular luxury train run (*3. Form!* = *betrieben*) by Indian Railways. Its 14 coaches were once used by the rulers of British India and are decorated in the rich style of that period. During their week-long journey the passengers travel in saloons looked after by a Khidmatgar, a special kind of personal attendant. The train departs from New Delhi and stops at many fascinating places, including the Taj Mahal. It returns to New Delhi on the morning of the eighth day.

2. **India**, with a population of over 1.1 billion, is the world's second most populous country and its largest democracy. India's largest cities are **Mumbai** (formerly Bombay), **Delhi** (not the capital New Delhi!), and **Kolkata** (formerly Calcutta). While **Hindi**, with the largest number of speakers, is the official language, **English** is regularly used in business, administration as well as in the legal system, the armed forces, and the media. In fact, with between 50 and 100 million English speakers, India is the second or third largest English-speaking country in the world.

run a train = einen Zug „betreiben"
railway = Eisenbahn
coach = (Eisenbahn-)Wagen
ruler = Herrscher(in)
decorate = ausschmücken
passenger = Fahrgast
saloon = Salon
look after = betreuen
attendant = Betreuer(in)
depart = abfahren
fascinating = faszinierend
return = zurückkehren
billion = Milliarde
most populous = bevölkerungsreichste
democracy = Demokratie
formerly = früher
official language = Amtssprache
regularly = regelmäßig
business = Geschäft(sleben)
administration = Verwaltung
legal system = Justiz
armed forces = Streitkräfte

137

Unit 11G Test yourself

Fortune Teller's Puzzle

(A = ACROSS, D = DOWN)

curious =
 neugierig
what's in store =
 was bevorsteht
imagine =
 stell dir vor
many times =
 viele Male
this time =
 diesmal

1D   Many people, when they have a _____, go to see a fortune teller.
9D   They are curious about _____ is in store for them.
8A   The fortune teller will often tell them things that are easy to _____.
13A By the way, have you ever _____ to see a fortune teller?
6D   I _____ to see a fortune teller yesterday.
3A   One of the things the woman said _____ that …
14D … I _____ been in love many times.
4D   But that's of _____ true of most men my age.
7A   So it's no _____ that she "knew" it.
12D But imagine, she also said I hadn't found my true love _____.
5D   Isn't that _____? You see, I'm 61 years old.
10D Now I'm thinking hard _____ that true love might be.
2A   Maybe I'll meet _____ when I go on a train journey in December.
14A I _____ booked a seven-day journey on the Palace on Wheels train in India.
13D That trip in a luxury train must _____ an unforgettable experience.
11A Up to now I've never come across _____ interesting on a train.
6A   But perhaps it _____ be different this time.
3D   Seven days on a train is enough time to get to know a person really _____.

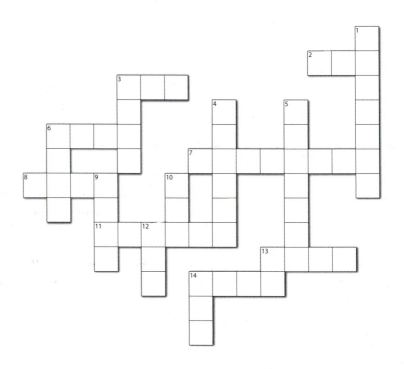

Theft

Unit 12

> Passiv
> Bedingungssätze
> *Would*
> Frageanhängsel
> *-ing*-Konstruktionen
> *-self*-Pronomen
> Gebrauch der Zeiten
> *… and the English sense of humour*

Unit 12A Dialogue

2/16

■ = Ken
● = Jean

car theft =
  Autodiebstahl
smile = lächeln
as usual =
  wie gewöhnlich
wrong = falsch
awful =
  schrecklich
take – took =
  nehmen – nahm
catch – caught –
  caught = fangen
  – fing – gefangen
crash into =
  prallen gegen
arrest = verhaften
crime =
  Verbrechen
remember =
  sich erinnern
anyway =
  wie dem auch sei
it seems =
  es scheint
relaxed =
  entspannt
lesson = Lektion
slap =
  Klaps, Schlag
probably =
  wahrscheinlich
misbehave =
  sich schlecht
  benehmen
sue = verklagen
cause =
  verursachen

A car theft

■ Hello Jean, not smiling as usual, is anything wrong?
● No, not really, it's just that my car was stolen over the weekend.
■ How awful! … I am sorry. Has it been found?
● Well, it was found yesterday – crashed. Some teenagers took it for a joyride …
■ Oh goodness … were they caught?
● Yes. They were chased by the police, crashed into a tree and were arrested.
■ Hmm. I don't know … these youngsters nowadays … They're all into crime and drugs and that sort of thing. I remember when we were young …
● Come off it, Ken, they aren't all bad, are they? Anyway, I heard that two of the kids were taken to hospital, but nothing serious it seems. I'm glad they weren't killed or injured seriously, that would have been terrible.
■ If this had happened to me, I wouldn't be as relaxed about it as you are. But let's hope they learn their lesson from it.
● I'm sure a few days in hospital and a slap on the wrist by the magistrate will make them think.
■ I suspect the slap will probably be just a gentle tap, they'll be told not to misbehave again and the police will be lucky if they aren't sued for chasing the kids and causing them to crash.

Ein Autodiebstahl

■ Hallo, Jean, nicht lächelnd wie sonst, stimmt etwas nicht?
● Nein, eigentlich nicht, nur ist mein Auto am Wochenende gestohlen worden.
■ Wie schrecklich! … Das tut mir aber leid. Ist es gefunden worden?
● Nun, es wurde gestern gefunden – kaputt. Ein paar Teenager haben damit eine Spritztour gemacht…
■ Ach du meine Güte … wurden sie gefasst?
● Ja. Sie wurden von der Polizei gejagt / verfolgt, fuhren gegen einen Baum und wurden verhaftet.
■ Hm. Ich weiß nicht … diese Jugendlichen heutzutag … Sie haben es alle mit Kriminalität und Drogen und so was. Ich weiß noch, als wir jung waren …
● Hör bloß auf, Ken, sie sind doch nicht alle schlecht, oder? Ich hörte jedenfalls, dass zwei der Jungen ins Krankenhaus gebracht wurden, aber es ist wohl nichts Ernstes. Ich bin froh, dass sie nicht ums Leben gekommen oder ernstlich verletzt worden sind, das wäre schrecklich gewesen.
■ Wenn das mir passiert wäre, würde ich das nicht so locker sehen wie du. Aber hoffen wir, sie lernen daraus.
● Ich bin sicher, ein paar Tage im Krankenhaus und „ein Schlag aufs Handgelenk" vom Richter werden ihnen zu denken geben.
■ Ich vermute, der Schlag wird wohl nur ein sanfter Klaps sein, ihnen wird gesagt werden, dass sie es nicht wieder tun sollen, und die Polizisten werden Glück haben, wenn sie nicht verklagt werden dafür, dass sie die Jungen verfolgten und „veranlassten zu verunglücken".

Unit 12B

...unktion des Passivs klargemacht. Letztlich geht es um die ..., das Subjekt oder das Objekt. Aufgrund dieser Entscheidung ... der Konstruktion: Aktiv oder Passiv. Setzen meine Gedanken bei *my car* an, ... e ich mit *My car* … und setze die Aussage notwendigerweise mit einer Passivkonstruktion fort; gehe ich von den „Tätern" aus, so muss eine Aktivkonstruktion folgen:

My car **was stolen** (by some teenagers).	*Mein Auto wurde (von einigen Teenagern) gestohlen.*
Some teenagers **stole** my car.	*Einige Teenager stahlen mein Auto.*

Durch die Klammern veranschaulichen wir, dass im Passivsatz der „Verursacher" der Handlung (*some teenagers*) weggelassen werden kann – und in der Regel wird, denn wenn seine Erwähnung wichtig ist, wählen wir meistens die Aktivkonstruktion.

✎ Verwandeln Sie die folgenden Sätze aus dem Aktiv ins Passiv. Wenn Ihnen der „Verursacher" nicht wichtig erscheint oder seine Nennung den Passivsatz „überfrachtet", lassen Sie ihn einfach weg. (Zu den unregelmäßigen Verben vgl. S. 219.)

a Someone has stolen my car. _____
b They steal a lot of cars these days. _____
c The police will find the car. _____
d Police found the car in a car park in Bridge Street. _____
e They have found the car. _____
f The kids had taken it for a joyride. _____
g Youngsters often steal cars just for a joyride. _____

someone = jemand
these days = heutzutage
police = Polizei, Polizisten
car park = Parkplatz
often = oft
chase (scharfes s!) = jagen

141

Unit 12B

police officer = Polizist(in)
prevent = verhindern
car theft = Autodiebstahl

h A police car chased the youngsters. _____
i A police officer arrested one of the youngsters in a bar. _____
j How can we prevent car thefts? _____

2 Nun verwandeln Sie bitte die folgenden Passivsätze ins Aktiv.

a He was seen by a police officer. _____
b The debate was watched by millions of people. _____

watch sth = (sich) etw ansehen
police ist immer Plural!
call = (an)rufen
people = Menschen
neighbour = Nachbar(in)
attack = anfallen
climb (Ausspr. „klaim") = besteigen
several = mehrere
miss = vermissen
concierge = Portier

c The police were called by a neighbour. _____
d Golf is played by millions of people. _____
e What do you do if you are attacked by a dog? _____
f Everest has been climbed by several thousand people. _____
g She will be missed by many people. _____
h Theatre tickets, sightseeing and transportation can be arranged by the concierge. _____

3 If this had happened to me … = „Wenn das mir passiert wäre …"

Beachten Sie, dass der Vergangenheitsform *had* im *if*-Satz hier ein deutsches „wäre" entspricht. Die deutsche Entsprechung kann allerdings auch „hätte" lauten (→ 8B1):

| If they **had** found the car … | Wenn sie das Auto gefunden **hätten** … |

✎ Wir üben dieses „wäre" oder „hätte" durch Übersetzung einiger „wenn"-Sätze.

crash into a tree = gegen einen Baum fahren
arrest = festnehmen
kill = umbringen
follow = folgen
advice = Rat
die = sterben

a Wenn er ein Auto gestohlen hätte … *If he had stolen*
b Wenn die Polizei ihn gefasst hätte … *If the police had caught*
c Wenn er nicht gegen einen Baum gefahren wäre … *If he had crashed into*
d Wenn sie ihn nicht festgenommen hätten … *If they hadn't him arrested*
e Wenn er jemand umgebracht hätte … *If he had killed someone*
f Wenn er meinem Rat gefolgt wäre … *If he had adviced my*
g Wenn er gestorben wäre … *If he had died*

4 That would have been terrible = „Das wäre schrecklich gewesen"

Wir haben schon öfter *would* (= würde) verwendet und geübt (→ 9B2, 9B3). Sie kennen bereits Verwendungen wie diese:

you'd be	= you would be	= du würdest sein	= du wärest
you'd have	= you would have	= du würdest haben	= du hättest
you'd know	= you would know	= du würdest wissen	= du wüsstest

In diesen Verwendungen haben wir die Konstruktion *would* + **Grundform des Verbs** (hier: *be, have, know*). In 12A haben wir aber nicht diese Konstruktion, sondern die Fügung *would* + *have* + **3. Form des Verbs** (also z. B. *been, had, known*). Vergleichen Sie:

That would **be** terrible. = *Das würde schrecklich sein.*
  = *Das wäre schrecklich.*

That would **have been** terrible. = *Das würde schrecklich gewesen sein.*
  = *Das wäre schrecklich gewesen.*

would = würde
would be = würde sein = wäre
would have been = würde gewesen sein = wäre gewesen

✎ Übersetzen Sie entsprechend diesen Beispielen.

a Das wäre falsch.   *it would be wrong*
b Das wäre falsch gewesen.   *it would have been wrong*
c Wir würden das Auto finden.   *we would find the car*
d Wir hätten das Auto gefunden.   *we would have found*
e Du hättest ein kleines Problem.   *you would have a little pro*
f Du hättest ein kleines Problem gehabt.   *you would have had a little pro*

wrong = falsch
small = klein

5 Frageanhängsel (→ 1D4, 5D3, 7B3-4)

Auch in unserem Dialog 12A kommt wieder ein Satz mit Frageanhängsel vor:

They aren't all bad, **are they?**   *Sie sind doch nicht alle schlecht, oder?*

✎ Sprechen Sie die Sätze mit den passenden Frageanhängseln.

a These youngsters are all into crime and drugs, *aren't they*
b Jane's always smiling, *isn't she*
c Your car was stolen, *wasn't it*
d It hasn't been found yet, *has it*
e Let's go to the hospital, *shall we*
f The kids weren't injured seriously, *were they*
g You'll miss the car, *won't you*

not … yet = noch nicht
serious(ly) = ernst, schwer
sue = verklagen

Unit 12B

Unit 12C — Reading text

2/17

holiday =
 Ferien, Urlaub
experience =
 Erlebnis
happen =
 passieren
won't = will not =
 werde nicht
rightly = zu Recht
fly – flew – flown =
 fliegen – flog –
 geflogen
cruise (Ausspr.:
 langes „u", kein „i")
along = entlang
gorgeous =
 herrlich
pretty = hübsch
innocent =
 unschuldig
shy = schüchtern
glance = Blick
except = außer
way = Weg, Art
space =
 Platz, Raum
move =
 sich bewegen
closer („s" wie „ß")
the ones = the girls
notice = bemerken
empty = leer
jump = springen
board ship =
 an Bord gehen
wallet =
 Brieftasche
gone (reimt sich
 mit „on")

A holiday experience

Don't ask me where it happened. I won't tell you. I'll just say it was in a beautiful southern European city, one loved by tourists and rightly so. I had just flown in from London and had a few hours to kill before embarking on a cruise of the Mediterranean.

I went for a leisurely walk along the seaside promenade, it was a gorgeous, sunny afternoon. I sat down on a bench. I felt in harmony with myself and the world.

A group of girls came along the promenade. They were pretty, they were laughing, they were having innocent fun. Lovely. After a shy glance at me and a few giggles they sat down on my bench. Well, all except one, actually. The way we were sitting there wasn't quite enough space on the bench and so we all moved closer together to make room for her. "Where there's a will there's a way," I said paternally as the ones next to me moved up really close. I didn't notice that all the other benches were empty.

After a short while the girls all jumped up again, and giggling and dancing they had soon disappeared.

There's no fool like an old fool. When I was boarding ship, later that afternoon, I reached for my wallet. It was gone.

Ein Urlaubserlebnis

Fragen Sie mich nicht, wo es passiert ist. Ich werde es Ihnen nicht sagen. Ich werde nur sagen, es war in einer schönen südeuropäischen Stadt, einer, die von Touristen geliebt wird und mit Recht. Ich war gerade aus London mit dem Flugzeug angekommen und hatte noch ein paar Stunden („totzuschlagen") Zeit, bevor ich mich zu einer Mittelmeerkreuzfahrt einschiffte.

Ich machte einen gemächlichen Spaziergang entlang der Strandpromenade, es war ein herrlicher, sonniger Nachmittag. Ich setzte mich auf eine Bank. Ich fühlte mich in Einklang mit mir (selbst) und der Welt.

Eine Gruppe von Mädchen kam die Promenade entlang. Sie waren hübsch, sie lachten, sie hatten unschuldigen Spaß. Reizend. Nach einem schüchternen Blick auf mich und einigem Kichern setzten sie sich auf meine Bank. Also, alle außer einer, genau genommen. So wie wir saßen, war nicht vollkommen genug Platz auf der Bank, und deshalb rutschten wir alle enger zusammen, um Platz für sie zu schaffen. „Wo ein Wille ist, ist (auch) ein Weg", sagte ich väterlich, während die mir Nächstsitzenden wirklich eng an mich heranrutschten. Ich bemerkte nicht, dass alle anderen Bänke leer waren.

Nach kurzer Zeit sprangen die Mädchen alle wieder auf, und kichernd und tänzelnd waren sie bald verschwunden.

Kein Narr (so schlimm) wie ein alter Narr! (Alter schützt vor Torheit nicht.) Als ich später an diesem Nachmittag an Bord ging, griff ich nach meiner Brieftasche. Sie war weg.

Unit 12D

Rules and practice

1 *-ing*-Form oder eine andere Form?

a I had a few hours to kill before (embark) _embarking_ on a cruise of the Mediterranean.

b I had a few hours to kill before I (embark) _embark_ on a cruise of the Mediterranean.

c A caddie is a person who helps a golf player by (carry) _carrying_ their clubs.

d A caddie is a person who (carry) _carry_ a golf player's clubs.

e We were thinking of (buy) _buying_ a house.

f We were planning (buy) _buy_ a house.

g We wanted (buy) _to buy_ a house.

h Thank you for (tell) _telling_ us about St Andrews.

i I'm so glad you (tell) _told_ us about St Andrews.

j Thank you for (be) _beeing_ so relaxed about it.

k I was glad she (be) _was_ so relaxed about it.

l She used to be so fond of (listen) _listening_ to good music.

m When she had time she often (listen) _listen_ to good music.

club = (Golf-)Schläger
be fond of doing sth = etw gern tun

2 Before, after, while, when + *-ing*

Beachten Sie den eleganten satzverkürzenden Gebrauch der *-ing*-Form nach Wörtern wie *before*, *after*, *while* und *when*.

| I had a few hours to kill **before embarking** on a cruise. | Ich hatte noch ein paar Stunden übrig, bevor ich mich zu einer Kreuzfahrt einschiffte. |
| One shouldn't talk **while playing** chess. | Man sollte nicht reden, während man Schach spielt. |

Unit 12D

do some reading = lesen
try = versuchen
remember sth = sich an etw erinnern
leave = verlassen
need = benötigen
glasses = (eine) Brille

✏️ Verkürzen Sie den eingeklammerten Teil der Sätze mit Hilfe der *-ing*-Form.

a I think I'll do some reading before (I go) _____ to bed.
b He suffered a heart attack while (he was playing) _____ golf.
c Two teenagers were taken to hospital after (they crashed) _____ into a tree.
d When (I was boarding) _____ ship, later that afternoon, I reached for my wallet.
e Two teenagers crashed into a tree after (they were) _____ chased by police.
f What do you eat before (you run) _____ a race?
g A 19-year-old was arrested after (he stole) _____ a car.
h When (I'm trying) _____ to remember a name I go through the alphabet.
i She said she was attacked while (she was walking) _____ in the park.
j He always kisses his wife before (he leaves) _____ the house.
k She needs glasses when (she reads) _____ books or newspapers.

3 Gebrauch der *-self*-Pronomen (→ 9E11, 10D2). Setzen Sie in den folgenden Sätzen die passenden *-self*-Pronomen ein.

I felt in harmony with myself and the world.   Ich fühlte mich in Harmonie mit mir selbst und der Welt.

a She felt in harmony with _herS_ and the world.
b We felt in harmony with _ourS_ and the world.
c They felt in harmony with _themS_ and the world.
d He felt in harmony with _hisS_ and the world.
e Do you feel in harmony with _yourS_ and the world?.
f The world is no longer in harmony with _it's self_
g Do you guys feel in harmony with _yourS_ and the world?

you guys = Ihr (Leute)

4 Gebrauch der Verbzeiten

Der Text 12C eignet sich gut zum Üben der Vergangenheitszeiten. Die Haupterzählzeit ist die Vergangenheit, aus der gelegentlich in die Vergangenheit vor der Vergangenheit (*past perfect* / „*had*-Form" → 7D3) zurückgegangen wird.

Setzen Sie die passenden Verbformen (Vergangenheit oder „had-Form") ein und achten Sie auch darauf, ob die einfache Form oder die Verlaufsform (→5B1, 6D3) angebracht ist und ob die verneinte Form mit *did* gebildet werden muss.

Unit 12D

believe = glauben
those = jene, diese
steal – stole – stolen
feel – felt – felt
stupid = dumm

It happened in a beautiful southern European city, one loved by tourists and rightly so. I (just fly) __flown__ in from London and (have) __had__ a few hours to kill before embarking on a cruise of the Mediterranean.

I (go) _____ for a leisurely walk along the seaside promenade, it (be) __was__ a gorgeous, sunny afternoon. I (sit) __sat__ down on a bench. I (feel) __felled__ in harmony with myself and the world.

A group of girls (come) __came__ along the promenade. They (be) __were__ pretty, they (laugh) __were laughing__, they (have) __were having__ innocent fun. Lovely.

After a shy glance at me and a few giggles they (sit) __sat__ down on my bench. Well, all except one, actually. The way we (sit) __were sitting__ there (not be) _____ quite enough space on the bench and so we all (move) __moved__ closer together to make room for her. "Where there's a will there's a way," I (say) __said__ paternally as the ones next to me (move) __moved__ up really close. I (not notice) __didn't notice__ that all the other benches (be) __were__ empty.

After a short while the girls all (jump) __jumped__ up again, and giggling and dancing they (soon disappear) __disappeared__.

There's no fool like an old fool. When I (board) __boarding__ ship, later that afternoon, I (reach) __reached__ for my wallet. It (be) __has__ gone. I (not can) __couldn't__ believe what (happen) __had happend__. Those lovely, innocent girls (steal) __had stolen__ my wallet. There (be) __were__ thousands of pounds in it. I (never feel) __had never felt__ so stupid in all my life.

5 Hör-Sprech-Übung. Jetzt kommt eine recht schwierige Übung, die Sie deshalb am besten mehrmals machen. Sie sollen kurze Aktivsätze ins Passiv setzen. Zwei der vorkommenden Verben sind unregelmäßig: *eat – ate – eaten, see – saw – seen*.

2/18

Sie hören zum Beispiel: ....The queen visited the museum.
Sie sagen: ....The museum was visited by the queen.
Sie hören die richtige Antwort: ....The museum was visited by the queen.
Sie wiederholen die Antwort: ....The museum was visited by the queen.

Unit 12E Focus on words

1. *Steal – theft*:

steal – stole – stolen	stehlen – stahl – gestohlen
theft	Diebstahl
thief – thieves	Dieb – Diebe

something – anything

2. Is **anything** wrong? (= Ist irgendetwas „falsch", d. h. nicht in Ordnung?) Wir erinnern uns (→8E1, 11B6): *some* bei bejahendem, *any* bei verneinendem oder fragendem Sinn. *There's **something** wrong with my phone* wäre „mit meinem Telefon stimmt was nicht", und *There isn't **anything** wrong with your phone* bedeutet „An deinem Telefon ist nichts kaputt." – Interessant ist aber, dass man statt *Is **anything** wrong?* auch *Is **something** wrong?* fragen kann. Mit *something* drückt man die Vermutung aus, dass etwas nicht in Ordnung ist, es handelt sich also nicht um eine echte Frage. Wenn jemand weinend vor Ihnen steht, schlussfolgern Sie, dass etwas passiert ist, und fragen: *Is **something** wrong?*

worry = sich Sorgen machen
attack = angreifen

3. **Youngster** für *young person* ist heute *slightly old-fashioned* (= leicht altmodisch), wird also überwiegend von der älteren Generation (und oft „jugendkritisch") gebraucht. Der heute gängige Ausdruck für „Jugendliche(r)" ist *young person*, abwertend bzw. in Verbindung mit Straftaten auch *youth(s)*, wie zum Beispiel in *These **youths** don't worry if you're young or old, they'll attack you and run away.* (= Diesen Jugendlichen ist es egal, ob man jung oder alt ist, sie überfallen einen und rennen weg.)

a few days = ein paar Tage

4. *They were taken **to hospital*** (= sie wurden ins Krankenhaus gebracht), *a few days **in hospital***: Im AE in beiden Fällen **the hospital**: *They were taken to **the hospital**, a few days in **the hospital**.*

5. *The **police*** (= die Polizei): Anders als das deutsche „Polizei" kann *police* auch zählbar konstruiert werden und ist in jedem Fall Mehrzahl:

injure = verletzen
protester = Demonstrant(in)

More than 50 **police** were injured.	Mehr als 50 **Polizisten** wurden verletzt.
Police have (*nicht*: has!) arrested dozens of protesters.	**Die Polizei hat** Dutzende von Demonstranten verhaftet.

6. **Bench** (= Bank zum Sitzen), **bank** (= Bank fürs Geld). *[Sch]*

7. **Wallet** ist das Wort für „Brieftasche", und das manchmal damit verwechselte **briefcase** heißt „Aktentasche".

8. *The **ones** next to me* (≈ die direkt neben mir Sitzenden): **Ones** ist „Stellvertreter" für ein zuvor genanntes Substantiv, in diesem Fall das Wort *girls*. Hätte der Mann am Rand der Bank gesessen und also nur ein Mädchen neben sich gehabt, so hätte er gesagt: *The one next to me.*

9. Zwei **proverbs** (= Sprichwörter) enthält der Dialog 12A:

fool = Narr

Where there's a will there's a way.	Wo ein Wille ist, da ist auch ein Weg.
There's no fool like an old fool.	„Kein Narr (so schlimm) wie ein alter Narr." Alter schützt vor Torheit nicht.

Unit 12F

Focus on culture

1. *Magistrates' Courts* (= Magistratsgerichte) bilden in *England* und *Wales* die unterste Stufe der Strafgerichtsbarkeit (= *criminal court system*). Sie sind zuständig für (= *deal with*) leichtere Straftaten (= *minor crimes*) wie Diebstahl (= *theft*), Ladendiebstahl (= *shoplifting*), Betrug (= *fraud*), Fahren trotz Führerscheinentzugs (= *driving while disqualified*), öffentliche Ruhestörung (= *breach of the peace*), Drogenbesitz (= *drug possession*) und leichtere Fälle von Einbruchsdiebstahl (= *burglary*).
Für schwerere Strafsachen (= *more serious crimes*) wie (= *such as*) Mord (= *murder*), Vergewaltigung (= *rape*) und Raub (= *robbery*) sind die **Crown Courts** zuständig.
Die allgemeine Bezeichnung für „Richter" ist *judge*, das allgemeine Wort für „(Rechts-)Anwalt" ist *lawyer*.

breach = Bruch
peace = Frieden
burglar = Einbrecher

2. *The English sense of humour:* Den Engländern wird ein besonderer Sinn für Humor nachgesagt. Dieser äußert sich nicht in der Zahl der Witze (= *jokes*), die sie erfinden, sondern in der Art, wie sie ernste Dinge nicht dramatisieren, sondern herunterspielen. In ihrer *conversation* ereifern sich die Engländer nicht über die großen Lebensfragen, sondern gehen scheinbar leicht über sie hin mit Ironie (= *irony*), Witz (= *wit*), Untertreibung (= *understatement*), Herabminderung der eigenen Bedeutung (= *self-deprecation*) und manchmal auch schierer Albernheit (= *sheer silliness*). Beim *small talk* ist Ernsthaftigkeit (= *seriousness*) tabu.
In 12C wie auch in einigen anderen Texten dieses Buches (11A, 9C, 8A, 6A, 5A, 1A) finden Sie diese Art sich selbst nicht ernst nehmenden und den Gesprächspartner sanft frotzelnden (= *gently teasing*) Humors.
Understatement, also das bewusste, oft witzige Herunterspielen (= *playing down*) bedeutender Dinge, ist vielleicht die typischste englische Sprachkonvention, die zu entschlüsseln dem Kontinentaleuropäer nicht immer leicht fällt.
So entspricht etwa *not (at all) bad* einem deutschen „ausgezeichnet!", *we're having a small problem* umschreibt eine Katastrophe erster Güte und *not very clever* bezeichnet eine Dummheit erheblichen Ausmaßes.
King George V (= *King George the Fifth*, 1865–1936) bittet die um sein Sterbebett (= *deathbed*) versammelten Würdenträger (= *dignitaries*) um Nachsicht mit den Worten: *Gentlemen, I am so sorry for keeping you waiting like this. I am unable to concentrate.* (= Meine Herren, es tut mir sehr leid, dass ich Sie so warten lasse. Ich bin außerstande, mich zu konzentrieren.)

sense of humour = Sinn für Humor

not at all bad = gar nicht schlecht
clever = klug, schlau

Unit 12G — Test yourself

Frustration Crossword

Hier ist eine kleine Geschichte mit Lücken. Ergänzen Sie die fehlenden Wörter und setzen Sie sie in das *crossword* ein. *Don't get frustrated!* (Eine Übersetzung des Textes finden Sie auf Seite 204. Außerdem ist der Text auf der CD.)

Two strangers were sitting over a (14D) _____ of wine in a London bar. One of (17A) _____ looked bored and unhappy. "Life is dull, and (13A) _____ in the world bores me," he said.

"How can you say (19D) _____ a thing?" said the other. "Life is wonderful, and the world is an exciting (1A) _____. Just take Italy. It's a delightful (2D) _____. Have you ever (16D) _____ there?"

"Oh yes, I've been to Italy. I was (12D) _____ last year. I didn't like it."

"Then go to Norway and see the midnight sun. Have you ever done that?"

"Yes, I've been to Norway, and I've (9D) _____ the midnight sun. That was a few years (7A) _____. It didn't impress me."

"Have you (10A) _____ thought about a hobby?" asked his companion.

"I've tried (3D) _____ of hobbies in my life," was the answer. "I've collected stamps and coins, I've (4D) _____ chess, golf, and the flute, I've painted in oils and watercolours. How terribly boring it all (8A) _____!"

"It (18A) _____ to me," said the other man, "that you have a serious problem. Go and (6D) _____ Dr Greenberg in Harley Street. They (11A) _____ he's the best psychiatrist in London."

"I am Dr Greenberg," was the sad man's (5D) _____.

frustrated = frustriert
stranger = Fremde(r)
bored = gelangweilt
dull = langweilig
bore = langweilen
exciting = spannend
delightful = reizend
Norway = Norwegen
impress = beeindrucken
think about = nachdenken über
answer = Antwort
collect = sammeln
stamp = Briefmarke
coin = Münze
flute = Flöte
paint = malen
boring = langweilig
serious = ernst
go and see = aufsuchen
psychiatrist (Ausspr.: „ßai<u>kai</u>etrist")
sad = traurig

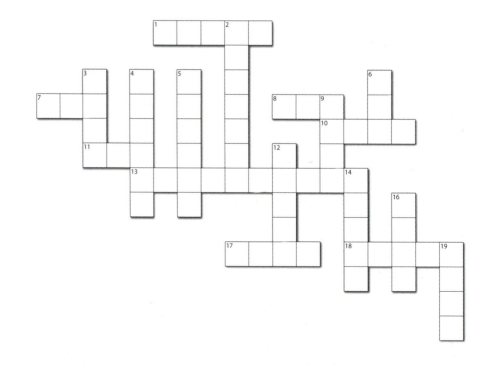

Education

Unit 13

› Present perfect "unfinished"
› „Seit" = *since* oder *for*?
› Frageanhängsel
› *-ing-*Form *oder to-*Form?
› Betonung durch Relativsatz
› Passiv
› Fragen mit *wh-*Wörtern
› … *and have a look at the Gherkin!*

Unit 13A

2/20

■ = man
● = woman

excellent = ausgezeichnet
take sth up = anfangen, etw zu betreiben
from scratch = von Grund auf
I'm sure = ich bin sicher
train as a hairdresser = Friseur(in) lernen
decide = entscheiden, beschließen
sell – sold – sold = verkaufen – verkaufte – verkauft
broad = breit
broaden = verbreitern, erweitern
wouldn't = würde nicht
talk about sth = über etw reden
gherkin = Gewürzgurke
the kind of place = die Art von Ort
(can) afford = sich leisten (können)
not … yet = noch nicht
things to do = zu erledigende Dinge

152

Dialogue

The second life

■ Your English is excellent. Have you lived in Britain or America?
● No I haven't, actually. I took it up when I retired.
■ But you didn't start from scratch, did you? I'm sure you learned some English at school.
● Well, not really. You see, I trained as a hairdresser, had my own shop, and at 58 I decided I'd had enough. I sold my house with the shop, rented a flat and started my second life …

■ Your second life?
● Yes, broadening my education, learning English, checking out the global village – oh, and getting married again. I met my husband in our English class. We've been married for, um, five years now – time flies!

■ And you're still going to class?
● Oh yes, both of us, we wouldn't want to miss it. It's a really nice group. We've been doing English together for so many years, and our teacher, well, he's just great at bringing us interesting things to talk and write about. We're into modern architecture at the moment – the Gherkin in London, the Guggenheim Museum in Bilbao, the Sydney Opera House and what have you … all of them great architecture.

■ And that's the kind of place you visit when you travel?
● Well, yes, if we can afford them. We haven't been to Australia yet, but it's been on our "to do" list for some time. If we win the lottery, we'll fly out there first class, that's easier on the legs.

Das zweite Leben

■ Ihr Englisch ist exzellent. Haben Sie in Großbritannien oder Amerika gelebt?
● Nein, eigentlich nicht. Ich habe es angefangen, als ich in Rente ging.
■ Aber Sie haben doch nicht von Null angefangen(, oder)? Sie haben sicher etwas Englisch in der Schule gelernt.
● Also, eigentlich nicht. Sehn Sie, ich habe Friseurin gelernt, hatte mein eigenes Geschäft, und mit 58 entschied ich, dass es reichte. Ich verkaufte mein Haus mit dem Geschäft, mietete eine Wohnung und begann mein zweites Leben …

■ Ihr zweites Leben?
● Ja, meine Bildung zu erweitern, Englisch zu lernen, mir das globale Dorf näher anzusehen – ach ja, und wieder zu heiraten. Ich habe meinen Mann in unserm Englischkurs kennengelernt. Wir sind jetzt, äh, fünf Jahre verheiratet – die Zeit vergeht!

■ Und Sie gehen noch zum Unterricht?
● O ja, beide, wir möchten es nicht missen. Es ist eine wirklich nette Gruppe. Wir machen schon seit so vielen Jahren Englisch zusammen, und unser Lehrer – also, der ist einfach großartig darin, uns interessante Dinge mitzubringen, über die wir dann reden und schreiben. Im Moment machen wir gerade moderne Architektur – das Gherkin in London, das Guggenheim-Museum in Bilbao, das Opernhaus von Sydney und so weiter … alles große Architektur.

■ Und solche Orte besuchen Sie dann, wenn Sie reisen?
● Nun ja, wenn wir sie uns leisten können. In Australien sind wir noch nicht gewesen, aber es ist seit einiger Zeit auf unserer Liste (der zu erledigenden Dinge). Wenn wir in der Lotterie gewinnen, fliegen wir da erste Klasse hin, das ist leichter für die Beine.

Unit 13B

Rules and practice

1 Das *present perfect "unfinished"*

Das *present perfect* ist die uns schon bekannte „*have*-Form" (→8B1): *have lived, have interrupted, have become, have forgotten, haven't been*.
Bisher haben wir nur einen Gebrauch des *present perfect* kennengelernt, nämlich den für abgeschlossene (= *finished*) Handlungen, weshalb wir diesen Gebrauch auch *present perfect* **finished** nennen können:

Present perfect für abgeschlossene Handlungen

I know we'**ve met** before.	*Ich weiß, wir sind uns schon mal begegnet.*
I'**ve been** to Italy.	*In Italien bin ich schon mal gewesen.*

Wir wissen auch, in welchen Punkten der Gebrauch des *present perfect* **finished** vom Deutschen abweicht: Es wird immer mit *have* gebildet (*I have been* = „ich bin gewesen"), und es kann nicht mit einer Zeitbestimmung der Vergangenheit gebraucht werden:

I know we'**ve met** before. – I know we **met** in 2005.
I'**ve been** to Italy. – I **was** in Italy last year.

Das *present perfect* **unfinished** wird natürlich ebenfalls stets mit *have* gebildet. Aber – und das ist das Besondere – es wird für Handlungen oder Zustände gebraucht, die sich **aus der Vergangenheit in die Gegenwart** erstrecken (und für die im Deutschen oft die Gegenwartsform steht!):

Present perfect für noch nicht abgeschlossene Handlungen

We **have been** married for five years.	*Wir sind seit fünf Jahren verheiratet.*
We **have been doing** English together for many years.	*Wir machen seit vielen Jahren Englisch zusammen.*
Australia **has been** on our list for some time.	*Australien ist seit einiger Zeit auf unserer Liste.*

since 1999

Diese Gegenüberstellung ist „ein Hammer", nicht wahr? Englisch die *have*-Form (das *present perfect tense*), deutsch die Gegenwartsform.
Und sehen Sie sich an, welches englische Wort hier für das deutsche „seit" steht: *for*!

Unit 13B

Ja, wir haben auch schon eine andere englische Entsprechung für „seit" kennengelernt, nämlich *since* (9F1). Wir müssen also *since* und *for* zu unterscheiden lernen:
since bezeichnet den Anfang der Handlung, also einen Zeit**punkt**:
since Adam and Eve, since 2004, since I last saw them;
for bezeichnet die bisherige Dauer der Handlung, also einen Zeit**raum**:
for three years / months / weeks / days.

2/21

2 Hör-Sprech-Übung. Machen Sie jetzt eine kleine Übung mit der CD: Sie hören einen Ausdruck, den Sie durch die englische Entsprechung für „seit" – also *since* oder *for* – erweitern sollen.

Sie hören zum Beispiel:	Sunday
Sie sagen:	since Sunday
Sie hören die richtige Antwort:	since Sunday
Sie wiederholen die Antwort:	since Sunday

since 1995 = seit 1995
for 20 years = seit 20 Jahren

3 Übersetzen Sie nun einige Sätze, und entscheiden Sie sich dabei für *have*-Form oder Gegenwartsform, *since* oder *for*. Vergleichen Sie anschließend mit dem Schlüssel, und machen Sie die Übung dann am besten noch einmal.

married = verheiratet
play chess = Schach spielen
how long? = wie lange?
sit on a bench = auf einer Bank sitzen

a Wir sind in London. – Wir sind seit zwei Wochen in London.
  We are in London
  We are in ... for 2 w

b Wir lernen Tango Argentino. – Seit September lernen wir Tango Argentino.
  We learn TA
  We learn TA since Sep.1

c Wir leben jetzt in Amerika. – Wir leben jetzt seit fünf Jahren hier.
  We live in A
  for 5 y

d Sind Sie verheiratet? – Ja, ich bin verheiratet. – Ich bin seit einem Jahr verheiratet.
  are you married Yes I'm
  for 1 y

e Was macht ihr? – Wir spielen Schach. – Wie lange spielt ihr denn schon?

f Sie sitzen auf einer Bank im Park. – Wie lange sitzen sie da schon?

4 Frageanhängsel (→1D4, 5D3, 7B3-4, 12B5)

Sie erinnern sich an die verschiedenen Erklärungen zum Anhängen der Frageanhängsel. Immer wurde das vorne stehende Hilfsverb wiederholt: negativ, wenn es vorne positiv war; positiv, wenn es vorne negativ war. In unserem Dialog 13A kommt nun wieder ein solcher Satz vor. Diesmal ist das Hilfsverb *didn't*:

But you **didn't** start from scratch, **did you?** Aber du hast doch nicht bei Null angefangen, **oder?**

Wichtig ist nun, dass als Frageanhängsel ebenfalls eine Form von *do* kommt, wenn vorne nur ein Vollverb und kein Hilfsverb steht:

| You **started** from scratch, **didn't you?** | Du hast von Null angefangen, *nicht wahr?* |

Dieser Gebrauch der *do*-Umschreibung ist ja auch folgerichtig, da die Frageform und verneinte Form eines Vollverbs stets mit *do / does / did* umschrieben wird. Beispiele für die anderen Formen von *do* in positiven und negativen Frageanhängseln:

You **don't** live in London, **do you?**	Sie wohnen (doch) nicht in London, *oder?*
You **live** in London, **don't you?**	Sie wohnen (doch) in London, *nicht wahr?*
She **doesn't** remember me, **does she?**	Sie erinnert sich nicht an mich, *oder?*
She **remembers** me, **doesn't she?**	Sie erinnert sich (doch) an mich, *nicht wahr?*

Hier nun eine Übung, wo jeder Satz ein anderes Frageanhängsel erfordert. Kriegen Sie das hin? Es ist ja auch gemein: Im Deutschen kommen wir mit „nicht wahr" und „oder" aus, im Englischen diese verwirrende Vielfalt. Daher dieser Tipp: Sie können im Zweifel einfach *right?* anhängen – das bleibt stets gleich und erfüllt ungefähr den gleichen Zweck: *You (don't) live in London, right?*

Unit 13B

✏️ **Versuchen Sie, die folgenden Sätze schnell und flüssig zu sprechen und dabei das passende Frageanhängsel anzuhängen.**

a You didn't learn your English at school, _did you_
b Sandra trained as a hairdresser, _didn't she_
c They've sold their house, _haven't they_
d He's rented a flat, _hasn't he_   _didn't he_
e You're still going to class, _aren't you_
f Dr Brown writes about modern architecture, _doesn't he_
g You haven't been to Sydney, _have you_
h We can't afford a five-star hotel, _can we_
i You'd like to win the lottery, _wouldn't you_
j Your wife doesn't want it, _does she_
k There isn't much we can do, _is there_   _can't we_ (Betonung)
l The police don't always help, _do they_

at school =
  in der Schule
flat =
  (Etagen-) Wohnung
Dr = doctor =
  Dr. / Doktor
can't afford =
  können uns nicht leisten
police ist Plural!

Unit 13C — Reading text

sentence = Satz
retirement = Pensionierung, Ruhestand
ceremony = Feier
look forward to = sich freuen auf
impatient(ly) = ungeduldig
however = aber, jedoch
common = häufig
valuable = wertvoll
lose = verlieren
may do sth = vielleicht etw tun
go on doing sth = weiterhin etw tun
though = obwohl
play a sport = einen Sport betreiben
science = (Natur-)Wissenschaft
voluntary = freiwillig, ehrenamtlich
ability = Fähigkeit
surprised = überrascht
worry about sth = sich Sorgen um etw machen

Contentment

An imaginary sentence spoken by the boss at an imaginary retirement ceremony: "I know this is a day you've been looking forward to for some years now, but, believe me, not half as much as we have."

Nobody would ever dream of saying it openly, but this is the way employer and employee often feel when their relationship ends: The worker has been waiting impatiently for the last day to arrive, and the boss is happy to see him go.

However, the opposite scenario is also common: If you have been valuable to your company because of your dedication and competence, they will not want to lose you and may offer you an arrangement under which you go on working for them, though perhaps only part-time and with a measure of flexibility. That way you will have the best of both worlds: the respect and extra income that comes with your work, and enough time to do things you have always wanted to do – play a sport or a musical instrument, take up painting, tango dancing or creative writing, lead a more active social life, learn a language or study a science, do voluntary work in the community, or travel and just enjoy life.

In any case, being active, trying to learn new things every day, never losing the ability to be surprised, and not worrying about your age are a sure recipe for contentment.

Zufriedenheit

Ein imaginärer Satz, vom Chef / von der Chefin bei einer imaginären Verabschiedungsfeier gesprochen: „Ich weiß, dass dies ein Tag ist, auf den Sie sich schon seit einigen Jahren freuen, aber, glauben Sie mir, nicht halb so sehr, wie wir es getan haben."
Niemand würde je im Traum daran denken, es offen zu sagen, aber dies ist die Art, wie Arbeitgeber und Arbeitnehmer es oft empfinden, wenn ihre Beziehung endet. Der Mitarbeiter hat ungeduldig darauf gewartet, dass der letzte Tag kommt, und der Chef / die Chefin ist glücklich, ihn gehen zu sehen.
Aber auch das entgegengesetzte Szenario kommt häufig vor: Wenn Sie für Ihre Firma wertvoll gewesen sind wegen Ihres Engagements und Ihrer Kompetenz, wird man Sie nicht verlieren wollen und bietet Ihnen vielleicht eine Vereinbarung / Regelung an, bei der Sie weiter für sie arbeiten, wenn auch vielleicht nur auf Teilzeitbasis und mit einem gewissen Maß an Flexibilität. Auf diese Weise werden Sie das Beste beider Welten haben: die Anerkennung und das zusätzliche Einkommen durch Ihre Arbeit und genug Zeit, Dinge zu tun, die Sie schon immer tun wollten – einen Sport betreiben oder ein Musikinstrument spielen, Malen, Tangotanzen oder kreatives Schreiben lernen, ein aktiveres gesellschaftliches Leben führen, eine Sprache lernen oder eine Wissenschaft studieren, ehrenamtlich in der Gemeinschaft arbeiten oder reisen und einfach das Leben genießen.
Auf jeden Fall sind Aktivbleiben, jeden Tag Neues zu lernen versuchen, nie die Fähigkeit verlieren, sich überraschen zu lassen, und sich nicht über das Alter Gedanken machen ein sicheres Rezept für Zufriedenheit.

Unit 13D

Rules and practice

1 Präposition + -ing-Form, nur -ing-Form oder to + Grundform des Verbs? Setzen Sie wie in den Beispielen jeweils die passende Form ein.

Präposition + -ing-Form: I'm not fond (walk) *of walking* around this area at night.
Nur -ing-Form: I try to avoid (walk) *walking* around this area at night.
To + Grundform des Verbs: I don't want (walk) *to walk* around this area at night.

a I'd never dream (say) *saying* such a thing.
b He's waiting impatiently for her (come) _____ back.
c You must avoid (travel) _____ on Friday nights.
d The boss was happy (see) _____ him go.
e There are some tricks (remember) _____ names.
f They may offer you an arrangement under which you go on (work) _____ for them.
g She now has enough time (do) _____ things she has always wanted to do.
h I started (eat) _____ less, cut out junk food and reduced my alcohol intake.
i I'd like (take) _____ up (paint) _____.
j We were thinking (buy) _____ a house.
k Seven days should be long enough (see) _____ a lot of the city.
l We don't spend much time (travel) _____ in trains these days.
m They will not want (lose) _____ you.
n Thank you (tell) _____ us about it.
o When are you coming (see) _____ us again?
p We must do all we can to prevent that (happen) _____ again.
q You must never lose the ability (be) _____ surprised.
r I'm looking forward (play) *playing* golf in St Andrews.

area = Gegend
such a thing = so etwas
avoid = vermeiden
on Friday nights = freitagabends
cut out = verzichten auf
intake = Aufnahme
food (langes u!)
take sth up = etw anfangen
buy (Ausspr.: „bai") = kaufen
prevent sth = etw verhindern
look forward to sth = sich auf etw freuen

Unit 13D

2 Besondere Betonung durch Relativsatz (→ 8D4)

In unserem Text 13C kommt diese Konstruktion vor:

| This is a day you've been looking forward to for some years now. | *Dies ist ein Tag, auf den Sie sich nun schon seit einigen Jahren freuen.* |

Hier ist *This is a day …* durch die Voranstellung besonders betont. Die Frontstellung von *This is a day …* ist wiederum nur möglich, wenn der Rest des Satzes als Relativsatz an *a day* angehängt wird. Ohne diese besondere Betonung würde der Satz so lauten:

| You've been looking forward to this day for some years now. | *Sie freuen sich nun schon seit einigen Jahren auf diesen Tag.* |

✎ Üben Sie nun die betonte Konstruktion durch Umwandlung aus der unbetonten.

She wants to marry this man. → This is the man she wants to marry.

a I met this woman on the train. _____
b They want to rent this flat. _____
c I told you about this man. _____
d I've been waiting for this letter. _____
e The king travelled in this train. _____
f We stayed at this hotel last summer. _____
g I had lunch with this man the other day. _____

meet = kennenlernen
rent = mieten
tell = erzählen
wait for = warten auf
stay = (z. B. in Hotel) wohnen
the other day = neulich

3 Wiederholung: das Passiv (→ 12B1).
Setzen Sie aus dem Aktiv ins Passiv. Achten Sie dabei auf die Beibehaltung der Zeitform, und lassen Sie den „Verursacher" weg, wenn seine Nennung Ihnen nicht angebracht erscheint.

Shakespeare's King Lear spoke these words. → These words were spoken by Shakespeare's King Lear.

a They didn't say it openly. _____
b People play and watch football all over the world. _____
c Millions of people learn English. _____
d They have sold the house. _____
e People have written a lot about this problem. _____
f Tourists love the city. _____

sell – sold – sold = verkaufen – verkaufte – verkauft
write about sth = über etw schreiben

g Terrorists have killed a UN peacekeeper. _____

h They took the two kids to hospital. _____

4 Fragen mit *wh*-Wörtern. Fragen Sie nach dem fett gedruckten Satzteil.

She married **her boss**. – **Who** did she marry?
She studied **architecture**. – **What** did she study?
She lives **in Glasgow**. – **Where** does she live?

a She met her husband **in her English class**. _____

b He trained as **a hairdresser**. _____

c She remembers **her first kiss**. _____

d They sued **the police**. _____

e The police chased **the car thieves**. _____

f He played golf **in St Andrews**. _____

g She'll meet her true love **on a train journey**. _____

h He likes **cheesecake**. _____

i She had lunch with **her great-uncle**. _____

j His girlfriend calls him **a pot-bellied couch potato**. _____

5 Übersetzen Sie.

a Ich habe Friseur gelernt. _____

b Ich habe meinen Mann in unserem Englischkurs kennengelernt. _____

c Wir sind jetzt fünf Jahre verheiratet. _____

d Wir machen seit vielen Jahren Englisch zusammen. _____

e Im Moment beschäftigen wir uns mit moderner Architektur. — *We are into modern Arch*

f Ich habe genug Zeit, um Dinge zu tun, die ich schon immer tun wollte. — *I have enough time to do things which I always want to do*

tidy up = ausmisten
tidying up my place

Unit 13D

peacekeeper = Blauhelm, UN-Soldat(in)

study = studieren
chase = jagen, verfolgen
cheesecake = Käsekuchen
pot-bellied = spitzbäuchig

meet = kennenlernen
do English = Englisch machen
at the moment = im Moment
be into sth = sich mit etw beschäftigen

Unit 13E   Focus on words

1. *Your English is* **excellent:** Statt *excellent* auch *very good, great, superb, fantastic* und natürlich *perfect*. Das Gegenteil (= *the opposite*) wäre *His English is poor / bad / terrible / pathetic*.

2. *Education* ist „Bildung", aber auch „Erziehung" oder „Pädagogik". *He was educated at University College London* heißt so viel wie „er studierte am University College London". *Educated* als Adjektiv ist „gebildet", *uneducated* „ungebildet". *A clever man (B. F. Skinner, 1904–90) once said: Education is what survives* (= überlebt) *when what has been learned has been forgotten*.

3. **Checking out the global village:** Für *global village* gibt es keine direkte deutsche Entsprechung. Gemeint ist *the world seen as a community in which people are connected by computers, television, etc*. – *Check out* ist ein relativ neues Verb mit der Bedeutung: „sich (jemand oder etwas Interessantes und/oder Neues) näher ansehen":

Thousands have **checked out** our new website.	*Tausende haben sich unsere neue Website angesehen.*
Let's **check out** the new Indian restaurant.	*Probieren wir doch mal das neue indische Restaurant.*
They're still **checking** her **out**.	*Sie versuchen immer noch, sich ein Bild von ihr zu machen.*

4. **Do English** (= Englisch machen / haben): „Haben Sie Englisch in der Schule gehabt?" wird nicht mit *have* übersetzt, sondern man sagt: *Did you do English at school?*

5. *If we* **win the lottery:** nicht *win in the lottery*! *Win the pools* heißt „im Toto gewinnen".

6. **Look forward to something** heißt „sich auf etwas freuen". Das *to* ist hier nicht das kleine Wörtchen bei der Grundform des Verbs (*try to do something* = etwas zu tun versuchen), sondern eine **Präposition**, auf die deshalb die *-ing-*Form und nicht die Grundform des Verbs folgt (→ 8D3c): *We're looking forward* **to seeing** *you* (= wir freuen uns darauf, euch zu sehen).

7. *Employ* = „beschäftigen, anstellen"

The company **employs** 500 people.	*Die Firma beschäftigt 500 Menschen.*
employer – employee	*Arbeitgeber(in) – Arbeitnehmer(in)*
She's looking for **employment**.	*Sie sucht eine Anstellung.*
unemployed – unemployment	*arbeitslos – (die) Arbeitslosigkeit*

8. **Play a sport** (= einen Sport betreiben): *Do you play a sport?* (= Betreibst du einen Sport?), *He does a lot of sport*. (= Er macht / treibt viel Sport.) *What's your favourite sport?* (= Was ist dein Lieblingssport?) *My favourite sports are table tennis and swimming*. (= Meine Lieblingssportarten sind Tischtennis und Schwimmen.)

9. **Creative writing** ist „kreatives / literarisches / schriftstellerisches Schreiben", in den deutschsprachigen Ländern vor allem in „Schreibwerkstätten" (= *writing workshops*) betrieben.

Focus on culture

Unit 13F

1. **English the world language:** About 380 million people speak English as their first language and over a billion use it as their second language. The United States, the United Kingdom, Canada and Australia have the largest numbers of native English speakers while India (→ 11F2), Nigeria and the Philippines each have tens of millions of second-language English speakers.
English is an official language in India, Pakistan, the Philippines and many African countries, but not in Britain or the United States, because these countries don't have an official language. It is, however, an official language of the United Nations and many other international organizations.
Of all the world's languages, English is the one most often studied as a foreign language. In Europe, the percentage of competent English speakers is particularly high in the Netherlands, Sweden, Denmark, and Luxembourg.
You will hear English spoken with a great variety of accents: British and American, Irish and Australian, African and Indian. Germans, too, speak English with a recognizable German accent, and it is equally easy to recognize Italian or French speakers of English. Nobody should worry about their accent. Though the English "invented" the language, it now belongs to the world for everyone to use to the best of their ability.

2. **The Gherkin** (= *Gewürzgurke*) is a famous skyscraper officially called St Mary Axe, after the street on which it stands in the City of London. "The City" is London's financial district. Opened in 2004, the Gherkin has quickly become one of London's most famous buildings and a major tourist attraction. It can be seen from all over London and looks best when viewed from a distance.

3. There are several **Guggenheim museums** in the world. The first one, in New York, designed by Frank Lloyd Wright and completed in 1959, has become an icon of modern architecture, but Frank Gehry's Guggenheim Museum Bilbao, opened in 1997, is no less spectacular and has greatly added to the attractiveness of this northern Spanish city.

2/23

billion = Milliarde
first = erste(r, s)
second = zweite(r, s)
native speaker = Muttersprachler(in)
official language = Amtssprache
most often = am häufigsten
study = lernen
percentage = Prozentsatz
particularly = besonders
variety = Vielfalt
recognizable = erkennbar
equally easy = genauso leicht
recognize = erkennen
invent = erfinden
ability = Fähigkeit

famous = berühmt
skyscraper = Wolkenkratzer
view = sehen, betrachten
distance = Ferne

several = mehrere
design = entwerfen
an icon = eine Ikone
less = weniger
add to sth = etw vergrößern
attractiveness = Attraktivität

Unit 13G Test yourself

Education Crossword

ACROSS
2 A Latin-American dance.
5 A British explorer who died returning from the South Pole.
7 The art and science of designing buildings.
8 Today's name of the city that used to be called Bombay.
9 London's financial district.
10 A place where people learn.
13 The UK minus Northern Ireland.
14 An island that is also a country and a continent.
17 One thousand million (1,000,000,000).
18 The country north of the United States.
19 The most populous country in Africa.

DOWN
1 The name of some famous museums of modern art.
2 A person we learn from.
3 A very small but politically and financially important country in western Europe.
4 Mozart's *The Marriage of Figaro* is an …
6 A judge in a court for minor crimes.
11 The work of a writer.
12 A large country in Asia, west of India and east of Afghanistan.
15 Medicine is a …
16 A musical instrument.

explorer = Forschungsreisende(r)
die = sterben
return = zurückkehren
South Pole = Südpol
art = Kunst
used to be called = hieß früher einmal
financial = Finanz-
district = Bezirk
island (das „s" ist stumm!)
most populous = bevölkerungsreichste
judge = Richter(in)
court = Gericht
minor = kleiner, leichter
crime = Straftat
writer = Schriftsteller(in)

162

Shakespeare

Unit 14

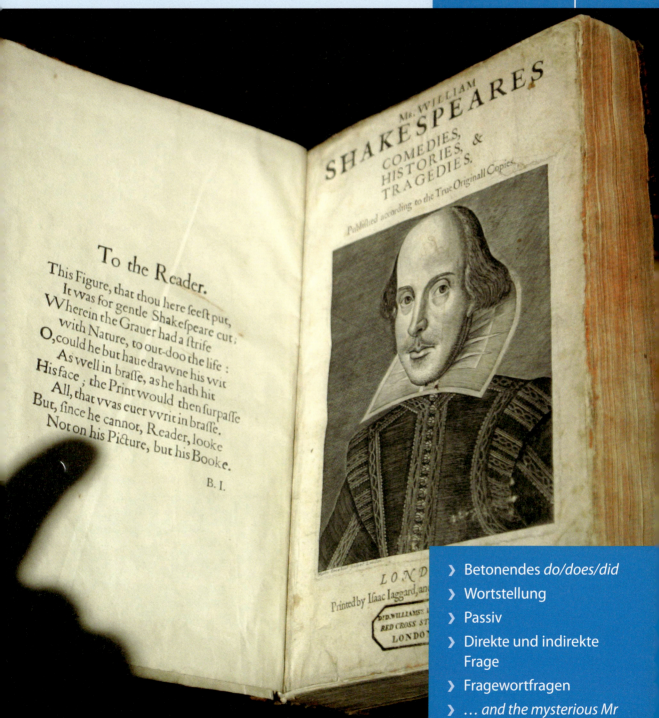

- Betonendes *do/does/did*
- Wortstellung
- Passiv
- Direkte und indirekte Frage
- Fragewortfragen
- *… and the mysterious Mr Shakespeare*

Unit 14A — Dialogue

2/24

■ = man
● = woman

go to see = besuchen (gehen)
in a way = in gewisser Weise
get closer = näherkommen
associated = verbunden
spend – spent = verbringen – verbrachte
childhood = Kindheit
marriage = Ehe
uneducated = ungebildet
rich = reich
allusion to = Anspielung auf
history = (die) Geschichte
grammar school = Gymnasium
whether = ob
hard = hart
become = werden (!)
play = (Theater-)Stück
what was it like? = wie war es (beschaffen)?
indeed (dient der Verstärkung)
mysterious = geheimnisvoll, rätselhaft
certainly = bestimmt

Back from Stratford-upon-Avon

■ So you went to see Shakespeare? Did you find him?

● Well, in a way yes. You do get a bit closer to Shakespeare as a person when you're in Stratford-upon-Avon.

■ You walk the streets he walked …

● … and you see places that are associated with his life, yes. There's the house where he spent his childhood and youth and the first years of his marriage …

■ I've heard that he was quite uneducated.

● Well, he can't have been, can he, with the rich language of his plays, the allusions to history and so on. Anyway, the grammar school he probably went to is still there.

■ You say "probably". Don't we know whether he went to grammar school or not?

● We don't. We have very few hard facts about Shakespeare's life.

■ But he did go to London, didn't he?

● Yes, and he became an actor and he wrote plays. But we don't know when he went to London, where he lived there, what friends he had, where he got his ideas from, how often he visited his family in Stratford, what indeed his private life was like.

■ Hmm. There are those portraits one always sees – he does look a bit mysterious there, don't you think?

● Well, I don't know about the man, but the pictures certainly are mysterious. Nobody knows if they really are Shakespeare.

Zurück aus Stratford-upon-Avon

■ Du wolltest also Shakespeare besuchen. Hast du ihn gefunden?

● Also, in gewisser Weise ja. Man kommt Shakespeare als Menschen schon ein bisschen näher, wenn man in Stratford-upon-Avon ist.

■ Man geht auf den Straßen, auf denen er ging …

● … und man sieht Orte, die mit seinem Leben zu tun haben – ja. Da ist das Haus, wo er seine Kindheit und Jugend und die ersten Jahre seiner Ehe verbrachte …

■ Ich habe gehört, dass er recht ungebildet war.

● Nun, das kann er doch wohl nicht gewesen sein bei der reichen Sprache seiner Stücke, den Anspielungen auf die Geschichte und so weiter. Jedenfalls ist das Gymnasium, auf das er wahrscheinlich ging, noch da.

■ Du sagst „wahrscheinlich". Wissen wir denn nicht, ob er aufs Gymnasium gegangen ist oder nicht?

● Nein. Wir haben sehr wenig harte Fakten über Shakespeares Leben.

■ Aber er ging doch nach London, oder?

● Ja, und er wurde Schauspieler und er schrieb Stücke. Aber wir wissen nicht, wann er nach London ging, wo er dort wohnte, was für Freunde er hatte, wo er seine Ideen herbekam, wie oft er seine Familie in Stratford besuchte, wie überhaupt sein Privatleben war.

■ Hm. Es gibt da diese Porträts, die man immer sieht – er sieht da schon ein bisschen mysteriös aus, meinst du nicht?

● Also, ich weiß nicht, ob das für den Menschen gilt, aber die Bilder sind sicher mysteriös. Niemand weiß, ob sie wirklich Shakespeare darstellen.

Unit 14B

Rules and practice

1 Betonendes *do/does/did*

Wir erinnern uns daran (→ 11B4), dass die Umschreibung mit *do/does/did* außer zur Bildung von Frage und Verneinung auch zur Betonung bzw. Verstärkung einer Aussage gebraucht werden kann:

You **do get** a bit closer to Shakespeare as a person when you're in Stratford-upon-Avon.	Man kommt Shakespeare als Menschen schon ein bisschen näher, wenn man in Stratford-upon-Avon ist.
But he **did go** to London, didn't he?	Aber er ging doch nach London, oder?

Ohne dieses verstärkende *do* (*you get a bit closer, he went to London*) klingen diese Sätze unvermittelter, d. h. sie stellen keinen so starken Bezug zum Vorhergehenden her wie mit der Verstärkung. Entsprechend unvermittelt können Sie natürlich sagen: *I love you*. Hat aber die angesprochene Person vorher Zweifel an Ihrer Liebe geäußert, so könnte man verstärken: *But I do love you, Emily*. (= Aber ich liebe dich doch wirklich, Emily.)

✎ Wir machen nun eine Übung, in der der hier gegebene Ausgangssatz einen Tatbestand verneint oder in Zweifel zieht. Sie widersprechen mit einem verstärkenden (und betont gesprochenen) *do/does/did*.

You don't want to go to Stratford, I suppose. → But I **do** want to go to Stratford!
Why didn't he go to grammar school? → But he **did** go to grammar school!

a You don't like her, I suppose.
b She doesn't believe me, I suppose.
c I suppose he never thanked you.
d I suppose your teacher didn't notice it.
e I'm sure she didn't start from scratch.
f Why didn't they arrest them?
g Why don't you play golf?
h Why didn't you follow my advice?

like = mögen
believe = glauben
teacher = Lehrer(in)
notice = bemerken
advice = Rat(schläge)

Unit 14B

play = (Theater-)Stück
spend – spent = verbringen – verbrachte
childhood = Kindheit
sit down = sich setzen
shy = schüchtern
glance = Blick

2 Wortstellung (→ 2D4, 8B1, 9B2)

Wir haben schon mehrfach festgestellt, dass die englische Wortstellung starrer ist als die deutsche. Einen wesentlichen Unterschied illustriert das folgende Satzpaar:

a. **Er war** recht ungebildet.
b. Ich habe gehört, dass **er** recht ungebildet **war**.

Im Englischen dagegen verändert sich die Wortstellung nicht, wenn dem Satztyp a wie in Satztyp b eine Wortgruppe vorangestellt ist:

a. **He was** quite uneducated.
b. I have heard that **he was** quite uneducated.

✏️ Achten Sie auf die im Englischen gleichbleibende Wortstellung bei der Übersetzung der folgenden Satzpaare.

a Er schrieb Theaterstücke. — *He wrote a play*
   In London schrieb er Theaterstücke. — *He wrote plays in L.*

b Er verbrachte seine Kindheit in diesem Haus. — *in this house he spent his childhood*
   In diesem Haus verbrachte er seine Kindheit.

c Er ging nach London. — *He went to L.*
   Wir wissen nicht, wann er nach London ging. — *We don't know when*

d Er besuchte seine Familie in Stratford. — *He visited*
   Wir wissen nicht, wie oft er seine Familie in Stratford besuchte. — *how often he v's*

e Sie setzten sich auf meine Bank. — *They sit down on my bench*
   Nach einem schüchternen Blick auf mich setzten sie sich auf meine Bank. — *After shy glance to me they sit down on my bench*

3 Stellung der Häufigkeitsadverbien (→ 8D1, 8D2)

Die folgenden Adverbien drücken aus, wie häufig etwas geschieht. Sie sind in der Regel unbetont, und unbetonte Adverbien stehen – anders als im Deutschen – vor dem Verb:

She **always / often / sometimes / regularly / usually / never** <u>visits</u> us on Sundays.	*Sie <u>besucht</u> uns **immer / oft / manchmal / regelmäßig / meistens / nie** sonntags.*

Unit 14B

✏️ Setzen Sie die eingeklammerten Adverbien entsprechend dieser Regel ein.

a Shakespeare uses unusual words. (often) _S. often uses unusual_
b I travel to work by car. (never) _I never travel_
c He has something interesting to say. (always) _he always_
d She walks her dog in the park. (regularly) _She regulary walks_
e We go on holiday in winter. (sometimes) _We sometime go_
f My mother goes to bed at eleven. (usually) _My mother usually goes_
g Nobody asked me that question. (ever) _Nobody ever asked_

unusual = ausgefallen
by car = mit dem Auto
regularly = regelmäßig
go on holiday = in Urlaub fahren
ever = je(mals)

4 Bringen Sie die Satzteile in eine korrekte Reihenfolge. (Keine Fragesätze!)

a are / delighted / we // that / you / here / are
   We are delighted that you are here

b always / I / say // that / we / a family of runners / are

c the famous Harbour Bridge / right behind our hotel / is
   the famous HB is right behind our hotel

d he / me / told // that / his sister / a delicatessen / runs

e in the summer / I / go / often / to Hyde Park / a book / to read

f one day / during a training race / felt / I / suddenly / a pain in my chest

g at the hospital / showed / tests // that / I / a heart attack / suffered / had
   test at the h. showed

h from our window / can / I / the Opera House / in the evening light / see
   from our w. I can see th. OH in

i if / in politics / are / interested / you // can / you / a debate in the Commons / watch
   if you are inter in polit you can watch a debate in th. C

j at the Eden Hotel / can / you / all the excitement of New York / at attractive prices / enjoy
   at the EH you can enjoy all the excitem. of NY at attr. prices

k of course / can / you / in the lake / go swimming // but / the hotel / has / too / an indoor pool
   Of course you can go swim. in the lake but the hotel has an indoor p. too

delighted = sehr erfreut
runner = Läufer(in)
right behind = direkt hinter
run a shop = ein Geschäft führen
training race = Trainingslauf
suddenly = plötzlich
pain = Schmerz(en)
chest = Brust
suffer = erleiden
excitement = Aufregung
enjoy = genießen
of course = natürlich

Unit 14C   Reading text

2/25

among = unter
few = wenige
pregnant = schwanger
eight years his senior = acht Jahre älter als er
actor = Schauspieler
about = etwa (um)
denounce = anprangern
upstart = Emporkömmling
crow = Krähe
publish = veröffentlichen
buy – bought = kaufen – kaufte
sue = verklagen
owe = schulden
a total of = insgesamt
revise = revidieren
will = Testament
prosperous = wohlhabend
leave = hinterlassen
bury (Ausspr.: „berri") = bestatten
grave = Grab
human being = Mensch
express = ausdrücken
poetry = Dichtung
beauty = Schönheit
contemporary = Zeitgenosse
perform = aufführen
vote = wählen (zu)
millennium = Jahrtausend

Shakespeare

Among the few facts we know about William Shakespeare is that he was born in Stratford-upon-Avon in 1564, married a pregnant woman eight years his senior in 1582, had three children with her (1583 and 1585), went to London in or about 1587 to become an actor, started writing plays about 1590, was denounced as an "upstart crow" in a book published in 1592, bought a house called New Place in Stratford in 1597, had his first plays published in 1598, sued neighbours for money owed to him in 1604 and 1608, wrote a total of about 37 plays and 154 sonnets, returned to Stratford between 1610 and 1612, revised his will in March 1616, and died as a prosperous man on 23 April 1616, leaving his wife his "second-best bed". Shakespeare was buried in Holy Trinity Church in Stratford, where his grave can be visited to this day.
Nothing of importance is known about Shakespeare's life and character, but he knew everything that's important in the lives and characters of human beings, and expressed it in poetry of timeless beauty. "He was not of an age, but for all time," said Shakespeare's contemporary Ben Jonson. Today, Shakespeare's work is still being performed and read all over the world, and at the end of the 20th century the poet from Stratford-upon-Avon was voted Man of the Millennium.

Shakespeare

Zu den wenigen Fakten, die wir über über William Shakespeare kennen, gehört, dass er 1564 in Stratford-upon-Avon geboren wurde, 1582 eine acht Jahre ältere, schwangere Frau heiratete, mit ihr drei Kinder hatte (1583 und 1585), im oder um das Jahr 1587 nach London ging, um Schauspieler zu werden, um 1590 Stücke zu schreiben begann, in einem 1592 erschienenen Buch als „emporgekommene Krähe" angeprangert wurde, 1597 in Stratford ein Haus namens New Place kaufte, seine ersten Stücke 1598 erscheinen ließ, 1604 und 1608 Nachbarn wegen ihm geschuldeten Geldes verklagte, insgesamt 37 Stücke und 154 Sonnette schrieb, zwischen 1610 und 1612 nach Stratford zurückkehrte, im März 1616 sein Testament änderte und als wohlhabender Mann am 23. April 1616 starb und seiner Frau sein „zweitbestes Bett" hinterließ. Shakespeare wurde in der Holy Trinity Church („Heiligen Dreifaltigkeitskirche") in Stratford bestattet, wo sein Grab bis heute besucht werden kann.
Über Shakespeares Leben und Charakter ist nichts von Bedeutung bekannt, aber er kannte alles, was in Leben und Charakter der Menschen bedeutsam ist, und drückte es in Dichtung von zeitloser Schönheit aus. „Er gehörte nicht einem Zeitalter, sondern aller Zeit", sagte Shakespeares Zeitgenosse Ben Jonson. Heute wird Shakespeares Werk in der ganzen Welt immer noch aufgeführt und gelesen, und am Ende des 20. Jahrhunderts wurde der Dichter aus Stratford-upon-Avon zum Mann des Jahrtausends gewählt.

Unit 14D

Rules and practice

1   Und noch einmal: das Passiv (→ 11D3, 12B1, 13D3)

Auf die Gefahr hin, dass Sie uns die Freundschaft aufkündigen, hier noch einmal zwei Beispiele zum Passiv und eine Übung dazu:

a. His grave **can be visited** to this day.	*Sein Grab kann bis zum heutigen Tag besucht werden.*
b. Shakespeare's work **is** still **being performed**.	*Shakespeares Werk wird immer noch aufgeführt.*

In Satz a haben wir das Passiv der Konstruktion **Hilfsverb + Vollverb**. Weitere häufig im Passiv gebrauchte Hilfsverben sind *could*, *must*, *should*, *may*, *might*, *will*, *would* und auch die Zukunftsform *be going to*.
In Satz b sehen Sie das Passiv der Verlaufsform, eine nicht ganz einfache Konstruktion, die Sie vielleicht nicht selbst benutzen, aber doch immerhin verstehen wollen.
Wenn wir Passivsätze ins Aktiv setzen wollen, müssen wir – das wissen wir bereits – einen „Verursacher" hinzufügen, also für Satz a zum Beispiel *people* und für Satz b *theatres all over the world*:

a. People **can visit** his grave to this day.	*Man kann sein Grab bis zum heutigen Tag besuchen.*
b. Theatres all over the world **are** still **performing** his work.	*Theater in der ganzen Welt führen immer noch sein Werk auf.*

Verwandeln Sie die Aktivsätze ins Passiv und die Passivsätze ins Aktiv (ggf. unter Verwendung der eingeklammerten „Verursacher").

a   Transportation can be arranged by the concierge.   _____

b   If you don't do that, you will be killed. (the king's men)   _____

c   He said that she would be killed. (the king's men)   _____

d   She will be missed by many people.   _____

concierge = Portier
miss = vermissen
be missed = (auch:) fehlen

169

Unit 14D

tell – told = sagen – sagte / gesagt
misbehave = ungezogen sein
watch = beobachten
toe = Zeh(e)
everywhere = überall

e They'll be told not to misbehave again. (the magistrate) _____
f You can see the Gherkin from all over London. _____
g They're going to open the new museum in April. _____
h The police are watching you. _____
i The grandchildren are keeping us on our toes. _____
j People are talking about her everywhere. _____
k English is being learned by hundreds of millions of people. _____

2 Direkte Frage – indirekte Frage. Wandeln Sie die direkten Fragen entsprechend den Beispielen in indirekte Fragen um.

> "When did Shakespeare go to London?" → We don't know when Shakespeare went to London.
> "Did he go to grammar school?" → We don't know whether he went to grammar school.

whether = ob
what friends? = was für Freunde?

a "Was Shakespeare's marriage happy?" *We don't know whether has been*
b "Where did Shakespeare live in London?" *We don't k. where S. lived in L*
c "What friends did Shakespeare have?" *What friends S had*
d "Where did he get his ideas from?" *Where he got his i. from*

3 So, jetzt machen Sie die Übung anders herum. Verwandeln Sie die indirekten Fragen in direkte Fragen.

what is it like? = wie ist es (beschaffen)?
write – wrote = schreiben – schrieb
return = zurückkehren

a We don't know what his private life was like. *What was his life like*
b We don't know how often he visited his family in Stratford. _____
c Nobody knows if the portraits really show Shakespeare. *do the p. really show S.*
d We don't know when Shakespeare wrote *Hamlet*. _____
e We don't know when exactly he returned to Stratford. _____

Unit 14D

4 Fragen Sie nach dem fett gedruckten Satzteil. Benutzen Sie die Fragewörter *how many, what, when, who, why*.

Shakespeare was born in **Stratford-upon-Avon**. → Where was Shakespeare born?

a He married **Anne Hathaway**. — *Who did he marry*
b They had **three** children. — *How many c.*
c He went to London **in or about 1587**. — *When did he go*
d Another writer called him **an "upstart crow"**. — *Who did another wr. call him*
e Shakespeare bought New Place **in 1597**. — *When did S. buy*
f He wrote **154** sonnets. — *How many s. did he write*
g He sued a neighbour **because he owed him money**. —
h Shakespeare died **in 1616**. — *When did S. die*
i He left **his "second-best bed"** to his wife. — *What did he leave his wife*

marry = heiraten
writer = Schriftsteller(in)
buy – bought = kaufen – kaufte
owe = schulden
bury (Ausspr.: „berri")

5 How good is your memory? Fill in the missing names and words.

a Shakespeare lived from _____ to *1616*.
b He was born and died in _____.
c The town where Shakespeare was born is on the river _____.
d Shakespeare probably went to a very good _____ school.
e The woman he married was much _____ than him.
f At the time they married she was _____ – in other words, she was expecting a baby.
g In the late 1580s Shakespeare went to _____.
h Shakespeare became an _____ and started writing _____.
i In 1598 his first plays were _____.
j Shakespeare wrote a total of 37 plays and 154 _____.
k There are many allusions to _____ in Shakespeare's plays.
l Towards the end of his life Shakespeare returned to _____.
m He lived in a house called _____.
n In his will, he left his wife _____.
o Shakespeare was buried in _____.

expect = erwarten
go – went = gehen – ging
become = werden
allusion = Anspielung
towards the end of his life = gegen Ende seines Lebens
bury (Ausspr.: „berrid") = bestatten

Unit 14E

Focus on words

all in all =
  alles in allem
invent = erfinden
in use =
  in Gebrauch

1. **Stratford-upon-Avon:** *Upon* ist eine ältere und heute förmliche bzw. das Historische bewahrende Form von *on*. Man kann also auch *Stratford-on-Avon* sagen, aber die Stadt legt Wert auf die alte, „würdevollere" Form.

2. **Uneducated** (= ungebildet) ist ein von Shakespeare geprägtes Wort, wie auch das Gegenteil *well-educated* (= gebildet). Alles in allem (*all in all*) hat Shakespeare etwa 1500 Wörter erfunden (*invented*), von denen etwa 800 noch heute in Gebrauch (*in use*) sind. So zum Beispiel:

accessible	*zugänglich*	fortune teller	*Wahrsager(in)*
birthplace	*Geburtsort, Geburtshaus*	impressed	*beeindruckt*
characterless	*charakterlos*	marriage bed	*Ehebett*
delighted	*erfreut, entzückt*	never-ending	*endlos*
employer	*Arbeitgeber, Dienstherr*	noiseless	*geräuschlos*
excitement	*Aufregung*	well-behaved	*wohlerzogen*

3. **Actor** (= Schauspieler): Die weibliche Form ist *actress* (= Schauspielerin), ganz davon abgesehen, dass zu Shakespeares Zeit (*in Shakespeare's time*) die weiblichen Rollen (*female parts*) von Männern – insbesondere Knaben vor dem Stimmbruch – gespielt wurden.

4. **Play** ist ein „(Theater-)Stück", „die Dramen Shakespeares" sind *Shakespeare's plays* oder *the plays of Shakespeare*; *playwright* ist „Stückeschreiber(in) / Dramatiker(in)".

5. **Eight years his / her senior** = *eight years older than him / her*.

6. **An upstart crow** (= eine emporgekommene Krähe): *An upstart* ist „ein Emporkömmling", „ein Neureicher". Robert Greene (1558–92), der Shakespeare so unfreundlich charakterisierte, war ebenfalls ein *playwright and poet*, der allerdings schon mit 34 Jahren starb, nachdem er angeblich zu sehr dem *Rhenish wine* (= Rheinwein) *and pickled herring* (= Salzhering) zugesprochen hatte.

7. **He had his first plays published** (= er ließ seine ersten Stücke erscheinen): *Have something done* heißt „etwas tun lassen", „veranlassen, dass etwas getan wird":

She had her hair done.	*Sie ließ sich die Haare machen.*
I had my car repaired.	*Ich ließ mein Auto reparieren.*
We're having new windows installed.	*Wir lassen neue Fenster einbauen.*

Aber mit dieser Konstruktion kann man auch ausdrücken, dass einem etwas zugefügt wurde:

I had my car stolen.	*Mir wurde mein Auto gestohlen.*

8. **A sonnet** ist „ein Sonett", d. h. ein 14-zeiliges Gedicht (*poem*) mit einem genau festgelegten Reimschema (*rhyme scheme* [Ausspr.: „skiem"]). *Shakespeare's sonnets are the most famous in the English language.*

Focus on culture

1. **Stratford-upon-Avon:** Beautifully situated on the west bank of the River Avon, this old market town is one of Britain's most visited tourist attractions. In spite of this, Stratford is a delightful place with half-timbered houses, pleasant streets, a lot of green, three excellent theatres and charming restaurants, cafés and tea rooms. Important Shakespeare sights are his birthplace in Henley Street, Nash's house (the home of Shakespeare's granddaughter Elizabeth and her husband Thomas Nash), Hall's Croft (the home of Shakespeare's daughter Susanna and her husband, the physician Dr John Hall), the grammar school in Church Street, and Holy Trinity Church with the graves of Shakespeare, his widow Anne and other members of his family. New Place, the house where Shakespeare died, was unfortunately pulled down in the 18th century, but its foundations are still there, within a beautiful Elizabethan garden.

2. *Shakespeare* or *Shakspe(a)re?* We have only six signatures in Shakespeare's own hand, and they are all different to the way we spell his name today. Five of them have *Shak...*, not *Shake...*, so it is quite possible that he pronounced the first half of his name as in *back*, and not as in *cake*.

3. **Ben Jonson** (1572–1637): English dramatist, poet and actor who, after a turbulent early life (he killed a fellow actor in a duel and narrowly escaped hanging) wrote many successful plays. He was a rival, friend and admirer of Shakespeare, who acted in at least two of Jonson's plays.

Unit 14F

2/26

situated = gelegen
bank = Ufer
in spite of this = trotzdem
half-timbered = Fachwerk-
charming = reizend
croft = (ursprüngl.:) kleiner Pachtbauernhof
physician = Arzt
grave = Grab
widow = Witwe
unfortunately = leider
pull down = abreißen
foundations = Fundamente
within = in(nerhalb)
Elizabethan = elisabethanisch (Elizabeth I, 1533–1603)

hand = (hier:) Handschrift
spell = buchstabieren
quite = durchaus
possible = möglich
pronounce = aussprechen

fellow actor = Schauspielerkollege
duel = Duell
narrowly = nur knapp
escape = entgehen
hanging = Hinrichtung durch den Strang
admirer = Bewunderer
act = (mit)spielen

Unit 14G Test yourself

Shakespeare Crossword

ACROSS
1. The river in which Shakespeare swam as a boy.
2. Where a dead person is buried.
5. A more formal word for *on*.
7. The prince who said, "To be, or not to be: that is the question..."
9. A black general who kills his wife and later takes his own life.
15. Shakespeare's granddaughter.
16. What a poet writes.
17. Shakespeare's daughter.
18. A writer of plays.

DOWN
1. The name of Shakespeare's wife.
3. One of the things Shakespeare was.
4. A woman whose husband has died.
6. A medical doctor.
8. The general who murders his king and becomes king.
10. A woman who acts in a play or film.
11. The poems Shakespeare wrote.
12. The town where Shakespeare was born and died.
13. A friend and rival of Shakespeare.
14. The rival who called Shakespeare an "upstart crow".
16. The things Shakespeare wrote.

swim – swam = schwimmen – schwamm
formal = förmlich
to be = (zu) sein
medical doctor = Doktor der Medizin
murder = ermorden
poem = Gedicht

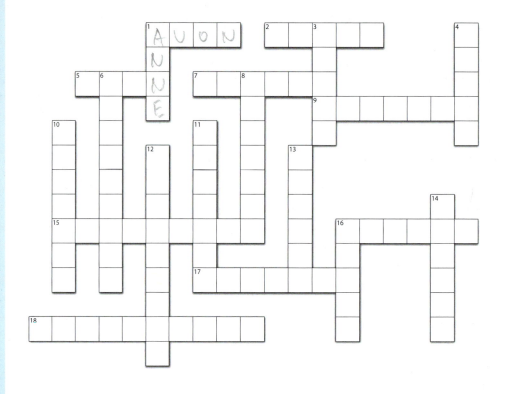

Victoria

Unit 15

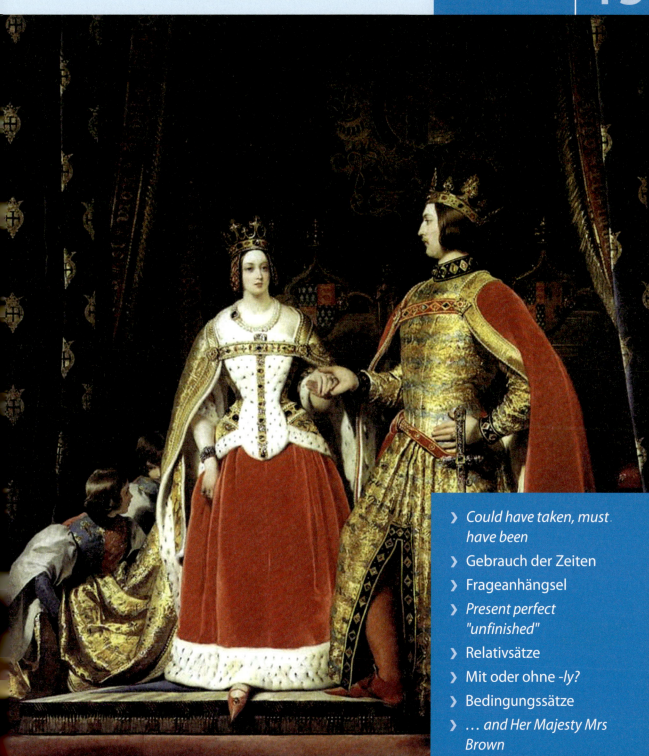

› *Could have taken, must have been*
› Gebrauch der Zeiten
› Frageanhängsel
› *Present perfect "unfinished"*
› Relativsätze
› Mit oder ohne *-ly*?
› Bedingungssätze
› *… and Her Majesty Mrs Brown*

Unit 15A — Dialogue

2/27

■ = London woman
● = German man

strike – struck – struck = auffallen – auffiel – aufgefallen
come across = begegnen
mention = erwähnen
somewhere = irgendwo
stay = (z. B. in Hotel) wohnen
dozen = Dutzend
avenue = Allee
and what have you = und was sonst noch
once = einmal
furniture = Möbel
jewellery = Schmuck
clothes = Kleidung
certain(ly) = gewiss
another 40 years = weitere 40 Jahre
mourn = (be)trauern
mourning = Trauer
although = obwohl
at the time = damals
close („s" wie „ß") = nahe(stehend)
suspect = vermuten
secret(ly) = heimlich

Victoria

■ Has it ever struck you how often you come across the name "Victoria" in London?
● Uh-huh, well, yes – now you mention it. The first time I came here I arrived at Victoria Station …
■ Quite. And from there you could have taken the Victoria Line to a Victoria Hotel somewhere on a Victoria Road …
● I never stayed at a Victoria Hotel.
■ But you might have done. There are probably hundreds of them.
● Okay, but is there a Victoria Road?
■ Of course there is – not just one but dozens, and there are Victoria Avenues, Victoria Streets and what have you.
● Hmm. I remember now, I once visited the Victoria and Albert Museum – furniture, jewellery, clothes, photography. I was fascinated by the early photographs. – Albert was Victoria's husband, wasn't he?
■ He was. She had nine children with him.
● Wow! Must have been a love match.
■ It certainly was. He died young, in 1861, but she lived another forty years, always in mourning for her beloved Albert.
● Didn't she marry again?
■ Oh no, although there were rumours at the time …
● Rumours? You mean of a marriage?
■ Yes, she had a personal servant who was very close to her for many years. His name was John Brown. Some people suspected that she had secretly married him, and they started calling her Mrs Brown …

Victoria

● Ist dir schon mal aufgefallen, wie oft einem in London der Name „Victoria" begegnet?
■ Ja schon – jetzt, wo du's erwähnst. Als ich das erste Mal herkam, kam ich an der Victoria Station an …
● Genau! Und von dort hättest du die Victoria-Linie zu einem Victoria Hotel irgendwo auf einer Victoria Road nehmen können …
■ Ich habe nie in einem Victoria Hotel gewohnt.
● Du hättest es aber können. Es gibt wahrscheinlich hunderte davon.
■ Okay, aber gibt es eine Victoria Road?
● Natürlich gibt es die – nicht nur eine, sondern Dutzende, und es gibt Victoria Avenues, Victoria Streets und was sonst noch.
■ Hm. Mir fällt gerade ein, ich habe mal das Victoria and Albert Museum besucht – Möbel, Schmuck, Kleidung, Fotografie. Von den frühen Fotografien war ich fasziniert. – Albert war doch Victorias Mann, nicht wahr?
● Ja. Sie hatte neun Kinder mit ihm.
■ Donnerwetter! Muss 'ne Liebesheirat gewesen sein.
● War es ganz gewiss. Er ist jung gestorben, 1861, aber sie hat noch 40 Jahre gelebt, immer in Trauer um ihren geliebten Albert.
■ Hat sie denn nicht wieder geheiratet?
● Ach was! Obwohl es damals Gerüchte gab …
■ Gerüchte? Du meinst, um eine Heirat?
● Ja, sie hatte viele Jahre lang einen persönlichen Diener, der ihr sehr nahestand. Er hieß John Brown. Manche Leute vermuteten, dass sie ihn heimlich geheiratet hätte, und sie fingen an, sie Frau Brown zu nennen …

Unit 15B

Rules and practice

1 *Could / might / must + have + 3. Form des Verbs* (→ 9D1, 10B4, 12B4)

You **could have taken** the Victoria Line.	Du **hättest** die Victoria-Linie **nehmen können**.
But you **might have done**.	Aber du **hättest** es **tun können**.
It **must have been** a love match.	Es **muss** eine Liebesheirat **gewesen sein**.

Diese nicht ganz einfache, aber wichtige Konstruktion findet sich auch häufig mit:
can't: *can't have been* (= kann nicht gewesen sein) (14A)
should: *should have known* (= hätte wissen sollen / müssen) (10A)
shouldn't: *shouldn't have done* (= hätte nicht tun sollen / dürfen)

Sowohl *could* als auch *might* können wir im Deutschen mit „könnte" übersetzen, aber es handelt sich um ein unterschiedliches „könnte":

could = „könnte" im Sinn „die Fähigkeit, die Gelegenheit, die Mittel haben"

They **could take** a taxi.	Sie könnten ein Taxi nehmen.
They **could have taken** a taxi.	Sie hätten ein Taxi nehmen können.

might = „könnte" im Sinn „es besteht die Möglichkeit"   (möge) (vielleicht eventuell)

They **might take** a taxi.	Sie könnten ein Taxi nehmen. / Vielleicht nehmen sie ein Taxi.
They **might have taken** a taxi.	Sie könnten ein Taxi genommen haben. / Vielleicht haben sie ein Taxi genommen.

Wenn Sie im Zweifel sind, nehmen Sie besser *could*.

 Übersetzen Sie.

a Ihr hättet im Victoria Hotel wohnen können. *you could have stayed / you might ste*

b Wir hätten die Nationalgalerie besuchen sollen. *we should have visited*

Unit 15B

know – knew – known = wissen – wusste – gewusst
easy / easily = leicht

c Sie muss fasziniert gewesen sein.
d Er hätte sie nicht heiraten sollen.
e Das hättet ihr wissen müssen.
f Das kann er nicht gewusst haben.
g Das hätte leicht passieren können.

2 Wiederholung der Verbzeiten: Setzen Sie das Verb in die passende Zeitform.

die = sterben
died = starb / gestorben
dead = tot
survive = überleben
yesterday = gestern
tomorrow = morgen
anything = (irgend)etwas
ever = je(mals)
already = schon

a Victoria (die) _died_ in 1901.
b Victoria (be) _has been_ dead for over a hundred years.
c Shakespeare's plays (still be) _are still_ performed today.
d Shakespeare's work (survive) _have survived_ to this day.
e In Stratford you can see the school Shakespeare (probably go) _might have_ to.
f I (retire) _will retire_ next year.
g (you go) _did you go_ to the gym yesterday?
h (you go) _will you go_ to the gym tomorrow?
i (you know) _do you know_ anything about Shakespeare's life?
j (you ever be) _been_ to Australia?
k My son is sixteen but (already write) _he already_ a play.
l I (write) _have written_ 37 books.
m Shakespeare (write) _wrote_ 37 plays.
n I (often visit) _visited_ the Victoria and Albert Museum when I lived in London.

king = König

3 Hör-Sprech-Übung. *Albert was Victoria's husband, wasn't he?* (= Albert war doch Victorias Gatte, nicht wahr?) Sie wissen inzwischen „verstandesmäßig", wie die Frageanhängsel (→ 1D4, 5D3, 7B3-4, 12B5, 13B4) gebildet werden. Eine andere Frage ist, ob Sie sie beim Sprechen auch immer schnell genug aus dem Vorderteil des Satzes „ableiten" können. Im Interesse dieser Geläufigkeit machen Sie diese Übung am besten mehrmals.

Sie hören zum Beispiel:	Albert wasn't king.
Sie sagen:	Albert wasn't king, was he?
Sie hören die richtige Antwort:	Albert wasn't king, was he?
Sie wiederholen die Antwort:	Albert wasn't king, was he?

Unit 15B

4 Vom Deutschen abweichender Gebrauch des *present perfect* für Handlungen, Zustände usw., die sich aus der Vergangenheit in die Gegenwart erstrecken (→13B1). Unterschied zwischen *since* und *for* als Entsprechungen für „seit". Beides können Sie bei der Übersetzung der folgenden Sätze üben.

a Sie ist seit Sonntag in London. _____

b Sie wohnt seit drei Tagen im Victoria Hotel. _____

c Sie kennt Colin seit Jahren. _____

d Colin wohnt schon immer in London. _____

e Sie wartet seit einer Stunde auf ihn. _____

f Er versucht seit Tagen, sie anzurufen. _____

5 Die folgenden Sätze bilden zusammen einen kleinen Text, mit dem Sie die Verbzeiten üben können. Setzen Sie die eingeklammerten Verben in die passende Zeit.

Tom is Ann's husband. They (be) _____ married for six years and their marriage is still happy.

They first (meet) _____ in the Victoria and Albert Museum. Ann (look) _____ at some Victorian photographs.

They (talk) _____ about the photos and she (tell) _____ him that she (always be) _____ interested in Queen Victoria and her times.

He (ask) _____ her to have lunch with him and they (go) _____ to an Indian restaurant in Soho.

Three months later they (get) _____ married.

Up to now they (live) _____ in a flat but now they (decide) _____ that they (buy) _____ a house.

At the moment they (still live) _____ in London but in future they (live) _____ in a village about 100 miles from London.

first meet = sich kennenlernen
be interested in = sich interessieren für
up to now = bis jetzt, bisher

6 Setzen Sie die fehlenden Präpositionen ein.

a In London you'll often come _____ the name Victoria.

b You may arrive _____ Victoria Station and stay _____ a hotel situated _____ Victoria Road.

c _____ the Victoria and Albert Museum you may be fascinated _____ the beautiful old furniture.

179

Unit 15C   Reading text

2/29

craft = (Wasser-, Luft-, Raum-) Fahrzeug
narrator = Erzähler(in)
grumble = murren
invisible = unsichtbar
loads of = Unmengen von
high time = höchste Zeit
ill = krank
ghillie = Jagdhelfer
rule = herrschen über
empire = Weltreich
the sun set = die Sonne ging unter
reign = Regierungszeit
double = sich verdoppeln
factory = Fabrik
sewer = Abwasserkanal
build – built – built = bauen – baute – gebaut
discover = entdecken
origin = Ursprung
species = Art(en)
enormous = enorm
progress = Fortschritte
beginning = Anfang
era = Ära, Zeit(alter)
eye = Auge
reclusive = einsiedlerisch

```
Victorians

An idea that has always fascinated me is that of the time machine –
a craft in which you can travel to the past or to the future. Like
the narrator in the story by H. G. Wells, most time travellers have
travelled to the future. I would travel to the past. I would visit
England in the 19th century, the England of Queen Victoria.
Imagine me going to a pub in the early 1870s. People are grumbling
about their invisible queen: "We pay her loads of money and what do
we get for it? Nothing! She's been in mourning for years, high time
she came out and did something for the nation. Too ill to open
Parliament but not too ill to dance with John Brown at the Ghillies'
Ball. Mrs Brown, ha-ha!"
If I had arrived at the time of the Queen's death, in 1901, I would
have heard her talked about quite differently. She had been on the
throne for over 63 years, she was the greatest monarch the nation
had ever known, she had ruled an empire on which the sun never set,
she had become "the grandmother of Europe". During her reign the
British population had doubled to 30 million; the middle classes had
become prosperous; factories, railways and sewers had been built,
and Darwin had discovered "the Origin of Species". It had been a
time of enormous progress, indeed the beginning of the modern era.
Somehow, in the eyes of her people, the reclusive "Widow of Windsor"
had become a symbol of all that.
```

Viktorianer

Eine Idee, die mich immer fasziniert hat, ist die der Zeitmaschine – ein Fahrzeug, mit dem man in die Vergangenheit oder Zukunft reisen kann. Gleich dem Erzähler in der Geschichte von H. G. Wells sind die meisten Zeitreisenden in die Zukunft gereist. Ich würde in die Vergangenheit reisen. Ich würde England im 19. Jahrhundert besuchen, das England der Königin Victoria.

Stell dir mich vor, wie ich in den frühen 1870er-Jahren in einen Pub gehe. Die Leute murren über ihre unsichtbare Königin: „Wir zahlen ihr jede Menge Geld und was kriegen wir dafür? Nichts! Seit Jahren ist sie in Trauer – höchste Zeit, dass sie rauskommt und etwas für die Nation tut. Zu krank, um das Parlament zu eröffnen, aber nicht zu krank, um mit John Brown auf dem Ball der Jagdhelfer zu tanzen. Frau Brown, haha!"

Wenn ich zur Zeit des Todes der Königin, 1901, (an)gekommen wäre, hätte ich ganz anders von ihr reden gehört. Sie war seit über 63 Jahren auf dem Thron gewesen, sie war die größte Monarchin, die das Land je erlebt hatte, sie hatte ein Imperium regiert, über dem die Sonne nie unterging, sie war die „Großmutter Europas" geworden. In ihrer Regierungszeit hatte sich die britische Bevölkerung auf 30 Millionen verdoppelt; der Mittelstand war wohlhabend geworden; Fabriken, Eisenbahnen und Abwasserkanäle waren gebaut worden und Darwin hatte den „Ursprung der Arten" entdeckt. Es war eine Zeit enormer Fortschritte gewesen, ja der Beginn des modernen Zeitalters. In den Augen ihres Volkes war die einsiedlerische „Witwe von Windsor" irgendwie zu einem Symbol für all dies geworden.

Unit 15D

Rules and practice

1 Noch ein letztes Mal: Relativsätze

Mit Relativsätzen haben wir uns schon mehrfach beschäftigt (→ 8D4, 9D4, 10B2, 10B5, 13D2). Wir haben festgestellt, dass diese nützliche Konstruktion
- mit **who** eingeleitet wird, wenn sie sich auf **Personen** bzw. auf „etwas Personifiziertes" (wie z. B. Tiere) bezieht,
- mit **that** oder **which** eingeleitet wird, wenn sie sich auf **Sachen** bezieht,
- und häufig **ohne** einleitendes *who/that/which* angehängt wird, wenn die Konstruktion auch ohne diese Relativpronomen gut verständlich ist.

Jetzt lernen wir noch eine kleine „Verfeinerung" dieser Regel hinzu:
Das Relativpronomen *that* können Sie **nicht nach einer Präposition** (wie z. B. *in* oder *on*) benutzen – es geht nur *which*:

Victoria ruled an empire **on which** the sun never set.	*Victoria herrschte über ein Imperium, **über welchem** die Sonne nie unterging.*

 Setzen Sie ein passendes Relativpronomen ein. Überlegen Sie, in welchen Sätzen Sie das Relativpronomen weglassen können.

a Victoria had a personal servant _who_ was very close to her.
b An idea _that/which_ has always fascinated me is that of the time machine.
c The time machine is a craft in _which_ you can travel to the past or to the future.
d To Victorians, their queen was the greatest monarch _who_ the nation had ever known.
e Nobody likes a person _who_ grumbles all the time.
f Victoria is a name _which_ you often come across in British cities.
g The hotel _which_ we stayed at was near Victoria Station.
h A man _who_ the queen was very close to was John Brown.
i The time in _which_ Victoria reigned is called the Victorian Era.
j The man _who_ wrote *The Time Machine* also wrote many short stories.

grumble = murren, schimpfen
reign = herrschen

Unit 15D

different(ly) =
  anders
situated =
  gelegen

2 Adjektiv (ohne *-ly*) – Adverb (mit *-ly*) (→8D1, 8D2, 14B3)

a	An American cheesecake is **different** from a German cheesecake.	Ein amerikanischer Käsekuchen ist **anders** als ein deutscher Käsekuchen.
b	They now talked about her quite **differently**.	Sie redeten jetzt ganz **anders** über sie.
c	The town is **beautiful**.	Die Stadt ist **wunderschön**.
d	The town is **beautifully** situated on the River Avon.	Die Stadt ist **wunderschön** am Fluss Avon gelegen.

Sehen Sie sich diese beiden Satzpaare a-b und c-d genau an:
Die fett gedruckten Wörter **ohne** *-ly* sind **Adjektive**.
Die fett gedruckten Wörter **mit** *-ly* sind **Adverbien**.
Adjektive (also die Form ohne *-ly*) benutzt man mit Bezug auf ein **Substantiv** (*cheesecake* bzw. *the town*) bzw. eine Wortgruppe, deren Kern ein Substantiv ist (*an American cheesecake*), wobei das Substantiv auch durch ein Pronomen ersetzt sein kann (*It is different from a German cheesecake, It is beautiful*).
Adverbien (also die Form mit *-ly*) benutzt man in allen anderen Fällen, also z. B. in Satz b mit Bezug auf eine Wortgruppe, deren Kern ein **Verb** (*talked*) ist, und in Satz d mit Bezug auf ein **Adjektiv** (*situated*).
Beachten Sie, dass bei Wörtern wie *easy* das *-y* zu *-i-* wird: *easily*.

 Entscheiden Sie nun, welche Form angebracht ist – mit *-ly* oder ohne *-ly*.

a Was Victoria (secret) _____ married to John Brown?

b Some people thought that there was a (secret) _____ marriage between them.

c Was the old woman a (real) _____ fortune teller?

d Was the old woman (real) _____ a fortune teller?

e English is not an (easy) _____ language.

f It is not (easy) _____ to learn a foreign language (real) _____ well.

foreign language =
  Fremdsprache

g Most jokes are (easy) _____ forgotten.

h Some people can talk (endless) _____ about things they know nothing about.

i History is an (endless) _____ story of war and aggression.

3 *Would travel – would have travelled* (→ 12B3, 12B4)

I **would travel** to the past. I **would have travelled** to the past.	Ich würde in die Vergangenheit reisen. Ich wäre in die Vergangenheit gereist.
You **would arrive** at Victoria Station. You **would have arrived** at Victoria Station.	Du würdest am V.-Bahnhof ankommen. Du wärest am Victoria-Bahnhof angekommen.

182

Unit 15D

Ausdrücke mit *would* benutzen wir oft in Bedingungssätzen, wobei wir zwei Typen mit *would*-Konstruktionen unterscheiden:

1. If you **wrote** the name down, you **would remember** it better.
   *Wenn du den Namen **aufschriebst**, **würdest** du ihn besser **behalten**.*
2. If you **had written** the name down, you **would have remembered** it better.
   *Wenn du den Namen **aufgeschrieben hättest**, **hättest** du ihn besser **behalten**.*

Satztyp 1 hat im *if*-Satz die Vergangenheitsform und im Hauptsatz *would* + Grundform des Verbs. Dieser Satztyp drückt eine Bedingung aus, die offenbar nicht erfüllt wird, aber erfüllt werden könnte.
Satztyp 2 hat im *if*-Satz die „*had*-Form" (→ 7D3, 12B3) und im Hauptsatz *would have* + 3. Form des Verbs (→ 12B4). Dieser Satztyp drückt eine Bedingung aus, die nicht mehr erfüllt werden kann, da die Gelegenheit dazu verstrichen ist.

✎ Setzen Sie nun in den folgenden Sätzen jeweils die Zeitform ein, die der Zeitform im anderen Teil des Satzes logisch entspricht. (Übersetzung → S. 208.)

a If you (travel) _____ by train, you would probably arrive at Victoria Station.

b If I had a time machine, I (travel) _____ to the past.

c What would you do if a dog (attack) _____ you?

d Where (you go) _____ if you were able to travel to the past?

e My girlfriend wouldn't call me a pot-bellied couch potato even if my stomach (not be) _____ as flat as it is now.

f If this had happened to me, I (call) _____ the police.

g If I had gone to London, I (stay) _____ at the Victoria Hotel.

h What (happen) _____ if the queen had married her servant?

i It would have been terrible if the thieves (be) _____ killed.

j If Queen Victoria hadn't had so many children, she (not become) _____ "the grandmother of Europe".

k If I (arrive) _____ at the time of the Queen's death, I would have heard her talked about quite differently.

be able to do sth = etw tun können

4 *It's high time* + Vergangenheitsform

Vom Deutschen her eigenartig erscheint die Vergangenheitsform nach *it's high time*:

It's high time she **came** out and **did** something for the nation.
*Es wird höchste Zeit, dass sie **rauskommt** und etwas für die Nation **tut**.*

Unit 15E

Focus on words

1. **Live – stay:** Beides kann „wohnen" heißen, aber *live* bedeutet „dauerhaft", *stay* hingegen „vorübergehend":

She **lives** in London.	*Sie wohnt in London.*
She **is staying** at the Queen's Hotel.	*Sie wohnt im Queen's Hotel.*

2. **Avenue** (= Allee, Boulevard): Das englische Wort *alley* hingegen ist ein „falscher Freund" (*false friend*), denn es bezeichnet keine „Allee", sondern eine enge Passage zwischen Gebäuden.

3. **Photography** (Betonung auf *tog*) ist „Fotografie" als „Lichtbildkunst bzw. -technik", *photograph/photo* (Betonung auf *pho*) ist „Fotografie" als „einzelnes Lichtbild", und „Fotograf(in)" ist *photographer* (Betonung auf *tog*).

4. They **started calling** her Mrs Brown (= sie fingen an, sie Mrs Brown zu nennen): Nach dem Verb *start* ist grundsätzlich auch die *to*-Form möglich: *they* **started to call** *her Mrs Brown*, aber das Gegensatzverb *stop* lässt sich nur mit der *-ing*-Form verbinden: *he stopped talking* (= er hörte auf zu reden).

5. **Craft** ist eine Kollektivbezeichnung für „Boot(e)" und jegliche Art von Luft- und Weltraumfahrzeug(en); der Plural ist ebenfalls *craft*: *the light craft in the cove* (= die leichten Boote in der kleinen Bucht), *one/two aircraft* (= ein Flugzeug / zwei Flugzeuge), *spacecraft* (= Raumfahrzeug[e]).

6. **19th century / nineteenth century** (= 19. Jahrhundert): Durch Anhängen von *-th* werden aus den Grundzahlen über 3 die Ordnungszahlen gebildet (→ S. 217):

   four – **fourth** (= vierte), *six* – **sixth** (= sechste) usw.
   Kleine Unregelmäßigkeiten sind *five* – **fifth**, *eight* – **eighth**, *nine* – **ninth**,
     twelve – **twelfth** und die Zehnerzahlen *twenty* – **twentieth**, *thirty* – **thirtieth** usw.
   Echte Ausnahmen sind **first** (= erste), **second** (= zweite) und **third** (= dritte).

7. **Ghillie** bezeichnet in Schottland einen Jagdhelfer, und auch heute noch veranstaltet die königliche Familie (*the Royal Family*), wenn sie im Sommer *at Balmoral Castle* ist, am Ende der Jagdsaison (*at the end of the hunting season*) einen *Ghillies' Ball*.

8. **1901** am besten *nineteen oh one* gesprochen, aber Sie können auch förmlicher *nineteen hundred and one* sagen. Weitere Muster für die Aussprache von Jahreszahlen: *1837* (*eighteen thirty-seven*), *2009* (*two thousand and nine*), *2013* (*twenty thirteen*).

Focus on culture

1. **Victoria** was born in 1819. She was queen of Great Britain and Ireland from 1837 to 1901 and empress of India from 1876 to 1901. In 1840 she married her German cousin Prince Albert (1819–61), with whom she had nine children. Queen Victoria became the "grandmother of Europe" by marrying off her children and grandchildren into most of Europe's ruling houses. Her eldest daughter, Victoria (1840–1901), married Prince Frederick William of Prussia, who was German emperor for 99 days in 1888. Their eldest son was William II (1859–1941), the last German emperor (1888–1918).

2. **Victoria Station**, today London's second busiest railway station and busiest underground station, was opened in 1860. "London Victoria", as the railway station is now officially called, serves the south of England and some European destinations.

3. The **Victoria Line** is a tube line running from the southwest to the northeast of London. (Londoners usually say "the tube" when they mean "the underground".)

4. **The Victoria and Albert Museum** has some of the world's finest collections of furniture, ceramics and glass, metalwork, jewellery and clothes.

5. The Scotsman **John Brown** (1826–1883) was Queen Victoria's personal servant and close personal friend for many years. Their relationship is the subject of a 1997 BBC film, *Her Majesty Mrs Brown*.

6. *The Time Machine* (1895) is a short science-fiction novel by H. G. Wells (1866–1946).

7. At the **State Opening of Parliament** the king or queen reads the Speech from the Throne written for him/her by the government. Unlike her great-great-grandmother Queen Victoria, Queen Elizabeth II has opened parliament every year since she came to the throne in 1952, except for two years when she was pregnant.

8. **Charles Darwin** (1809–82): In his book *On the Origin of Species* (= Über den Ursprung der Arten) (1859), Charles Darwin explained that plants and animals develop gradually from simpler to more complicated forms by natural selection.

Unit 15F

2/30

empress = Kaiserin
with whom = mit dem
ruling house = Herrscherhaus
eldest daughter / son = älteste(r) Tochter / Sohn
Frederick = Friedrich
William = Wilhelm
Prussia = Preußen
emperor = Kaiser

busiest = mit dem höchsten Verkehrsaufkommen
destination = Bestimmungsort
tube = **underground** = U-Bahn
ceramics = Keramik
metalwork = Metall(arbeit)

2/31

Scotsman = Schotte
subject = Thema
novel = Roman
speech = Rede
unlike = im Gegensatz zu
except for = mit Ausnahme von
explain = erklären
plant = Pflanze
develop = sich entwickeln
gradual(ly) = allmählich
simple(r) = einfach(er)
complicated = kompliziert
selection = Auslese

Unit 15G Test yourself

Farewell Crossword

farewell = Abschied

ACROSS
1 The country where golf was born.
5 The architect who built the Guggenheim Museum in New York.
8 Queen Victoria's husband.
13 The town where the greatest English poet was born.
14 The people who lived in the Victorian Era.
15 A famous Greek storyteller.
17 The largest country in Africa, by population.
20 An island in New York City.
21 The US state Boston is the capital of.

DOWN
2 The river that flows through London.
3 A country which is also an island and a continent.
4 The man who developed the theory of evolution by natural selection.
5 The man who wrote *The Time Machine*.
6 The man who said, "To be, or not to be: that is the question ..."
7 An area in Britain from which a pudding and a terrier come.
9 The family name of the British royal family.
10 An English poet who was almost hanged.
11 The United Kingdom minus Northern Ireland.
12 A famous great-great-granddaughter of Queen Victoria.
13 The man who invented the word "fortune teller".
16 The biggest city down under.
18 The land of delicious curries.
19 First name of a man Queen Victoria was very fond of.

186

Schlüssel

Unit 1

1B1
a I'm. b you're. c she's. d They're. e that's; He's. f We're; It's.

1B3
You're Tom. – You're Tom, I suppose.
And you're Janet. – And you're Janet, I suppose.
They're very happy. – They're very happy, I suppose.
She's on holiday. – She's on holiday, I suppose.
Sarah is his granddaughter. – Sarah is his granddaughter, I suppose.
Toby has made a mess. – Toby has made a mess, I suppose.
The dog isn't house-trained. – The dog isn't house-trained, I suppose.

1B4
a came. b meet. c Make. d let. e forgot. f tell. g made. h get.

1B5
a These are our dogs Ben and Toby.
b This is Tom with his wife Janet.
c This is the new member of our family.
d This is Sarah with Toby on her arm.
e This is our best rug.
f These rugs are very nice.
g These dogs are all house-trained.

1B6
a And I suppose you're Janet. / And you're Janet, I suppose.
b We're delighted / We're very glad (that) you're here.
c Toby is a new member of our family.
d He's only ten weeks old.

1D1
a runners. b granddaughters. c dog; runner. d member; family. e weeks. f sister; delicatessen. g biscuits; cakes. h brothers; hotel. i hundreds; goats. j Goats; hobby; business.

1D2
a introduces. b runs; gets. c says. d run. e runs f believe. g live; lives.

1D3
a have. b has. c has. d have. e has. f has. g has; have.

1D5
Tom is retired now. – Tom is retired now, isn't he?
Uncle Fred is a strange man. – Uncle Fred is a strange man, isn't he?
Rachel is nice. – Rachel is nice, isn't she?
The pudding is very good. – The pudding is very good, isn't it?
Toby is only ten weeks old. – Toby is only ten weeks old, isn't he?
The hotel is called The Blue Danube. – The hotel is called The Blue Danube, isn't it?
That's a funny name. – That's a funny name, isn't it?
Janet is your daughter. – Janet is your daughter, isn't she?
That's your dog. – That's your dog, isn't it?

1D6
a The hotel hasn't got a spa.
b The family hasn't got a dog.
c The goat hasn't got a name.
d My sister hasn't got a hobby.
e John hasn't got a sister in London.
f She hasn't got a good computer.

1D7
a to. b at. c with; for. d to. e of. f on. g from. h of. i of. j on.

1G

187

Schlüssel

Unit 2

2B1
a It's over there.
b They're lovely.
c It's just a stone's throw from here.
d They're just a stone's throw from here.
e It's good.
f It isn't far away from here.
g They're free.

2B2
a Isn't Buckingham Palace over there?
b Isn't everything expensive here?
c Isn't Westminster Abbey just a stone's throw from here?
d Isn't there a good Indian restaurant in Denman Street?
e Aren't the government buildings of Whitehall just a stone's throw from here?
f Aren't the squirrels lovely?
g Aren't we right in the middle of London?
h Aren't you hungry?

2B3
a The squirrels in St James's Park are lovely.
b There's a pelican on the lake.
c You can walk to Piccadilly Circus.
d Trafalgar Square isn't far away either.
e We're right in the middle of London.
f The Houses of Parliament are just a stone's throw from here.
g You can walk to Trafalgar Square and Piccadilly Circus.
h There's a good Indian restaurant in Denman Street.
i Most of the museums in London are free.

2B5
The Houses of Parliament are beautiful. They are not far from St James's Park and the government buildings of Whitehall.
St James's Park is one of the beautiful parks right in the middle of London. It is a peaceful place with fine old trees and a lovely lake.
From St James's Park it is a nice walk to Soho with its restaurants, bars and clubs.
You are hungry? Then let's go and have a curry at an Indian restaurant. There are three or four Indian restaurants in Denman Street.
Restaurants are expensive in London, everything is expensive, but most of the museums are free.
Ruth and Marion run a German delicatessen in London. Their frankfurters, puddings and biscuits are popular. They live on a boat on the Thames.

2D1
a they're. b stone's; aren't. c It's; isn't.
d they're; We're. e he's. f You'll. g there's. h let's.
i Ruth's; city's. j Speakers'; aren't.

2D3
lots of dogs in our street – There are lots of dogs in our street.
lots of beautiful paintings in the National Gallery – There are lots of beautiful paintings in the National Gallery.
many Indian restaurants in Soho – There are many Indian restaurants in Soho.
a German delicatessen in Old Street – There's a German delicatessen in Old Street.
some ducks on the lake – There are some ducks on the lake.
a dog in this house – There's a dog in this house.
many government buildings in Whitehall – There are many government buildings in Whitehall.
no squirrels in Trafalgar Square – There are no squirrels in Trafalgar Square.
no Indian restaurant in Martin Street – There's no Indian restaurant in Martin Street.

2D4
a You can watch a trial at the Old Bailey.
b You can watch a debate in the Commons.
c You can watch the Changing of the Guard at Buckingham Palace.
d You can look at the beautiful paintings in the National Gallery.
e You can listen to the speakers in Hyde Park.
f You can listen to free concerts in the Church of St-Martin-in-the-Fields.

Schlüssel

2D5
a hundreds of goats. b the government buildings of Whitehall. c the south bank of the Thames. d the middle / centre of London. e most of the museums. f the Houses of Parliament. g a new member of our family. h a lot of interesting things. i one of the best ways to see London. j if you're fond of walking / if you like to walk. k the Church of St-Martin-in-the-Fields. l the Changing of the Guard.

2D6
a The National Gallery is in Trafalgar Square.
b We can look at the beautiful paintings there.
c At the weekend we can listen to the speakers in Hyde Park.
d Are you interested in politics?
e We can go to Buckingham Palace or watch a trial at the Old Bailey.
f We can walk along the south bank of the Thames from Westminster Bridge to Tower Bridge.

2G

Unit 3

3B1
The hotel is old and it has charm and character. It's on a hill overlooking a lake. It's nice and quiet and you can go for long walks. Of course, you can go swimming in the lake, but the hotel has an indoor pool too. My room is bright and cheerful and you have a view of the valley with the lake and the mountains beyond. The TV has a thousand channels, there's DVD and Internet, and what's really important: the bed has a duvet. The hotel is old but it has all the mod cons. It's absolutely state of the art.

3B2
a has. b have. c has. d have. e has. f has.
g have. h have. i has. j have. k has. l have. m have.

3B3
a a. b an. c a. d an. e a. f an. g an. h a.

3B4
a What's St James's Park like? – It's beautiful.
b What's the room like? – It's bright and cheerful.
c What's Tom like? – He's very nice.
d What's Sarah like? – She's a lovely girl.
e What's the Bombay Restaurant like? – It's good.
f What's Uncle Fred like? – He's a strange man.
g What are the paintings like? – They're very interesting.
h What are the concerts like? – They're just wonderful.
i What's the lake like? – It's very large and deep.
j What's the hotel like? – It has charm and character.

3B6
Where's the hotel? – It's on a hill.
Where's the National Gallery? – It's in Trafalgar Square.
Where's Speakers' Corner? – It's in Hyde Park.
Where's the duvet? – It's on the bed.
Where's Uncle Fred? – He's in New Zealand.
Where's the Queen? – She's in Buckingham Palace.
Where are the ducks? – They're on the lake.
Where are the government buildings? – They're in Whitehall.

189

Schlüssel

Where are the free lunchtime concerts? – They're in the Church of St-Martin-in-the-Fields.

3D1

a Broadway. b Fifth Avenue. c museum. d airports. e (*BE* railway) station / (*AE* train) station / (*AE*) terminal station. f old / attractive / expensive / important. g sight. h far. i restaurants.

3D2

a It's in New York (City) / in Manhattan.
b It's a museum / an art museum in New York (City) / in Manhattan.
c They're in London.
d They're airports in New York (City).
e It's a (famous) street in New York (City) (where there are many theatres).
f There are many expensive shops on Fifth Avenue.
g You can get souvenirs at the hotel gift shop / at the Eden Gift Shop.

3D3

We can take a bus to the Empire State Building.
We can eat / have a nice hamburger in Times Square.
We can go for a walk in Central Park.
We can have lunch at a Manhattan restaurant.
We can visit MoMA and the Met.
We can go shopping on Fifth Avenue.
We can buy souvenirs in the hotel gift shop.
We can go swimming in the hotel pool.
We can go to a Broadway theatre.

3D4

Beachten Sie: Statt We will … *können Sie hier auch immer* We'll … *sagen.*
We will take a bus to the Empire State Building.
We will eat / have a nice hamburger in Times Square.
We will go for a walk in Central Park.
We will have lunch at a Manhattan restaurant.
We will visit MoMA and the Met.
We will go shopping on Fifth Avenue.
We will buy souvenirs in the hotel gift shop.
We will go swimming in the hotel pool.
We will go to a Broadway theatre.

3D5

■ What's the Eden Hotel like?
● Oh, it's a good hotel, and it's right in the middle of Manhattan, within walking distance of a lot of New York sights. Many Broadway theatres are close by.
■ Good. What about your room? Is it quiet?
● Well, it isn't very/too quiet. Manhattan isn't a quiet place. But the room is OK. It's quite large actually, and it's bright and cheerful. There's Internet access, a DVD player, and the TV has a thousand channels.
■ Great. Is it expensive?
● The hotel? No, it isn't very expensive. And the prices in the gift shop are OK too.
■ Lovely. Well, have a good time in New York!
● Thanks.

3D6

a Let's walk.
b Let's have a curry.
c Let's go to the British Museum.
d Let's listen to the speakers.
e Let's go for a walk.
f Let's go swimming.
g Let's take the bus.

3D7

go shopping on Fifth Avenue – Let's go shopping on Fifth Avenue.
buy a souvenir for Anna – Let's buy a souvenir for Anna.
go to the Met today – Let's go to the Met today.
take a bus to Times Square – Let's take a bus to Times Square.
walk up to Central Park – Let's walk up to Central Park.
have lunch at a restaurant – Let's have lunch at a restaurant.
buy some postcards in the gift shop – Let's buy some postcards in the gift shop.
get tickets for a Broadway musical – Let's get tickets for a Broadway musical.
take the train from Penn Station – Let's take the train from Penn Station.

Schlüssel

3D

```
        N
      MUSEUM
   C    W
   H  SHOP   H   V
   U  O      O   A
   RESTAURANT   L
   C  E      P   L
   HILL    THEATRE
            R    Y
```

Across/Down: MUSEUM, SHOP, RESTAURANT, HILL, THEATRE, CHURCH, NEWS(?), HOSPITAL, VALLEY

3G

1. NYC is the largest (= *größte*) city in the USA.
2. NYC is about (= *etwa*) 400 years old.
3. The population of NYC is about 8 million.
4. NYC has about 2,000 bridges.
5. Manhattan is a borough of NYC.
6. The Empire State Building is the tallest (= *höchste*) skyscraper (= *Wolkenkratzer*) in NYC.
7. NYC taxis are yellow (= *gelb*).
8. The Statue of Liberty is on an island.
9. Grand Central Terminal is a station in NYC.
10. No (= *keine*) Avenue runs (= *verläuft*) through (= *durch*) Central Park. (5th = fifth = *fünfte*, 12th = twelfth = *zwölfte*)
11. MoMA is a museum.
12. Mammon City is not a nickname of NYC. *Den Spitznamen Gotham verdankt New York dem Schriftsteller Washington Irving (1783–1859), der ihn in 1807–8 erschienenen satirischen Schriften über das Leben in New York verwendete.*

Unit 4

4B1

- ■ Lovejoy Bed and Breakfast. Can I help you?
- ● Yes, hello. Do you have a vacancy for three nights from next Monday?
- ■ Single or double?
- ● Actually I need two rooms – a single and a double.
- ■ Oh I see. Let me just check … I don't have a single, but I can do two doubles – for 130 dollars, and 110 dollars.
- ● Hmm. – Are they non-smoking?
- ■ We only have non-smoking rooms.
- ● Good. What about TV? Can we watch the New York Jets?
- ■ Absolutely! We don't have TVs in the rooms, but there's a large television in the living room exclusively for our guests.
- ● Uh-huh. And … by the way, do you allow children?
- ■ No, I'm afraid we don't.
- ● But do you take dogs? We have a Yorkshire terrier.
- ■ Yes, if it's well-behaved. We have a German shepherd …
- ● Hmm. – You say in your ad you're right in the heart / middle of Manhattan. How far are you from Grand Central Station?
- ■ About 1,300 miles.
- ● My goodness! What do you mean?
- ■ We're in Manhattan, Kansas.

4B2

a. Is the room quiet?
b. Is it a non-smoking room?
c. Can we watch TV?
d. Is there a television in the living room?
e. Do you like children?
f. Do they have a dog?
g. Do you mean Grand Central Station?
h. Can we go swimming in the lake?
i. Do they only have non-smoking rooms?

4B3

a. The tickets aren't expensive.
b. He isn't very well-behaved.
c. I can't help you.
d. I don't watch TV a lot.
e. They don't have a TV.
f. We don't allow dogs.
g. We aren't / We're not in Manhattan.
h. You can't swim in the lake.
i. We don't go to concerts a lot.

4B5

Are you hungry? – No I'm not.
Are you interested in politics? – No I'm not.
Is Tom in the house? – No he isn't.

Schlüssel

Is that a German wine? – No it isn't.
Is there a TV in the room? – No there isn't.
Are the biscuits good? – No they aren't.
Can you swim? – No I can't.
Can we watch TV here? – No we can't.
Do you like dogs? – No I don't.
Do they drink wine? – No they don't.
Has Uncle Fred got a house? – No he hasn't.

4B6
a on. b about; from. c for; from. d of. e within; of.
f at. g at / from.

4D1
a walks. b have. c can. d listens. e overlooks. f don't.
g doesn't. h will. i like. j Does. k Does. l doesn't.

4D4
a A double room is a room with one large bed for two people (in a hotel or B&B). / A double room is a bedroom for two people. / A double room has one large bed for two people.
b A twin room is a room with two single beds (in a hotel or B&B).
c A Yorkshire terrier is a small dog (with long hair).
d Grand Central is a station in New York City / in Manhattan.
e Kansas is a state in/of the USA / in/of the United States.
f A manhattan is a cocktail (whisky mixed with vermouth, or vermouth mixed with whisky).
g B&B means "bed and breakfast".
h Dogs bark.
i Westminster Abbey is a very large / big and important church in London.
j You can watch trials at the Old Bailey.

4D5
a This B&B only has non-smoking rooms / has non-smoking rooms only.
b Carol doesn't like children's noise.
c The B&B allows / takes dogs but it doesn't allow / take children.
d Carol doesn't want a twin (room).
e Carol's dog doesn't bark very much / a lot.

f Does the hotel have an indoor pool?
g Does it have a sauna?
h Do the dogs make a lot of noise?
i Does she like to go to the theatre?
j Do they like to go to the theatre?
k Do you like to go to the theatre?

4D
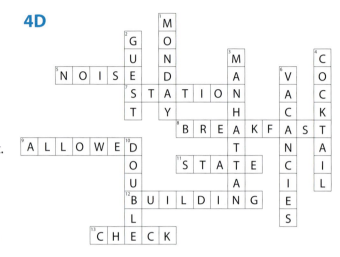

4G
Dialogtext:
Woman: The Bailey House Hotel. Can I help you?
Man: Yes, hello! Do you have a single room for two nights from next Friday?
Woman: Let me see. Yes, I have a room. It's a double but I can let you have it at the price of a single.
Man: Great. – Er … how much is it?
Woman: Eighty pounds per night …
Man: … That's including breakfast I suppose?
Woman: Yes indeed, the price includes a full English breakfast.
Man: And does the room have a bath?
Woman: Yes … it has an en-suite bathroom (= ein eigenes Badezimmer) with both bath and shower, a hairdryer, minibar, direct-dial telephone, Internet access, TV with DVD …
Man: … Never mind the DVD. I have my movies on my laptop.

Schlüssel

Antworten:
The man wants to book a single room.
He wants the room from Friday to Sunday.
The hotel has a double room.
The hotel offers a double room.
The price per night of a single room is £80.
The price includes a big breakfast.
The room has a private bathroom.
The man doesn't want a DVD player.

Unit 5

5B1
a calls. b Are you calling; are you doing. c watch.
d are you watching; are winning. e sometimes have.
f never take. g am reading. h is the dog barking.
i bark. j are you calling. k Do all the rooms have. l are making; are getting.

5B2
a her. b their. c its. d our. e her. f its. g my. h his.
i your.

5D1
a They are going swimming this afternoon.
b They are watching TV tonight.
c They are going to the British Museum tomorrow.
d They are taking a break this weekend.
e They are getting married next month.
f They are serving breakfast in half an hour.

5D2
a at; while. b across; from. c behind. d climb; did.
e view; in. f its; around. g on; below. h top; metres. i don't.

5D3
a isn't he? b is it? c is she? d isn't it? e isn't it? f isn't she? g isn't he? h is he? i is there?

5D4
Manhattan is an island. – Manhattan is an island, isn't it?
130 dollars is quite expensive. – 130 dollars is quite expensive, isn't it?
Children's noise isn't really a problem. – Children's noise isn't really a problem, is it?
Colin's your uncle. – Colin's your uncle, isn't he?
Tom's not very busy. – Tom's not very busy, is he?
Sarah's keeping you on your toes. – Sarah's keeping you on your toes, isn't she?
The daughter isn't very nice. – The daughter isn't very nice, is she?
There's a TV in the living room. – There's a TV in the living room, isn't there?
There isn't much time. – There isn't much time, is there?
This is Jessica. – This is Jessica, isn't it?

5D5
a Steve is working out in the gym (right now / just now).
b The hotel is just fantastic / great / terrific.
c From our window we can see the opera house.
d Right behind our hotel is the famous Sydney Harbour Bridge.
e The view from the bridge is fantastic.
f You (can) see the beautiful city with its many coves.
g The Sydney Harbour Bridge is the largest steel-arch bridge in the world.
h Tomorrow we are flying back. / We are flying back tomorrow.
i The flight from Sydney to London takes 22 hours.

5D

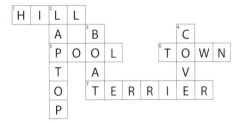

5G
1. 200 years. 2. 9pm on Saturday 10 January. 3. Canberra. 4. Montreal. 5. About 22 million. 6. In December. 7. The British Queen. 8. In the southeast. 9. English.

Schlüssel

Unit 6

6B1
a She looked happy.
b She enjoyed her holiday.
c She wanted to go for a walk.
d She loved the lake.
e She went swimming every morning.
f She always waited for me.
g There were some ducks in the lake.
h She had some food for the ducks.
i The hotel was very nice but it didn't allow dogs.
j It was very quiet.

6B2
a Carol wanted to book a double room for three nights.
b The Lovejoy B&B didn't allow children.
c That was all right with Carol because she didn't like children's noise.
d Carol's Yorkshire terrier, however, was welcome as long as it didn't bark too much and didn't attack other dogs.
e But there was a small problem.
f Carol wanted a room in Manhattan, New York, but the Lovejoy B&B was in Manhattan, Kansas.
g It was a little too far from Grand Central Station.

6B4
We watched a lot of TV. – We had to watch a lot of TV.
We waited endlessly at airports. – We had to wait endlessly at airports.
We walked to the hotel. – We had to walk to the hotel.
We carried our heavy bags. – We had to carry our heavy bags.
We climbed a high mountain. – We had to climb a high mountain.
We did a lot of sightseeing. – We had to do a lot of sightseeing.
We listened to a lot of loud music. – We had to listen to a lot of loud music.

6B5
a John didn't enjoy his holiday.
b The pilots were on strike and he had to wait endlessly at airports.
c When he arrived, there were no taxis.
d He had to walk to the hotel / had to go to the hotel on foot.
e He had to carry two heavy bags.
f The hotel staff didn't speak (any) English.
g Breakfast was terrible.
h The restaurant food was appalling.

6B6
a Why did they call the police?
b Why did they go to a B&B?
c Why did they want to get married in Australia?
d Why did they go to Soho?
e Why didn't they take a taxi?
f Why didn't they enjoy their holiday?
g Why didn't they want to go?
h Why were there no taxis?
i Why weren't they happy?

6D1
a John doesn't want to go on holiday but his wife insists.
b A lot of things go wrong.
c The pilots are on strike, so they wait endlessly at airports.
d When they finally arrive, there are no taxis and they have to walk to the hotel.
e John has to carry their two heavy bags.
f Everything is a nightmare.
g The hotel staff doesn't / don't speak English.
h When John comes home, he is hungry for roast beef and fish and chips.

6D3
a arrived; were waiting. b were walking; attacked. c were; climbed. d was sitting; was working. e were listening; asked. f were enjoying; came. g were waiting; stopped; asked; were going.

6D4
a was. b wanted; lived. c asked; came. d answered; was; were. e said; would.

6D5
a The pilots will be on strike, so we'll wait endlessly at airports.

Schlüssel

b There'll be no taxis and we'll have to walk to the hotel.
c I'll have to carry our two heavy bags.
d There'll be no English food at all.
e Everything will be covered in garlic.
f It'll be a nightmare.
g But we'll survive.

6D6

a answered. b nice. c great / terrific / wonderful. d people. e very well, thank you. f very. g awful / appalling / dreadful / pathetic / lousy / very bad / really bad. h busy. i in Australia.

6G

a = 6. b = 4. c = 8. d = 7. e = 9. f = 10. g = 5. h = 2. i = 1. j = 3.
Wörtliche Übersetzungen der *idioms*:
a Sie schlug nicht um den Busch herum.
b Sie hat kein Bein, auf dem sie stehen kann gegen uns.
c Sie weiß, auf welcher Seite ihr Brot "gebuttert" ist.
d Sie sieht aus, als ob Butter nicht in ihrem Mund schmelzen würde.
e Sie läuft Ringe um ihn herum.
f Sie wird mich zum Frühstück verzehren, wenn ich das tue.
g Sie ist zwischen dem Teufel und der tiefen blauen See.
h Sie ist emporgekommen in der Welt.
i Sie ist im Fahrersitz.
j Sie ist über ihr Haltbarkeitsdatum hinaus.

Unit 7

7B1

Beachten Sie: Ist die Handlung mit einer „Unsicherheitsfloskel" wie *I think, maybe, I'm afraid, I'm sure* etc. verbunden, so ist einfaches *will* die wahrscheinlichste Variante.
a I'll miss / (*da going to außer Absicht auch Gewissheit ausdrücken kann, ist hier auch gut möglich*:) I'm going to miss. b I'll tell / (*Betonung der Absicht*:) I'm going to tell. c I'll take. d I'll take / (*Absicht*:) I'm going to take / (*aufgrund der Tagesplanung zu erwarten*:) I'll be taking. e I'll do. f I won't have to. g I won't miss / (*Gewissheit*:) I'm not going to miss. h I'll have to / I'm going to have to. i I'll take. j I'll run / (*Betonung der Absicht*:) I'm going to run. k We're flying / (*ist so geplant, vorgesehen*:) We'll be flying. l She'll retire / She's retiring / She'll be retiring / She's going to retire / (*möglich ist auch die seltenere und daher bei uns nicht aufgeführte „Fahrplan-"/„Programm"-Zukunft*:) She retires. m We'll be / We're going to be. n (*Neutral*:) we'll climb / (*Absicht*:) we're going to climb / (*ist so geplant*:) we're climbing / we'll be climbing. o (*Entschlossenheit, es nicht zu tun*:) I'm not going to climb. p you'll have to / you're going to have to. q (*geplant für einen genannten Termin*:) We're having / (*ist so vorgesehen*:) We'll be having / (*Absicht, Gewissheit*:) We're going to have; they'll keep. r are you doing / will you be doing / are you going to do.

7B2

a They arrived two hours ago.
b John called about three days ago.
c We lived here years ago.
d He visited us about six months ago.
e A few days ago he/it attacked a Yorkshire terrier. / He/It attacked a Yorkshire terrier a few days ago.
f Two years ago we climbed a high mountain in Malaysia. / We climbed a high mountain in Malaysia two years ago.

7B4

It's strange. – It's strange, isn't it?
It's your last day. – It's your last day, isn't it?
This isn't much fun. – This isn't much fun, is it?
You're into running. – You're into running, aren't you?
They aren't very nice. – They aren't very nice, are they?
We can relax a little. – We can relax a little, can't we?
She can't run a marathon. – She can't run a marathon, can she?
He'll retire next year. – He'll retire next year, won't he?
We won't have to wait. – We won't have to wait, will we?

Schlüssel

7D1
a run. b training. c felt. d during. e running. f didn't. g went. h sent. i suffered. j have. k followed. l became. m running. n ran. o finished.

7D2
a called. b finished. c suffered. d stopped. e he has / he'll have / he will have. f says. g sent. h ran. i went. j become. k shown. l felt.

7D3
a She had retired at the end of the year.
b She had relaxed a little.
c She had gone out with friends.
d She had improved her German.
e She had jogged a lot.
f She had climbed mountains.
g She had trained for the marathon.
h She had run the marathon.

7D4
a How often did she run the Boston Marathon?
b How did she feel?
c When did she run again?
d How long did she wait?
e Who did she go to see?
f Where did he send her?
g What did the tests show?
h When did she retire?

7D5
a I'm going to call you Gary.
b I'm not going to stop running.
c I'm going to run again tomorrow.
d I'm going to train for the marathon.
e I'm going to run the Boston Marathon.
f This year I'm going to be faster than last year.
g I'm going to be (as) fit as a fiddle.
h I'm not going to retire.
i I'm going to get married.

7G

Unit 8

8B1
a We have missed you.
b He has finished the game.
c She has improved her English.
d They have booked a double room.
e They haven't answered my email.

8B2
a He has waited too long.
b You have trained enough.
c They have stopped talking.
d I have always worked with young people.

8B3
a The letter has arrived.
b What has happened?
c She has retired.

8B4
a I have forgotten what it was.
b Their / Your / Her service has become terrible.
c He has run the marathon 34 times.
d You haven't got me yet.

8B5
a I wanted to get up early tomorrow.
b She wanted to go to the doctor yesterday.

Schlüssel

c He wanted to run the marathon but didn't.
d She wanted to retire at the end of the year.
e Did you want to play with the dogs?
f Did you want to walk to the hotel?

8B7

go to the theatre a lot – They used to go to the theatre a lot.
go for long walks – They used to go for long walks.
work out in a gym – They used to work out in a gym.
go swimming every day – They used to go swimming every day.
have a whisky before dinner – They used to have a whisky before dinner.
play chess every Sunday afternoon – They used to play chess every Sunday afternoon.
eat in expensive restaurants – They used to eat in expensive restaurants.
go to the mountains for their holidays – They used to go to the mountains for their holidays.

8D1

a When they finally arrived, there were no taxis.
b She will probably miss the people she worked with.
c He suddenly felt a pain in his chest. / Suddenly he felt …
d His doctor immediately sent him to the emergency room.
e I really don't want a new computer. / I don't really want …

8D2

a We had to wait endlessly at the airport.
b The food was absolutely / really disgusting.
c My memory really isn't what it used to be. / Especially my memory isn't what …
d There's an indoor pool exclusively / especially for our guests.
e I was a bit overweight and completely / absolutely unfit.
f A lot of people have difficulty remembering names, especially as they grow older.

8D3

a Speaking of restaurants, it's lunchtime and I'm hungry.
b At 65, and training for his 35th marathon, he felt fit as a fiddle.
c We can go shopping on Fifth Avenue.
d She's fond of watching reality TV shows.
e If you write a name down, you will remember it better.
f Writing a name down will help you remember it.
g Remembering the meaning of a name may be helpful.
h Fancy getting married in Sydney, ten thousand miles away.
i You should never eat junk food.
j You should avoid eating junk food.
k I think I'll do some reading before I go to bed.

8D4

a the room we booked
b the stories he tells
c the food we get here
d the bags I had to carry
e the house they live in

8G

Dialogtext:
Man   Oh hello, er …
Woman   … Jessica Peters …
Man   Oh yes, hello Jessica – I'm Martin Day … We met at the …
Woman   After the marathon!
Man   Yes I know … the bar of the hotel …
Woman   The Westminster Hotel.
Man   Right. Westminster Hotel. I'd forgotten the name. Small hotel, but rather nice …
Woman   I like small hotels.
Man   So do I. They often have more, er, character … they're often cheaper, too.
Woman   Often, not always.
Man   Yeah, that's right. But the Westminster wasn't … I mean, it wasn't expensive, was it?
Woman   Well, maybe not by London standards but … you know, everything is expensive to me here. I'm from Berlin you see …

Schlüssel

Man	Great! Lovely city, Berlin, from all I've heard. I've never been there myself.
Woman	Are you from London? Oh no, of course, you can't be … I mean, a Londoner doesn't stay in a London hotel.
Man	Correct. I'm from Sheffield, actually …

a (The woman's name is) Jessica Peters.
b She's from Berlin.
c (The man's name is) Martin Day.
d He's from Sheffield.
e (They first met) After the marathon.
f (Their first meeting was) In the bar of the Westminster Hotel.
g She says she likes small hotels.
h He says he likes small hotels too, and that they often have more character and are often cheaper, too.

Unit 9

9B1

a Let's take the bus. / Why don't we take the bus?
b Shall we play some chess? / Why don't we play some chess?
c Shall we relax a bit? / Let's relax a bit.
d Do you want me to stop here?
e Shall I get you a taxi?
f Why don't we get married?
g Do you want me to arrange theatre tickets?

9B2

a I would take / I'd take this table.
b I would wait / I'd wait two days.
c I would try / I'd try the Dundee pudding.
d I would be / I'd be frank.
e It would be / It'd be a mistake.
f We would have / We'd have a big problem.
g She would get / She'd get tickets for the concert.
h We would actually need / We'd actually need two rooms.

9B3

a It wouldn't be expensive.
b I wouldn't be interested.
c That wouldn't be unusual. / That would be nothing unusual.
d He wouldn't help me.
e I wouldn't go swimming here.
f I wouldn't say that.
g You wouldn't have to go to the office.
h She wouldn't be happy there.

9B4

a are. b is. c does. d do. e has. f did. g will. h won't. i can't. j they wouldn't. k I don't. l they didn't. m there weren't.

9B5

This building looks strange. – It does indeed.
The cheesecake looks good. – It does indeed.
He looks very happy. – He does indeed.
The Dundee pudding is tempting. – It is indeed.
Anne is very fit. – She is indeed.
The hotel people are all very nice. – They are indeed.
Breakfast was terrible. – It was indeed.
We should try the salmon. – We should indeed.
We've met before. – We have indeed.

9D1

a You could have started.
b You could have asked me.
c We could have avoided that.
d That couldn't have happened here.
e We could have played chess.
f I could have run faster.

9D2

a London is older than New York.
b She is nicer than her sister.
c My boyfriend is vainer / more vain than me.
d Kansas is flatter than a pancake.
e Many people are more overweight than me.
f London is more expensive than Berlin.
g Snow White is more beautiful than her stepmother.
h Nothing is better than love.

9D4

a who. b who. c which / that. d which / that. e who.
f which / that. g who. h which / that. i which (*auf eine Präposition wie z. B.* in, on *oder* from *kann nur* which *folgen!*). j who.

9D5

We didn't book online. – But we could have booked online.
We didn't walk. – But we could have walked.
He didn't wait. – But he could have waited.
He didn't call us. – But he could have called us.
She didn't see him. – But she could have seen him.
She didn't run the marathon. – But she could have run the marathon.
She didn't retire at 60. – But she could have retired at 60.
They didn't climb the bridge. – But they could have climbed the bridge.

9G

The speaker watches a lot of television. True.
The speaker often watches football. True.
He's a Portsmouth fan. False.
He likes to do the household shopping. False.
He regularly walks his dog. True.
He would like to go on holiday more often. False.
He would like to learn a foreign language. True.

Unit 10

10B1

■ Hi Alex, back from your holiday?
● Yes – back from heaven.
■ Heaven? What do you mean? Did you go to Bali? Someone once called it the nearest thing to heaven on earth.
● No, we went to Scotland, St Andrews to be exact.
■ St Andrews in Scotland? I've heard the name but I couldn't say what it's about. Not sunny beaches or palm trees, to be sure.
● Well, it was sunny as a matter of fact, but you don't go to St Andrews for the weather. Does golf ring a bell?
■ Ah, I should have known – when you talk of heaven you mean golf. But let me guess: St Andrews has a nice golf course that's easy to play because it's got a high wall around it so lousy players like you can't hit the ball out of bounds.
● Did I ever tell you that you're the nastiest friend I have? And the worst thing is you don't know a thing about golf, or you'd know that the Old Course at St Andrews is the oldest golf course in the world.
■ I'm impressed.
● You should be. Playing at St Andrews is one of the most wonderful experiences I had.

10B2

a the nicest / most pleasant restaurant I know
b the most attractive man I know
c the most unpleasant people I know
d the nastiest friend I have
e the most expensive city I know
f the heaviest bag we had
g the quietest / most quiet room the hotel has
h the biggest / greatest mistake I made
i the most wonderful experience I had

10B3

a the longest bridge in the world
b the best golf player / golfer in the world
c the worst pizza in the world
d the most delicious cheesecake in the world
e one of the most interesting museums in the world
f one of the most expensive paintings in the world

10B4

I didn't book online. – I should have booked online.
I didn't wait. – I should have waited.
I didn't walk. – I should have walked.
I didn't call her. – I should have called her.
I didn't play golf in Scotland. – I should have played golf in Scotland.
I didn't guess that Alex was on a golfing trip. – I should have guessed that Alex was on a golfing trip.
I didn't know that St Andrews was the home of golf. – I should have known that St Andrews was the home of golf.

Schlüssel

10B5
a the best friend I have. b which / that. c who.
d experiences a golfer can have. e people I work
with. f which / that. g names I just can't. h who.
i someone I know. j which / that.

10D1
(*Wir geben Ihnen hier jeweils nur das in dem betreffenden Zusammenhang üblichste -ly-Wort.*)
a pleasantly surprised. b delightfully old-fashioned.
c easily accessible. d absolutely state of the art.
e completely different. f extremely well-preserved.
g absolutely wonderful.

10D2
a itself. b themselves. c herself. d ourselves.
e himself. f myself. g itself. h yourself. i yourselves.

10D3
a I was surprised to hear that.
b It is important to stop global warming.
c When are you coming to see us? / When are you going to come and see/visit us?
d She would like to learn a foreign language.
e I would like to book a double room.
f He managed to avoid this mistake.
g They want to get married in Australia.

10D4
a from. b on / about. c from. d on. e into. f by.
g for. h in. i at. j to. k around.

10D5
stop global warming – It's important to stop global warming.
keep busy – It's important to keep busy.
relax from time to time – It's important to relax from time to time.
get enough exercise – It's important to get enough exercise.
keep in good shape – It's important to keep in good shape.
listen to your doctor – It's important to listen to your doctor.
follow your doctor's orders – It's important to follow your doctor's orders.
not to eat unhealthy fats – It's important not to eat unhealthy fats.
not to drink too much alcohol – It's important not to drink too much alcohol.

10D6
a It's lunchtime and I'm hungry.
b It's a very nice house, it's old and it's got charm and character, but it has its price.
c St Andrews is proud of its university.
d Melbourne is famous for its beautiful parks, fine restaurants and wide boulevards.
e It's happened again.
f You can't play a game if you don't know its rules.
g Living in a big city has its problems.

10D7
a for coming. b from happening. c of watching. d at remembering. e for remembering. f about going / of going. g of buying / about buying. h for reading.
i from eating.

10G

200

Schlüssel

Unit 11

11B1
a She arrived yesterday.
b Paul called yesterday.
c I visited him in hospital yesterday.
d We played chess yesterday.
e I booked our rooms yesterday.
f I ran my first marathon yesterday.

11B2
a What are the people of Athens like? (= Wie sind die Athener denn so?)
b Who were you having lunch with? (= Mit wem hast du Mittag gegessen?)
c How many nights do you want to book for? (= Für wie viele Nächte möchten Sie buchen?)
d What are you waiting for? (= Worauf wartest du [denn]?)
e What are you thinking about? (= Woran denkst du gerade? / Worüber denkst du nach?)
f I've no idea what you're talking about. (= Ich weiß nicht, wovon Sie reden.)
g Golf is something I know nothing about. (= Golf ist etwas, wovon ich nichts verstehe.)

11B3
a She said I was interested in music.
b She said I wasn't married.
c She said I had a fear of heights.
d She said I liked dogs.
e She said I didn't go to church.
f She said I couldn't swim.
g She said I would / I'd have five grandchildren.

11B5
I love you. – I do love you.
I love your cheesecake. – I do love your cheesecake.
We miss you. – We do miss you.
I remember that night. – I do remember that night.
Her new boyfriend looks nice. – Her new boyfriend does look nice.
Jack knows a lot about golf. – Jack does know a lot about golf.
We played some chess. – We did play some chess.
I followed your advice. – I did follow your advice.
They trained a lot. – They did train a lot.
We went to see him in hospital. – We did go to see him in hospital.

11B6
a. anyone. b someone. c anyone. d anyone.
e someone. f Someone. g someone. h anyone.
i anyone. j someone.

11D1
(*Alle Zeitangaben sind bezogen auf das Jahr 2010.*)
a Elizabeth became Queen 58 years ago / almost 60 years ago.
b John F. Kennedy was murdered 47 years ago.
c The Berlin Wall came down 21 years ago / over 20 years ago / more than 20 years ago.
d Digital cameras first came on the market about 20 years ago.
e Tony Blair became Prime Minister 13 (thirteen) years ago.
f The Google search engine was founded 12 (twelve) years ago.
g The Twin Towers were destroyed nine years ago.
h The Millennium Bridge over the Thames opened eight years ago.
i Germany got its first female chancellor five years ago.

11D2
a "I don't believe you."
b "Sarabaya is young and healthy."
c "I remember what you told me."
d "I'm convinced that you used your magical powers to kill Sarabaya."
e "It's my belief that you're a witch."
f "You'll / You will be killed."
g "I'll / I will let you live if you tell me when you yourself will die."

11D3
a were killed. b was founded. c will be published.
d were transplanted. e were made / have been made.
f will be needed. g were married. h was last invaded.
i will be used.

Schlüssel

11D4

A powerful king goes to see a fortune teller to hear what she has to say about the future. The old woman tells him that his favourite wife, Sarabaya, will die within a year.

The king doesn't believe the woman. After all, Sarabaya is young and healthy, why should she die? A few months later Sarabaya is dead and the king is devastated. He also remembers what the fortune teller told him and becomes convinced that she used her magical powers to kill Sarabaya.

He orders the woman to appear before him and tells her that it is his belief that she is not a fortune teller but a witch who used her power to kill his wife. If, however, she is really a fortune teller, she should tell him when she herself will die, or else she will be killed. The woman thinks carefully, and then says, "I will die three days before you, Your Majesty."

11D5

I don't know why the king visited a fortune teller. – Why did the king visit a fortune teller?
I don't know what the old woman told him. – What did the old woman tell him?
I don't know why the king's wife died. – Why did the king's wife die?
I don't know why the woman killed Sarabaya. – Why did the woman kill Sarabaya?
I don't know why the king didn't believe the woman. – Why didn't the king believe the woman?
I don't know why he said she was a witch. – Why did he say she was a witch?
I don't know why he wanted to kill the fortune teller. – Why did he want to kill the fortune teller?

11G

Unit 12

12B1

a My car has been stolen.
b A lot of cars are stolen these days.
c The car will be found.
d The car was found by police (= *Polizisten*!) in a car park in Bridge Street.
e The car has been found.
f It had been taken (by kids) for a joyride.
g Cars are often stolen (by youngsters) just for a joyride.
h The youngsters were chased by a police car.
i One of the youngsters was arrested in a bar.
j How can car thefts be prevented?

12B2

a A police officer saw him.
b Millions of people watched the debate.
c A neighbour called the police.
d Millions of people play golf.
e What do you do if a dog attacks you?
f Several thousand people have climbed Everest.
g Many people will miss her.
h The concierge can arrange theatre tickets, sightseeing and transportation.

12B3

a If he had stolen a car …
b If the police had caught him …
c If he hadn't crashed into a tree …
d If they hadn't arrested him …
e If he had killed someone …
f If he had followed my advice …
g If he had died …

12B4

a That would be wrong.
b That would have been wrong.
c We would / We'd find the car.
d We would have found the car.
e You would / You'd have a small / little problem.
f You would have had a small / little problem.

Schlüssel

12B5
a aren't they? b isn't she? c wasn't it? d has it?
e shall we? f were they? g won't you?

12D1
a embarking. b embarked. c carrying. d carries.
e buying. f to buy. g to buy. h telling. i (have) told / are telling. j being. k was. l listening. m listened.

12D2
a before going. b while playing. c after crashing.
d When boarding ship. e after being chased. f before running. g after stealing. h When trying. i while walking. j before leaving. k when reading.

12D3
a herself. b ourselves. c themselves. d himself.
e yourself / yourselves. f itself. g yourselves.

12D4
It happened in a beautiful southern European city, one loved by tourists and rightly so. I had just flown in from London and had a few hours to kill before embarking on a cruise of the Mediterranean.
I went for a leisurely walk along the seaside promenade, it was a gorgeous, sunny afternoon. I sat down on a bench. I felt in harmony with myself and the world. A group of girls came along the promenade. They were pretty, they were laughing, they were having innocent fun. Lovely.
After a shy glance at me and a few giggles they sat down on my bench. Well, all except one, actually. The way we were sitting / we sat there wasn't quite enough space on the bench and so we all moved closer together to make room for her. "Where there's a will there's a way," I said paternally as the ones next to me moved up really close. I didn't notice that all the other benches were empty.
After a short while the girls all jumped up again, and giggling and dancing they (had) soon disappeared. There's no fool like an old fool. When I boarded / was boarding ship, later that afternoon, I reached for my wallet. It was gone. I could not / couldn't believe what had happened. Those lovely, innocent girls had stolen my wallet. There had been thousands of pounds in it. I had never felt so stupid in all my life.

12D5
The queen visited the museum. – The museum was visited by the queen.
Carol booked the rooms. – The rooms were booked by Carol.
A neighbour saw the boys. – The boys were seen by a neighbour.
The concierge arranged our sightseeing tour. – Our sightseeing tour was arranged by the concierge.
The dog ate the biscuits. – The biscuits were eaten by the dog.
The police chased them. – They were chased by the police.
His father interrupted him. – He was interrupted by his father.
Her friends will miss her. – She will / She'll be missed by her friends.

12G

Vollständiger Text:
Two strangers were sitting over a glass of wine in a London bar. One of them looked bored and unhappy. "Life is dull, and everything in the world bores me," he said.
"How can you say such a thing?" said the other. "Life is wonderful, and the world is an exciting place. Just take Italy. It's a delightful country. Have you ever been there?"
"Oh yes, I've been to Italy. I was there last year. I didn't like it."
"Then go to Norway and see the midnight sun. Have you ever done that?"
"Yes, I've been to Norway, and I've seen the midnight sun. That was a few years ago. It didn't impress me."

Schlüssel

"Have you ever thought about a hobby?" asked his companion.
"I've tried lots of hobbies in my life," was the answer. "I've collected stamps and coins, I've played chess, golf, and the flute, I've painted in oils and watercolours. How terribly boring it all was!"
"It seems to me," said the other man, "that you have a serious problem. Go and see Dr Greenberg in Harley Street. They say he's the best psychiatrist in London."
"I am Dr Greenberg," was the sad man's answer.

Zwei Fremde saßen bei einem Glas Wein in einer Londoner Bar. Der eine von ihnen sah gelangweilt und unglücklich aus. „Das Leben ist langweilig, und alles auf der Welt langweilt mich", sagte er.
„Wie können Sie so etwas sagen?", sagte der andere. „Das Leben ist herrlich, und die Welt ist ein aufregender Ort. Nehmen Sie nur Italien. Es ist ein reizendes Land. Sind Sie schon mal dort gewesen?"
„O ja, ich bin in Italien gewesen. Ich war voriges Jahr dort. Es hat mir nicht gefallen."
Dann fahren Sie doch nach Norwegen und schauen Sie sich die Mitternachtssonne an. Haben Sie das schon mal getan?"
„Ja, ich bin in Norwegen gewesen und ich habe die Mitternachtssonne gesehen. Das war vor ein paar Jahren. Es hat mich nicht beeindruckt."
„Haben Sie schon mal an ein Hobby gedacht?", fragte sein Gefährte.
„Ich habe in meinem Leben schon viele Hobbys ausprobiert", war die Antwort. „Ich habe Briefmarken und Münzen gesammelt, ich habe Schach, Golf und Flöte gespielt, ich habe in Öl und Wasserfarben gemalt. Wie schrecklich langweilig das doch alles war!"
„Es scheint mir", sagte der andere Mann, „dass Sie ein ernstes Problem haben. Gehen Sie zu Dr. Greenberg in der Harley Street. Man sagt, er sei der beste Psychiater in London."
„Ich bin Dr. Greenberg", war des traurigen Mannes Antwort.

Unit 13

13B2
Sunday – since Sunday
our holidays – since our holidays
weeks – for weeks
a few days – for a few days
last year – since last year
the last hour – for the last hour
we boarded ship – since we boarded ship
twenty minutes – for twenty minutes
I retired – since I retired
we visited the Guggenheim Museum – since we visited the Guggenheim Museum
a long time – for a long time

13B3
a We are in London. – We have been in London for two weeks (now).
b We are learning the Tango Argentino. – Since September we have been learning the Tango Argentino.
c We are now living / We now live in America. – We have lived / have been living here for five years (now).
d Are you married? – Yes, I am married. – I have been married for a year (now).
e What are you doing? – We are playing chess. – How long have you been playing?
f They are sitting on a bench in the park. – How long have they been sitting there?

13B4
a did you? b didn't she? c haven't they? d hasn't he? e aren't you? f doesn't he? g have you? h can we? i wouldn't you? j does she? k is there? l do they?
(*Police* ist Mehrzahl!)

13D1
a of saying. b to come. c travelling. d to see. e for remembering. f working. g to do. h eating / to eat. i to take; painting. j of buying / about buying. k to see. l travelling. m to lose. n for telling. o to see. p (from) happening. q to be. r to playing. (*To* ist hier Präposition, nicht das Wörtchen, das vor der Grundform des Verbs steht, wie in *I want to play golf*.)

13D2
a This is the woman I met on the train.
b This is the flat they want to rent.
c This is the man I told you about.
d This is the letter I've been waiting for.
e This is the train the king travelled in.
f This is the hotel we stayed at last summer.
g This is the man I had lunch with the other day.

13D3
a It wasn't said openly.
b Football is played and watched all over the world.
c English is learned by millions of people.
d The house has been sold.
e A lot has been written about this problem.
f The city is loved by tourists.
g A UN peacekeeper has been killed by terrorists.
h The two kids were taken to hospital.

13D4
a Where did she meet her husband?
b What did he train as?
c What does she remember?
d Who did they sue?
e Who did the police chase?
f Where did he play golf?
g Where will she meet her true love?.
h What does he like?
i Who did she have lunch with?
j What does his girlfriend call him?

13D5
a I trained as a hairdresser.
b I (first) met my husband in our English class.
c We have been married (for) five years (now).
d We have been doing English together for many years.
e We are into modern architecture at the moment. / At the moment we are into modern architecture.
f I have enough time / I've got enough time to do things (that) I have always wanted to do.

13G

Unit 14

14B1
Das fett gedruckte *do/does/did* muss betont gesprochen werden.
a But I **do** like her!
b But she **does** believe you!
c But he **did** thank me!
d But he/she **did** notice it!
e But she **did** start from scratch!
f But they **did** arrest them!
g But I **do** play golf!
h But I **did** follow your advice!

14B2
a He wrote plays (for the theatre) / stage plays. In London he wrote plays (for the theatre) / stage plays.
b He spent his childhood in this house. In this house he spent his childhood.
c He went to London. We don't know when he went to London.
d He visited his family in Stratford. We don't know how often he visited his family in Stratford.
e They sat down on my bench. After a shy glance at me they sat down on my bench.

Schlüssel

14B3
a Shakespeare often uses unusual words.
b I never travel to work by car.
c He always has something interesting to say.
d She regularly walks her dog in the park.
e We sometimes go on holiday in winter.
f My mother usually goes to bed at eleven.
g Nobody ever asked me that question.

14B4
a We are delighted that you are here.
b I always say that we are a family of runners.
c The famous Harbour Bridge is right behind our hotel.
d He told me that his sister runs a delicatessen.
e In the summer I often go to Hyde Park to read a book.
f One day, during a training race, I suddenly felt a pain in my chest.
g At the hospital, tests / Tests at the hospital showed that I had suffered a heart attack.
h From our window I can see the Opera House in the evening light.
i If you are interested in politics, you can watch a debate in the Commons.
j At the Eden Hotel you can enjoy all the excitement of New York at attractive prices.
k Of course you can go / You can of course go swimming in the lake, but the hotel has an indoor pool too.

14D1
a The concierge can arrange transportation.
b If you don't do that, the king's men will kill you.
c He said that the king's men would kill her.
d Many people will miss her.
e The magistrate will tell them not to misbehave again.
f The Gherkin can be seen from all over London.
g The new museum is going to be opened in April.
h You are being watched by the police.
i We are being kept on our toes by the grandchildren.
j She is being talked about everywhere.
k Hundreds of millions of people are learning English.

14D2
a We don't know whether Shakespeare's marriage was happy.
b We don't know where Shakespeare lived in London.
c We don't know what friends Shakespeare had.
d We don't know where he got his ideas from.

14D3
a What was his private life like?
b How often did he visit his family in Stratford?
c Do the portraits really show Shakespeare?
d When did Shakespeare write Hamlet?
e When exactly did he return to Stratford?

14D4
a Who did he marry?
b How many children did they have?
c When did he go to London?
d What did another writer call him?
e When did Shakespeare buy New Place?
f How many sonnets did he write?
g Why did he sue a neighbour?
h When did Shakespeare die?
i What did he leave to his wife?

14D5
a Shakespeare lived from 1564 to 1616.
b He was born and died in Stratford-upon-Avon.
c The town where Shakespeare was born is on the river Avon.
d Shakespeare probably went to a very good grammar school.
e The woman he married was much older than him.
f At the time they married she was pregnant – in other words, she was expecting a baby.
g In the late 1580s Shakespeare went to London.
h Shakespeare became an actor and started writing plays.
i In 1598 his first plays were published.
j Shakespeare wrote a total of 37 plays and 154 sonnets.
k There are many allusions to history in Shakespeare's plays.
l Towards the end of his life Shakespeare returned to Stratford(-upon-Avon).

m He lived in a house called New Place.
n In his will, he left his wife his second-best bed.
o Shakespeare was buried in Holy Trinity Church in Stratford(-upon-Avon).

14G

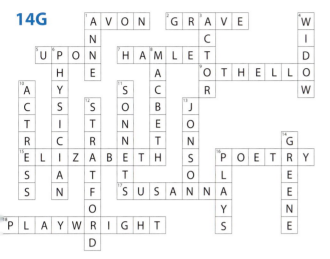

Unit 15

15B1

a You could have stayed at the Victoria Hotel.
b We should have visited the National Gallery.
c She must have been fascinated.
d He shouldn't have married her.
e You should have known that.
f He can't have known that.
g That could / might easily have happened.

15B2

a died. b has been. c are still (being) performed.
d has survived. e probably went. f I (will) retire / I'm retiring / I'm going to retire / I'll be retiring. g Did you go. h Are you going / Will you be going / Are you going to go. i Do you know. j Have you ever been.
k is already writing / has already written. l I have written. m wrote.
n I often visited.

15B3

Albert wasn't king. – Albert wasn't king, was he?
Victoria and Albert had nine children. – Victoria and Albert had nine children, didn't they?
Their marriage was a love match. – Their marriage was a love match, wasn't it?
Albert died very young. – Albert died very young, didn't he?
Victoria didn't marry again. – Victoria didn't marry again, did she?
We'll arrive at Victoria Station. – We'll arrive at Victoria Station, won't we?
The Victoria Hotel is on Victoria Road. – The Victoria Hotel is on Victoria Road, isn't it?
We could take the Victoria Line. – We could take the Victoria Line, couldn't we?
You've never stayed at the Victoria Hotel. – You've never stayed at the Victoria Hotel, have you?
There's also a Victoria Avenue. – There's also a Victoria Avenue, isn't there?
You remember. – You remember, don't you?

15B4

a She has been in London since Sunday.
b She has been staying at the Victoria Hotel for three days.
c She has known Colin for years.
d Colin has always lived in London.
e She has been waiting for him for an hour.
f He has been trying to call her for days / has been trying for days to call her.

15B5

Tom is Ann's husband. They have been married for six years and their marriage is still happy.
They first met in the Victoria and Albert Museum. Ann was looking at some Victorian photographs.
They talked about the photos and she told him that she had always been interested in Queen Victoria and her times.
He asked her to have lunch with him and they went to an Indian restaurant in Soho.
Three months later they got married.
Up to now they have lived / have been living in a flat but now they have decided that they are going to buy / that they will buy a house.
At the moment they are stilling living in London but in future they will live / will be living in a village about 100 miles from London.

Schlüssel

15B6
a In London you'll often come across the name Victoria.
b You may arrive at Victoria Station and stay at / in a hotel situated in / on Victoria Road.
c At the Victoria and Albert Museum you may be fascinated by the beautiful old furniture.

15D1
a who. b that / which. c which. d –. e who. f –. g –. h –. i which. j who.

15D2
a secretly. b secret. c real. d really. e easy. f easy; really. g easily. h endlessly. i endless.

15D3
a If you travelled by train, you would probably arrive at Victoria Station. (= Wenn Sie mit dem Zug reisen / reisen würden, würden Sie wahrscheinlich am Victoria-Bahnhof ankommen.)
b If I had a time machine, I would travel to the past. (= Wenn ich eine Zeitmaschine hätte, würde ich in die Vergangenheit reisen.)
c What would you do if a dog attacked you? (= Was würdest du tun, wenn dich ein Hund angriffe / angreifen würde?)
d Where would you go if you were able to travel to the past? (= Wohin würdest du fahren, wenn du in die Vergangenheit reisen könntest?)
e My girlfriend wouldn't call me a pot-bellied couch potato even if my stomach was not as flat as it is now. (= Meine Freundin würde mich auch dann nicht eine spitzbäuchige Couchkartoffel nennen, wenn mein Bauch nicht so flach wäre, wie er jetzt ist.)
f If this had happened to me, I would have called the police. (= Wenn das mir passiert wäre, hätte ich die Polizei gerufen).
g If I had gone to London, I would have stayed at the Victoria Hotel. (= Wenn ich nach London gefahren wäre, hätte ich im Victoria Hotel gewohnt.)
h What would have happened if the queen had married her servant? (= Was wäre passiert, wenn die Königin ihren Diener geheiratet hätte?)
i It would have been terrible if the thieves had been killed. (= Es wäre schrecklich gewesen, wenn die Diebe getötet worden wären / ums Leben gekommen wären.)
j If Queen Victoria hadn't had so many children, she would not have become "the grandmother of Europe". (= Wenn Königin Victoria nicht so viele Kinder gehabt hätte, wäre sie nicht „die Großmutter Europas" geworden.)
k If I had arrived at the time of the Queen's death, I would have heard her talked about quite differently. (= Wenn ich zur Zeit des Todes der Königin gekommen wäre, hätte ich ganz anders über sie reden hören.)

15G

Wortschatz

Der wichtigste Allgemeinwortschatz

Unser Buch vermittelt einen Wortschatz von ca. 1000 Wörtern. Verglichen mit dem Gesamtwortschatz des Englischen (ca. 500 000 Wörter) ist das eine verschwindend kleine Zahl, was Sie aber nicht beunruhigen muss, da der von den meisten Mitgliedern der Sprachgemeinschaft benutzte Alltagswortschatz nur ein paar tausend Wörter umfasst.

Die nachstehende Liste der 500 „wichtigsten" englischen Wörter stellt den notwendigen Allgemeinwortschatz dar, das heißt ein Vokabular, dessen häufiges Vorkommen nicht auf bestimmte Themen oder Situationen beschränkt, sondern übergreifend in allen Lebensbereichen anzutreffen ist. Die in dieser Auswahl enthaltenen 100 am häufigsten gebrauchten Wörter machen sage und schreibe 50 Prozent eines jeden beliebigen Textes aus. Es empfiehlt sich, dass Sie nach Durchnahme dieses Lehrbuches überprüfen, ob Sie alle in der Liste enthaltenen Wörter aktiv beherrschen. Wörter, mit denen Sie besondere Schwierigkeiten haben, könnten Sie auf Zettel DIN A7 schreiben – den englischen Ausdruck auf die eine Seite, den deutschen auf die andere – und sie dann so oft wiederholen, bis sie „sitzen". Auf diese Weise sichern Sie sich eine solide Wortschatzgrundlage, auf der Sie im praktischen Umgang mit der Sprache aufbauen können.

Natürlich können Sie diese Liste auch als ein erstes „Wörterbuch" zum Nachschlagen benutzen. Allerdings sollten Sie sich recht bald ein richtiges (zunächst nicht zu großes) Wörterbuch Englisch–Deutsch, Deutsch–Englisch zulegen. Wählen Sie ein *dictionary* aus, das möglichst viele Anwendungsbeispiele bietet.

A

a(n)	ein(e)
able	imstande
about	ungefähr; etwa
about: talk about sth.	über etw. reden
above	(dar)über; oberhalb
across (the street)	über (die Straße)
actually	an sich; eigentlich
after	nach; nachdem
again	wieder
against	gegen
ago: ten years ago	vor zehn Jahren
agree	der gleichen Meinung sein
air	Luft
all	all(e); alles
allow	erlauben
almost	fast; beinahe
along	entlang
already	schon
also	auch
although	obwohl
always	immer
am: 10am	10 Uhr (morgens) (→ pm)
among (friends etc.)	unter (Freunden etc.)
and (so on)	und (so weiter)
animal	Tier
another	noch ein(e)
answer	antworten; Antwort
any	irgendwelch
any: not any	kein(e)
anyone	(irgend)jemand
anyone: not anyone	niemand
anything	(irgend)etwas
anyway	sowieso; überhaupt; jedenfalls
appear	erscheinen
area	Gebiet
argue	argumentieren; sich streiten
argument	Argument; Auseinandersetzung
around	herum; umher
as (big) as	so (groß) wie
as if	als ob
as well as	sowie
ask	fragen
ask for	bitten um
at (the door)	an (der Tür)
at least	mindestens
at: not (good) at all	überhaupt nicht (gut)
away	weg

Wortschatz

B

back	zurück; Rückseite; Rücken
bad	schlecht; schlimm
be	sein; werden
be to	sollen
because	weil
because of	wegen
become	werden
before	vor; bevor; vorher
begin	anfangen
behind	hinter
believe	glauben
better	besser
between	zwischen
big	groß
bit	bisschen
body	Körper
book	Buch
both	beide
boy	Junge
break	brechen; kaputtmachen
bring	bringen
build	bauen
building	Gebäude
business	Geschäft(sleben)
but	aber; sondern
buy	kaufen
by (car)	mit (dem Auto)
by (Shakespeare)	von (Shakespeare)
by: (finish) by (5 o'clock)	bis (5 Uhr fertig sein)

C

call	rufen; anrufen
can	kann
cannot / can't	kann nicht
car	Auto
care	Sorgfalt; (Für-)Sorge
carry	tragen
case	Fall
catch	fangen; erwischen
cause	Ursache; verursachen
centre	Zentrum
century	Jahrhundert
certain(ly)	gewiss; bestimmt
chance	Chance; Möglichkeit
change	ändern; wechseln; (Ver-)Änderung; Wechsel
child – children	Kind – Kinder
choose	(aus)wählen
church	Kirche
city	(größere) Stadt
class	Klasse
clear	klar
colour	Farbe
come	kommen
company	Gesellschaft
condition	Bedingung; Zustand
consider	erwägen; halten für
continue (doing sth.)	fortfahren (etw. zu tun)
cost	kosten; Kosten
could	könnte; konnte
country	Land
cut	schneiden

D

date	Datum; Verabredung
day	Tag
dead	tot
death	(der) Tod
decide	entscheiden; beschließen
decision	Entscheidung; Entschluss
describe	beschreiben
die	sterben
difference	Unterschied
different	verschieden; anders
difficult	schwierig
difficulty	Schwierigkeit
discuss	diskutieren (über)
do	tun; machen
doctor	Arzt, Ärztin
dog	Hund
door	Tür
down	(he)runter; hinunter
drive	fahren; treiben
during	während

E

each	jede(r, s) (einzelne)
each other	einander; sich
early	früh

easy	leicht; einfach	food	Essen; Nahrung; Futter
eat	essen; fressen	foot	Fuß
either ... or	entweder ... oder	for	für
else	sonst	for (two years)	zwei Jahre lang; seit zwei Jahren
(someone) else	(jemand) anders		
end	Ende; enden	foreign	ausländisch
enjoy	genießen	forget	vergessen
enough	genug	free	frei; kostenlos
enter	betreten; eintreten	friend	Freund(in)
especially	besonders	from (nine to five)	von (neun bis fünf)
even	sogar	from (Italy)	aus (Italien)
evening	Abend	full	voll
event	Ereignis	further	weiter
ever	je(mals)	future	Zukunft
every	jede(r,s)		
everyone	jeder(mann); alle	**G**	
everything	alles	game	Spiel
example	Beispiel	garden	Garten
expect	erwarten	get	bekommen; kommen; werden
explain	erklären		
express	ausdrücken	girl	Mädchen
eye	Auge	give	geben; schenken
		glass	Glas
F		go	gehen; fahren
face	Gesicht	good	gut
fact	Tatsache	government	Regierung
fail	scheitern	great	groß(artig)
fall	fallen	group	Gruppe
family	Familie	grow (up)	(auf)wachsen
far	weit		
father	Vater	**H**	
feel	(sich) fühlen	hair	Haar(e)
few	wenige	half	halb
few: a few	ein paar	hand	Hand
field	Feld; Gebiet	happen	geschehen; passieren
fight	kämpfen; Kampf	happy	glücklich
finally	schließlich	hard	hart; (*Aufgabe*) schwer
find	finden	have (got)	haben
fine	schön	have (got) to	müssen
finish	beenden; fertig sein (mit)	he	er
finished	fertig	head	Kopf
fire	Feuer; Brand	health	Gesundheit
first	erste; zuerst	hear	hören
floor	(Fuß-)Boden; Stock(werk)	heart	Herz
follow(ing)	folgen(d)	help	helfen; Hilfe

Wortschatz

her	sie; ihr
here	hier
high	hoch
him	ihn; ihm
his	sein
hold	(ab)halten
home	Heim; Wohnung; Haus
home: at home	zu Hause
hope	hoffen; Hoffnung
horse	Pferd
hospital	Krankenhaus
hotel	Hotel
hour	Stunde
house	Haus
how	wie
however	jedoch

I

I	ich
idea	Idee
if	wenn; falls; ob
important	wichtig
in	in
including	einschließlich
income	Einkommen
indeed	wiklich; tatsächlich
information	Information(en)
interest	Interesse
international	international
into	in (hinein)
it	es; er; sie; ihn
its	sein; ihr

J

job	Arbeit; Job
join	beitreten; sich anschließen
just	gerade; genau; einfach; nur

K

keep	halten; behalten
kill	töten
kind	Art
know	wissen; kennen

L

land	Land
language	Sprache
large	groß
last	letzte(r, s)
late	spät
law	Recht; Gesetz
lead	führen
learn	lernen
leave	(ver)lassen
less	weniger
let	lassen
letter	Brief
lie	liegen
life	(das) Leben
light	Licht; leicht
like	wie; mögen; gern haben
line	Linie; Zeile
list	Liste
little	klein; wenig
live	leben; wohnen
long	lang(e)
look	schauen; Blick
lose	verlieren
lot: a lot of	viel(e)
love	lieben; Liebe
low	niedrig

M

main	Haupt-
make	machen
man	Mann
many	viele
market	Markt
matter	Sache
may	darf; mag; kann
me	mich; mir
mean	meinen
meet	(sich) treffen; kennenlernen
meeting	Sitzung; Begegnung
member	Mitglied
might	könnte (vielleicht)
mind	Kopf; Geist; Gedanken
minute	Minute
money	Geld

Wortschatz

month	Monat	only	nur
more	mehr	open	(er)öffnen; offen
morning	Morgen	or	oder
most	(die) meisten; höchst	order	Ordnung
mother	Mutter	order: in order to	um zu
move	(sich) bewegen	other	andere
much	viel	our	unser
music	(die) Musik	out	hinaus; (he)raus
must	muss	over	(her/hin)über
must not	darf nicht	own	eigen
my	mein		

N

name	Name
national	national
nature	(die) Natur
near	in der Nähe von
necessary	notwendig; nötig
need	brauchen; Notwendigkeit
never	nie(mals)
new	neu
news	Nachricht(en)
next	nächste(r, s)
nice	nett; hübsch
night	Nacht; Abend
no	nein; kein
no one	niemand
not	nicht
not anything	nichts
nothing	nichts
now	jetzt
number	Zahl; Anzahl

P

page	(Buch-)Seite
paper	Papier; Zeitung
part	Teil
party	Partei; Party
past	Vergangenheit
pay	(be)zahlen
people	Leute; Menschen
perhaps	vielleicht
person	Person; Mensch
picture	Bild
piece	Stück
place	Ort
plan	Plan; planen
play	spielen
please	bitte
pm: 10pm	22 Uhr (→ am)
point	Punkt
police	Polizei
political	politisch
poor	arm
possible	möglich
pound	Pfund
power	Macht
president	Präsident(in)
price	Preis
probably	wahrscheinlich
problem	Problem
produce	herstellen
product	Produkt
program(me)	Programm
public	öffentlich
put (it on the table)	(es auf den Tisch) tun

O

of	von
of course	selbstverständlich
off	weg; aus(geschaltet)
office	Büro; Amt
often	oft
old	alt
on	auf
on (the first of May)	am (ersten Mai)
once	einmal
one	ein(s)
one: a good one	ein(e) gute(r)

Wortschatz

Q
question	Frage
quick(ly)	schnell
quite (right)	ganz (richtig)

R
raise	erhöhen
rather	ziemlich
reach	erreichen
read	lesen
real(ly)	wirklich
reason	Grund
reduce	reduzieren
relationship	Beziehung
remain	bleiben
remember	sich erinnern (an)
report	Bericht; berichten
rest	Ruhe; ruhen; Rest
right	richtig; rechte(r, s)
rise	(an)steigen
road	Straße
room	Zimmer
round	rund; (rund)herum
rule	Regel
run	rennen; laufen

S
sale	Verkauf
same	selbe
say	sagen
school	Schule
sea: the sea	die See
see	sehen
seem	scheinen
sell	verkaufen
send	schicken
several	mehrere
shall	soll
she	sie
shop	Laden
short	kurz
should	sollte; müsste
show	Show; zeigen
side	Seite
similar	ähnlich
simple	einfach
since (May)	seit (Mai)
sit	sitzen
size	Größe
small	klein
so	so; sodass; damit
social	sozial
some	einige; etwas
someone	jemand
something	etwas
sometimes	manchmal
son	Sohn
soon	bald
sorry!	Entschuldigung!
sort	Art; Sorte
speak	sprechen
special	besondere(r,s)
spend	ausgeben; verbringen
stand	stehen
start	anfangen; Anfang
station	Bahnhof
stay	bleiben; wohnen
step	Schritt
still	(immer) noch
stop	(an)halten
story	Geschichte
street	Straße
strong	stark
student	Studierende(r)
study	studieren
success	Erfolg
such	solch(e,er,es)
such as	wie (zum Beispiel)
suggest	vorschlagen
sure	sicher

T
table	Tisch
take	nehmen; bringen
talk	reden; Gespräch
teacher	Lehrer(in)
tell	sagen; erzählen
than: bigger than	größer als
thank you	danke
that	dass; das; diese(r,s)

the	der; die; das
their	ihr
them	sie; ihnen
then	dann
there	dort
they	sie
thing	Ding; Sache
think	denken
this	dies(e,er,es)
though	obwohl
through	durch
time	Zeit
to	zu; nach
today	heute
together	zusammen
too	auch
too (much)	zu (viel)
town	(kleinere) Stadt
true	wahr
try	versuchen
turn	drehen

U

under	unter
understand	verstehen
union	Union
university	Universität
until	bis
up	hinauf; rauf
us	uns
use	Gebrauch; Nutzen; gebrauchen; benutzen
used to	pflegte zu
usually	meistens

V

very	sehr

W

wait	warten
walk	(zu Fuß) gehen
wall	Wand; Mauer
want (to)	wollen
war	Krieg
watch	beobachten
water	Wasser
way	Weg; Art und Weise
we	wir
week	Woche
well	gut
what	was
when	wann; wenn
where	wo(hin)
whether	ob
which	welche(r,s)
while	während
who	wer; der/die/das
whole	ganz
whose	wessen; dessen/deren
why	warum
wife	(Ehe-)Frau
will	wird
win	gewinnen
window	Fenster
wish	wünschen
with	mit
without	ohne
woman	Frau
word	Wort
work	arbeiten; Arbeit
world	Welt
would	würde
write	schreiben
wrong	falsch

Y

year	Jahr
yes	ja
yesterday	gestern
yet: not yet	noch nicht
you	du; Sie; ihr; dich; dir; Ihnen; euch
young	jung
your	dein; Ihr

Zahlen

Grundzahlen

1 one	7 seven	13 thirteen	19 nineteen	48 forty-eight
2 two	8 eight	14 fourteen	20 twenty	50 fifty
3 three	9 nine	15 fifteen	21 twenty-one	60 sixty
4 four	10 ten	16 sixteen	30 thirty	70 seventy
5 five	11 eleven	17 seventeen	35 thirty-five	80 eighty
6 six	12 twelve	18 eighteen	40 forty	90 ninety

100	one hundred / a hundred
101	one hundred and one / a hundred and one
102	one hundred and two / a hundred and two
200	two hundred
368	three hundred and sixty-eight
1,000	one thousand / a thousand
1,101	one thousand one hundred and one
3,000	three thousand
100,000	one hundred thousand / a hundred thousand
1,000,000	one million / a million
1,000,000,000	one billion / a billion

Ordnungszahlen

Die Ordnungszahl wird regelmäßig gebildet aus der Grundzahl + -th:

4th	(the) fourth	(der / die / das) Vierte
15th	(the) fifteenth	(der / die / das) Fünfzehnte
27th	(the) twenty-seventh	(der / die / das) Siebenundzwanzigste
100th	(the) hundredth	(der / die / das) Hundertste
110th	(the) hundred and tenth	(der / die / das) Hundertzehnte

Unregelmäßig gebildete Ordnungszahlen:

1st	(the) first	(der / die / das) Erste
2nd	(the) second	(der / die / das) Zweite
3rd	(the) third	(der / die / das) Dritte

Entsprechend auch bei zusammengesetzten Zahlen:

21st = twenty-first, 32nd = thirty-second, 43rd = forty-third etc.

Unregelmäßige Schreibung bzw. Aussprache:

five – fifth	twenty – twentieth	sixty – sixtieth
eight – eighth	thirty – thirtieth	seventy – seventieth
nine – ninth	forty – fortieth	eighty – eightieth
twelve – twelfth	fifty – fiftieth	ninety – ninetieth

Verben

Die wichtigsten unregelmäßigen Verben

Als unregelmäßig bezeichnet man Verben, deren 2. und/oder 3. Form nicht auf -ed endet.
Die drei in der Liste angegebenen Formen sind:

1. *infinitive* / Grundform: z. B. *fly* (= fliegen)
2. *past tense* / Vergangenheitsform: z. B. *flew* (= flog)
3. *past participle* / *-ed participle*: z. B. *flown* (= geflogen)

Das Sternchen * bedeutet: Auch die regelmäßige Form (auf -ed) ist gebräuchlich.

beat, beat, beaten	schlagen, schlug, geschlagen
become, became, become	werden, wurde, geworden
begin, began, begun	beginnen, begann, begonnen
bind, bound, bound	binden, band, gebunden
bite, bit, bitten	beißen, biss, gebissen
bleed, bled, bled	bluten, blutete, geblutet
blow, blew, blown	blasen, blies, geblasen
break, broke, broken	brechen, brach, gebrochen
bring, brought, brought	bringen, brachte, gebracht
build, built, built	bauen, baute, gebaut
burn, burnt*, burnt*	brennen, brannte, gebrannt
burst, burst, burst	platzen, platzte, geplatzt
buy, bought, bought	kaufen, kaufte, gekauft
catch, caught, caught	fangen, fing, gefangen
choose, chose, chosen	wählen, wählte, gewählt
come, came, come	kommen, kam, gekommen
cost, cost, cost	kosten, kostete, gekostet
cut, cut, cut	schneiden, schnitt, geschnitten
deal, dealt, dealt	handeln, handelte, gehandelt
dig, dug, dug	graben, grub, gegraben
do, did, done	tun, tat, getan
draw, drew, drawn	ziehen, zog, gezogen
dream, dreamt*, dreamt*	träumen, träumte, geträumt
drink, drank, drunk	trinken, trank, getrunken
drive, drove, driven	fahren, fuhr, gefahren
eat, ate, eaten	essen, aß, gegessen
fall, fell, fallen	fallen, fiel, gefallen
feed, fed, fed	füttern, fütterte, gefüttert
feel, felt, felt	fühlen, fühlte, gefühlt
fight, fought, fought	kämpfen, kämpfte, gekämpft
find, found, found	finden, fand, gefunden
flee, fled, fled	fliehen, floh, geflohen

Verben

fly, flew, flown	fliegen, flog, geflogen
forbid, forbade, forbidden	verbieten, verbot, verboten
forget, forgot, forgotten	vergessen, vergaß, vergessen
forgive, forgave, forgiven	vergeben, vergab, vergeben
freeze, froze, frozen	gefrieren, gefror, gefroren
get, got, got	kriegen, kriegte, gekriegt
give, gave, given	geben, gab, gegeben
go, went, gone	gehen, ging, gegangen
grow, grew, grown	wachsen, wuchs, gewachsen
hang, hung*, hung*	hängen, hängte, gehängt
hear, heard, heard	hören, hörte, gehört
hide, hid, hidden	verstecken, versteckte, versteckt
hit, hit, hit	treffen, traf, getroffen
hold, held, held	halten, hielt, gehalten
hurt, hurt, hurt	verletzen, verletzte, verletzt
keep, kept, kept	halten, hielt, gehalten
know, knew, known	wissen, wusste, gewusst
lay, laid, laid	legen, legte, gelegt
lead, led, led	führen, führte, geführt
lean, leant*, leant*	lehnen, lehnte, gelehnt
learn, learnt*, learnt*	lernen, lernte, gelernt
leave, left, left	verlassen, verließ, verlassen
lend, lent, lent	leihen, lieh, geliehen
let, let, let	lassen, ließ, gelassen
lie, lay, lain	liegen, lag, gelegen
light, lit*, lit*	anzünden, anzündete, angezündet
lose, lost, lost	verlieren, verlor, verloren
make, made, made	machen, machte, gemacht
mean, meant, meant	meinen, meinte, gemeint
meet, met, met	begegnen, begegnete, begegnet
pay, paid, paid	zahlen, zahlte, gezahlt
put, put, put	legen, legte, gelegt
read, read, read	lesen, las, gelesen
ride, rode, ridden	reiten, ritt, geritten
ring, rang, rung	läuten, läutete, geläutet
rise, rose, risen	steigen, stieg, gestiegen
run, ran, run	rennen, rannte, gerannt
say, said, said	sagen, sagte, gesagt
see, saw, seen	sehen, sah, gesehen
sell, sold, sold	verkaufen, verkaufte, verkauft
send, sent, sent	schicken, schickte, geschickt

Verben

set, set, set	setzen, setzte, gesetzt
shake, shook, shaken	schütteln, schüttelte, geschüttelt
shoot, shot, shot	schießen, schoss, geschossen
show, showed, shown	zeigen, zeigte, gezeigt
shut, shut, shut	schließen, schloss, geschlossen
sing, sang, sung	singen, sang, gesungen
sink, sank, sunk	sinken, sank, gesunken
sit, sat, sat	sitzen, saß, gesessen
sleep, slept, slept	schlafen, schlief, geschlafen
smell, smelt*, smelt*	riechen, roch, gerochen
speak, spoke, spoken	sprechen, sprach, gesprochen
spell, spelt*, spelt*	buchstabieren, buchstabierte, buchstabiert
spend, spent, spent	ausgeben, ausgab, ausgegeben
split, split, split	spalten, spaltete, gespalten
spread, spread, spread	ausbreiten, ausbreitete, ausgebreitet
stand, stood, stood	stehen, stand, gestanden
steal, stole, stolen	stehlen, stahl, gestohlen
strike, struck, struck	schlagen, schlug, geschlagen
swear, swore, sworn	schwören, schwor, geschworen
sweep, swept, swept	fegen, fegte, gefegt
swim, swam, swum	schwimmen, schwamm, geschwommen
take, took, taken	nehmen, nahm, genommen
teach, taught, taught	lehren, lehrte, gelehrt
tell, told, told	erzählen, erzählte, erzählt
think, thought, thought	denken, dachte, gedacht
throw, threw, thrown	werfen, warf, geworfen
understand, understood, understood	verstehen, verstand, verstanden
wake, woke, woken	wecken, weckte, geweckt
wear, wore, worn	tragen, trug, getragen
weep, wept, wept	weinen, weinte, geweint
win, won, won	gewinnen, gewann, gewonnen
write, wrote, written	schreiben, schrieb, geschrieben

Register

Die Zahlen bezeichnen die Seiten.

a oder *an*? 34
about 124
Abschiedsfloskeln 17
Adjektiv = Eigenschaftswort
Adjektiv 10, 28, 40, 110, 182
Adverb = Umstandswort
Adverb 10, 97, 166, 167
afraid 52, 76
ago 83, 133
Aktiv → Passiv
allow 52
„als" 110
also 28
am 9
an 34
Anredeformen 17
any – some 100
anyone – someone 131
anything – something 148
Apostroph 25
are 9, 11
Artikel *the* 22
„auch" 28
bag(s) 76
Bedingungssatz 142, 143, 183
Begrüßungsfloskeln 17
besitzanz. Pronomen 58, 59
bloody 28, 101
boyfriend 64
can 26, 37
check 52
check sth out 160
child(ren) 52
could 109
could have + 3. Form 109, 111, 177, 178
deli(catessen) 16
direkte Rede → indirekte Rede
do 46
do (zur Betonung) 130, 131, 165
does(n't) 49, 50
don't 46
Eigenschaftswort → Adjektiv
Einzahl → Singular
either 28
every 100
fancy 59
for 154, 179
Frageanhängsel 14, 62, 83, 143, 154, 155, 178
Frageform 46
fuck(ing) 101
Fürwort → Pronomen
Futur → Zukunft

get married 64
girlfriend 64
go – walk 40
going to 81, 82, 87, 94, 95
got 15
grand- 64
Grundzahlen 217
had-Form 86, 146, 147, 183
has – have 14, 33
hasn't got 15
„hätte" 142, 143
Häufigkeitsadverbien 166, 167
have – has 14, 33
have sth done 172
have to 70
have-Form 83, 86, 93, 94, 142, 153, 154, 179
high – tall 64
high time + Vergangenheit 183
Hilfsverben 107
hill – mountain 64
holiday – vacation 16, 124
hospital 148
how 76
how are you? 76
how many? 171
idioms 78, 88
if 28
if-Satz 142, 183
important 122
indeed 107
indirekte Frage 170
indirekte Rede 130, 133, 134
-ing-Form 98, 99, 123, 145, 146, 157, 160
interesting – interested 28
into 88
is 9, 11
it – they 21
it's – its 122, 123
Jahreszahlen 184
journey – trip 136
„kennenlernen" 136
Komma bei Zahlen 52, 113
„könnte" 177
Kraftausdrücke 28, 101
Kurzform – Vollform 9
lake – sea 64
Ländernamen 77
let's 39, 105
like 112
look forward to 160
love 136
-ly-Adverbien 97, 121, 166, 167, 182

may 100
Mehrzahl → Plural
-ment 88
mess 16
might 100
might have + 3. Form 177, 178
more 110
most 112, 118
mountain – hill 64
„müssen" 70
must 70
must have + 3. Form 177, 178
next – nearest 88
„nicht wahr?" → Frageanhängsel
of 27
ones 148
Ordnungszahlen 184, 217
Passiv 134, 135, 141, 142, 147, 158, 159, 169, 170
past perfect → Vorvergangenheit
past tense → Vergangenheit
Perfekt → *have*-Form
Plural = Mehrzahl
Plural 15, 21, 22, 23, 112
Plusquamperfekt → Vorvergangenheit
police 148
pound 113
Präposition = Verhältniswort
Präpositionen 15, 27, 47, 98, 99, 122, 123, 129, 157, 181
Präteritum → Vergangenheit
present perfect → *have*-Form
progressive form → Verlaufsform
Pronomen = Fürwort
Pronomen 9, 10, 23, 58, 59
Punkt bei Zahlen 52, 113
question tag → Frageanhängsel
Relativpronomen 111, 119
Relativsatz 99, 111, 118, 119, 158, 181
run 15
sea – lake 64
see 136
„seit" 154, 179
-self-Pronomen 112, 121, 146
-s-Form des Verbs 14, 15, 33, 49, 135
shall I/we? 105, 136
should 100
should have + 3. Form 119
since 154, 179
single 52
Singular = Einzahl
Singular oder Plural? 23
so 28

Register

so (that) 124
some – any 100
someone – anyone 131
something – anything 148
sorry 76
spa 16
speaking of 28
sport(s) 160
Städtenamen 77
start 184
Steigerung 111, 112, 118
Superlativ 118, 119
suppose 10
tall – high 64
-th 184, 217
than 110
that 111, 119, 181
the (Wegfall) 22, 148
there is/are 26
they – it 21
this – these 11
to + Grundform 157
to be exact 124

to be honest 124
to be sure 124
too 28
trip – journey 136
Umstandswort → Adverb
United States 53
unregelm. Verben 85, 87, 94, 219–221
used to 95
vacancy 52
vacation 16, 124
Verb = Zeitwort, Tätigkeitswort
Vergangenheit 69, 73, 83, 129, 130, 133, 135, 146, 147
Vergleich 88, 111, 112
Verlaufsform 57, 61, 74, 81, 82
verneinte Frage 21
Verneinung 23, 46
Vorvergangenheit 86, 87, 146, 147
walk 40
want me to 105
want to 95
„wäre" 142, 143
what 37, 159, 171

what a 76, 124
what ... like? 34
when 171
when to 124
where 27, 37, 159
which 111, 119, 181
who 111, 119, 159, 171, 181
why 71, 171
why don't you? 105
will 38, 75, 81, 82
„wohnen" 184
world 119
Wortstellung 26, 93, 94, 106, 122, 129, 166, 167
would 143, 182, 183
would have + 3. Form 143, 182, 183
would(n't) 106
yesterday 129
you 17
Zahlen 184, 217
Zukunft 75, 81, 82, 87

Quellenverzeichnis

Coverfoto: Brücke © Imagesource/Black; Paar © Corbis/Jupiterimages **Seite 7:** Familie © iStockphoto/Kevin Russ; Frau © iStockphoto/Neustockimages **Seite 9:** © iStockphoto/Neustockimages **Seite 12:** © Colourbox **Seite 17:** iStockphoto/Catherine Yeulet **Seite 19:** Big Ben © bildunion; St. James Park © fotolia/Jo Chambers **Seite 21:** © fotolia/Jo Chambers **Seite 24:** © fotolia/Dave Peck **Seite 29:** © iStockphoto/Shmulitk **Seite 31:** Rezeption © French Photographers Only/Jupiterimages; Landschaft © panthermedia/Jürgen von Wirth **Seite 32:** © panthermedia/Jürgen von Wirth **Seite 36:** © iStockphoto/Terraxplorer **Seite 41:** © fotolia/PhotographerOne **Seite 43:** Bed & Breakfast © panthermedia/Hermann Otto Feis; Frau © iStockphoto/Dan Wilton **Seite 45:** © iStockphoto/Dan Wilton **Seite 48:** © Village of Manhattan/Staff Photography **Seite 53:** © fotolia/Karin Lau **Seite 54:** © Colourbox **Seite 55:** Sydney © iStockphoto/Felix Alim; Hochzeit © iStockphoto/Leo Stanners **Seite 57:** © iStockphoto/Leo Stanners **Seite 60:** © irisblende.de **Seite 65:** © iStockphoto/iophoto **Seite 67:** Paar © fotolia/Yuri Arcurs; Flughafen © fotolia/Frank Eckgold **Seite 69:** © fotolia/Frank Eckgold **Seite 72:** MHV-Archiv **Seite 77:** © fotolia/Joe Gough **Seite 79:** Marathon © irisblende.de; Läufer © iStockphoto/photoGartner **Seite 81:** © iStockphoto/photoGartner **Seite 84:** © irisblende.de **Seite 89:** © iStockphoto/Stuart Berman **Seite 91:** Porträt © fotolia/dav820; Schach © Corbis UK Ltd/Jupiterimages **Seite 93:** © Corbis UK Ltd/Jupiterimages **Seite 96:** © Stockphotography/Ed Bock Photography **Seite 101:** © irisblende.de **Seite 102:** © fotolia/Yuri Arcurs **Seite 103:** Paar groß © getty images/Jochen Sand; Paar klein © MEV **Seite 105:** © MEV **Seite 109:** © fotolia/Monkey Business **Seite 113:** © fotolia/RoJo Images **Seite 115:** Golfplatz © St Andrews Links Trust/Donald Ford; Auto © irisblende.de **Seite 117:** © irisblende.de **Seite 121:** © fotolia/Monkey Business **Seite 125:** © fotolia/fried_lettuce **Seite 127:** Taj Mahal © panthermedia/Stephan Seybold; Wahrsagerin © fotolia/Scott Griessel **Seite 132:** © fotolia/Scott Griessel **Seite 137:** Delhi © Shotshop/Alexander Pöschel; Zug © Palace on Wheels **Seite 139:** Polizist © fotolia/Dawn; Polizeisperre © iStockphoto/pdtnc **Seite 141:** © iStockphoto/pdtnc **Seite 145:** © fotolia/redpole **Seite 149:** © Red Door VR Ltd. Leeds UK **Seite 151:** Porträt: © iStockphoto/William Britten; Kurs © fotolia/Monkey Business **Seite 153:** © fotolia/Monkey Business **Seite 157:** © iStockphoto/David Newton **Seite 161:** © fotolia/Daniel Tackley **Seite 163:** First Folio © Associated Press; Geburtshaus Shakespeare © iStockphoto/Mark Goddard **Seite 165:** © iStockphoto/Mark Goddard **Seite 169:** © fotolia/david hughes **Seite 173:** © fotolia/Igor Tarasov **Seite 175:** © MHV-Archiv **Seite 177:** © MHV-Archiv **Seite 181:** © fotolia/Monkey Business **Seite 185:** © fotolia/Alex Yeung